Fifth Edition

Steps to
SMALL BUSINESS
START-UP

Everything You Need
to Know to Turn
Your Idea into a
Successful Business

Linda Pinson • Jerry Jinnett

Dearborn™
Trade Publishing
A **Kaplan Professional** Company

Vice President and Publisher: Cynthia A. Zigmund
Acquisitions Editor: Jonathan Malysiak
Senior Managing Editor: Jack Kiburz
Interior Design: Eliot House Productions
Cover Design: Design Solutions
Typesetting: Eliot House Productions

Published by Dearborn Trade Publishing
A Kaplan Professional Company

Printed in the United States of America

03 04 05 10 9 8 7 6 5 4 3 2 1

Library of Congress Cataloging-in-Publication Data
Pinson, Linda.
        Steps to small business start-up: everything you need to know to turn your idea into a successful business/Linda Pinson and Jerry Jinnett.—5th ed.
        p.   cm.
    Includes bibliographical references and index.
    ISBN 0-7931-7927-0 (pbk.)
    1. New business enterprises—United States. 2. Small business—United States. 3. Success in business—United States. I. Jinnett, Jerry. II. Title.
    HD62.5.P565 2003
    658.1'1—dc21   2003011803

Dearborn Trade books are available at special quantity discounts to use for sales promotions, employee premiums, or educational purposes. Please call our Special Sales Department to order or for more information at 800-245-2665, e-mail us at trade@dearborn.com, or write to Dearborn Trade Publishing, 30 South Wacker Drive, Suite 2500, Chicago, IL 60606-7481.

TABLE OF CONTENTS

Introduction——vii

Acknowledgments——ix

CHAPTER 1   GETTING STARTED 1
Examining Your Personal Objectives——1
Exploring Business Ideas——2
Identifying Skills, Interests, and Personal Qualities——4
Evaluating Your Strengths and Weaknesses——4

CHAPTER 2   FINDING A BUSINESS. 9
Developing Your Own Business——9
Buying an Existing Business——10
Buying a Franchise——11

CHAPTER 3   DETERMINING BUSINESS FEASIBILITY. 17
Generating a Viable Business Idea——17
Researching Your Market——18
Finding Your Target Market——19
Collecting General (or Secondary) Data——20
Competition——21
Collecting Personal (or Primary) Data——22
Use of Questionnaires——23
Putting It Together——25

CHAPTER 4   CHOOSING A BUSINESS NAME 35
Narrowing the Search——37
Name Availability——38

CHAPTER 5   CHOOSING A BUSINESS LOCATION 39
Location Evaluation——39
Shopping Center——41
Business Incubators——41
Enterprise Zones——42
Lease Provisions——42

CHAPTER 6   DEVELOPING A HOME-BASED BUSINESS 47
How Does a Home-Based Business Differ from Other Businesses?——48
Do You Qualify for a Home-Office Deduction?——48
Calculating Your Deduction——50
Increasing Your Chances for Success——52

CHAPTER 7   CHOOSING A LEGAL STRUCTURE 59
Sole Proprietorship——60
Partnership——61
Partnership Agreements——62
Corporation——63
S Corporation——65
Limited Liability Company (LLC)——66
General Considerations——67

CHAPTER 8   PRESENTING YOUR BUSINESS. 69
Graphic Identity——69
Business Cards——70
Promotional Materials——71
Choosing a Printer——72

CHAPTER 9   PROTECTING YOUR BUSINESS 77
Disclosure Letter——77
Journal——77
Copyright——78
Trademark——80
Patent——81
Contracts——82
Hiring an Attorney——83

CHAPTER 10   SECURING A BUSINESS LICENSE 87
Location Considerations——87
Licensing a Home-Based Business——88
Applying for a Business License——89
Always Post Your Business License——90

CHAPTER 11   REGISTERING A FICTITIOUS NAME
(FILING A "DBA") 93
If You Fail to File——94
How to File a DBA——94
Renewal of Your DBA——95

CHAPTER 12   OBTAINING A SELLER'S PERMIT 99
Applying for a Seller's Permit——99
Purpose of a Seller's Permit——99
State Laws Vary——100
Misuse of Your Seller's Permit——100
Resale Certificate——101
Reporting Sales Tax——101

CHAPTER 13   SETTING UP A BANK ACCOUNT 109
Separate Business and Personal Finances——111
Open a Checking Account——111
Additional Accounts You May Wish to Consider——112

CHAPTER 14   SELECTING YOUR INSURANCE 115
Shopping for an Insurance Company——115
The Basic Kinds of Insurance——116
Property and Liability Insurance——116
Life Insurance——118
Health Insurance——118
Employee Benefits——118
Other Considerations——119

CHAPTER 15   FINANCING YOUR BUSINESS 121
Will You Need to Borrow Money?——121
How Much Do You Need and When Do You Need It?——122
What Are the Sources Available to You?——122
Which Type of Financing Costs the Most?——128

CHAPTER 16   KEEPING YOUR BOOKS 131
The Importance of Recordkeeping——131
Should You Hire an Accounting Professional?——132
When Do You Begin?——133
What Records Do You Need to Keep?——133
Keeping the Books on Schedule——137

CHAPTER 17   SUCCESS OR FAILURE: IT DEPENDS
                        ON YOUR CASH FLOW 151
What Is a Cash Flow Statement?——151
Preplanning Worksheets——152
Using the Worksheets to Build the Cash Flow Statement——158

CHAPTER 18   DEVELOPING A MARKETING PLAN 165
Product or Service——165
Place——166
Price——167
Promotion——167

CHAPTER 19   PROMOTING YOUR BUSINESS 171
Media Advertising——171
Publicity——174
Alternative Methods——174
Marketing on the Internet——177

CHAPTER 20   BUSINESS PLANNING: THE KEY
                TO YOUR SUCCESS 187
Why Should You Write a Business Plan?——188
Revising Your Business Plan——189
A Winning Business Plan Format——189
Anatomy of a Business Plan Outline——189

APPENDIX A   RESOURCES FOR SMALL BUSINESS 193
The Small Business Administration——193
Other Federal Resources——194
Associations and Agencies——194
Books——195
Library Resources——196

APPENDIX B   WORKSHEETS 199

Glossary——*233*
Index——*242*

INTRODUCTION

Now, more than at any time in our nation's history, the economy is being driven by the engine of small business. Hundreds of thousands of new businesses are started every year, and it is imperative that they are properly launched and given every chance to establish their niches in the marketplace of the new millennium.

We hope you are pleased with our new edition of *Steps to Small Business Start-Up*. This book has been written with the hope that it will provide you, the new small business entrepreneur, with the information, forms, and worksheets you will need to go through the process of starting your business and laying a proper foundation for the development of a successful business venture.

We have tried to present the information in a logical sequence so that you will have a guideline to follow as you get your business organized and legalized. However, the procedures and requirements may vary slightly according to your location and industry. We would suggest that you read through the entire book one time and then go back and begin the process of forming your business.

Forms, examples, and worksheets have been included in the book for your convenience. They may be duplicated for your own use but not for commercial purposes.

We have written *Steps to Small Business Start-Up* based on our experiences as business owners. We have also incorporated information and feedback from the many thousands of students, users of our books, business professionals, and other small business owners with whom we have been fortunate enough to interact over the last several years.

We hope that you will benefit from this book and that it will provide you with the motivation and knowledge to take your idea "out of your mind... and into the marketplace."

Best wishes for a very successful small business.

—Linda Pinson and Jerry Jinnett

ACKNOWLEDGMENTS

Dearborn would like to acknowledge the works of Small Business Development Centers (SBDCs) around the country for their untiring support of start-ups and small business owners. Many SBDCs provide high-quality materials, such as *Steps to Small Business Start-Up* and other titles, to enhance the training and counseling of entrepreneurs in their state. This is the type of public/private partnership that will make today's small businesses prosper.

Other books and software by Linda Pinson

Anatomy of a Business Plan

Automate Your Business Plan (software)

Keeping the Books

CHAPTER 1

GETTING STARTED

Everyone has dreamed of owning a business. At one time or another, we all have ideas that come into our minds but never quite make it into the marketplace. It has been said that an entrepreneur can best be defined by the following thought: All people have great ideas while in the shower. Most of us get out of the shower and forget about them. The entrepreneur is the person who gets out of the shower and acts on those ideas. However, you will increase your chances of success if you ask some tough questions before acting. What is my reason for starting a business? What type of business can I start? What skills, interests, and personal qualities will I be able to bring to the business? What are my strengths and weaknesses as a business owner?

• • • • •

EXAMINING YOUR PERSONAL OBJECTIVES

Begin with examining why you want to start a business. People come to business ownership for a variety of reasons. They want to "be their own boss," "build a future," "follow the American dream," "earn lots of money." Look closely at why you want to start and run a business. What are your motivating factors?

There seem to be two schools of thought regarding business ownership:

1. Choose a business with great profit potential. After all, why would you go into business if not to make a lot of money?

2. Choose a business that you love. If you can't enjoy the work, why do it?

If profit is your motivation, take a close look at what that means. A business must be able to cover all of its costs, pay for all of its expenses, cover the owners' personal financial needs, and have enough net revenue left to allow the business to grow. Focus on the role this business will play in your personal financial situation. Will this business provide you with a full income? Will the business supplement your current income? Before going much further, it is necessary to look at what your personal financial needs are. A **Personal Monthly Expense Worksheet** has been included on page 6 to help you determine your total living expenses. This will help determine your **owner equity** or **draw** as explained on page 154, the **Cash to Be Paid Out Worksheet** for your business.

If doing what you love is your motivation, try to analyze what that means. Is there a market out there to support your dream? Is there enough potential revenue to make this a profitable business and not just a folly? Is your business feasible? Chapter 3 will show you how to determine the profitability of your business before you devote time and money to its development.

A successful business allows you to make a profit while doing work that you enjoy. With careful research and planning you can develop a business that fills a need, brings you pleasure and pride, and earns enough revenue to meet your personal needs, pay for itself, and provide profits for future growth. The key words here are **research** and **planning**. Continue with some research into what you, the owner, will bring to this business.

EXPLORING BUSINESS IDEAS

Ideas for new businesses come from many sources. You may wish to turn an interest of yours into a business. Take a look at your hobbies, volunteer experience, and leisure activities. You could develop a line of specialty foods, do event planning, give golf lessons, or develop an antique locating and refinishing service.

Sell what you know. Any specialized knowledge or skill can be turned into a business. You can develop a newspaper column, write a book, present workshops, and conduct seminars in your area of expertise. An understanding of the Internet can lead to a business of designing, monitoring, and updating Web sites. This same knowledge can be used to retrieve information useful to other businesses. You can prepare demographic studies, databases, market surveys, and information resource lists.

You can put to work equipment and technology you already have. Desktop publishing, video recording of weddings, and photography of children's sports events are examples of businesses that make use of equipment you may already own and be proficient in using.

Many new businesses are started by individuals who utilize existing skills from their salaried jobs. Accountants, payroll administrators, technical writers, and computer specialists are examples of employees who have marketable skills that can be developed into service businesses. As companies **downsize** and **outsource**, new opportunities arise for entrepreneurs.

Any task or responsibility people don't like to do or don't have time to do for themselves can be the basis for a service business. Housecleaning, home repairs, gardening, proofreading, gift purchasing, and furniture refinishing may fill needs in your business community.

You may wish to explore an idea that is new to you. Take classes, apprentice, or work in an area dealing with your new field of interest. If you think you might be interested in catering or some other facet of the food industry, work at a restaurant. Learn all of the aspects of the business. How are supplies ordered, how are deliveries handled, how is inventory controlled, how is food handled, and how are invoices and purchase orders handled? What are the strengths of the restaurant? What would you improve? You are not going to steal their business plan! You are getting an education while moonlighting and earning extra money to put toward the start-up of your business. You will learn to feel comfortable with the terminology and procedures of the food industry. You will also find out if you really enjoy working with food.

An inventive entrepreneur can develop a new product or improve an existing one. Now is the time for the old adage, "find a need and fill it." New products are usually spawned out of the imagination. If you can't think of something new, remember that many existing products can be improved upon. A welder we know has designed an improved version of a jack used for leveling mobile homes. He used his creative talent in designing the new jack and his welding skill in manufacturing his product. He has created a double need for his talents. His product is timely, and today he is a busy, happy, and prosperous man.

TECH TIP 1

ACCESS START-UP INFORMATION VIA THE INTERNET

Technological advances enable you to quickly and easily access up-to-the-minute information on business start-up. The Small Business Administration's Web site at <www.sba/gov> is an excellent source of business information. Access the site and click on "Starting a Business" on the home page. Then check out "Your First Steps" and "Start-Up Kit." The latter provides a table of contents for the SBA Small Business Resource Guide. Clicking on individual topics will yield specific information on business development, and the text contains hotlinks to additional sites and information. Through this site, you can also access special interest groups and electronic mail forums, and you will find a searchable database of SBA publications and resources.

Another site is maintained by *Entrepreneur* magazine and can be accessed at <www.entrepreneur.com>. Click on "Start-Ups" on the home page for information, articles, and links covering the start-up process.

It is also worth checking a site maintained by the *Wall Street Journal* Center for Entrepreneurs. It can be accessed at <www.startupjournal.com>. Click on "How-To" and "Ideas" for a listing of current articles.

When you are accessing information over the Internet, it is a good idea to "bookmark" key sites. The most useful sites are updated and changed frequently. The key article or information you find today may not be there tomorrow, so it is a good idea to download or print articles and information of use when first located.

IDENTIFYING SKILLS, INTERESTS, AND PERSONAL QUALITIES

Now is a good time to step back and take an objective look at what lies ahead. Business ownership is not for everyone. While some people may have the motivation and desire for business ownership, they may not have taken the time to properly investigate and research their abilities and business ideas. A careful evaluation of your skills, interests, and personal qualities can help you determine the business you are best suited for. Skills are your abilities to use your knowledge and training proficiently. Interests are those things you enjoy doing and that bring you pleasure. Personal qualities are those traits and characteristics that make you unique.

The **Personal Assessment Worksheet 1** on page 7 has been provided to help you analyze your skills, interests, and personal qualities and determine the types of businesses you may be suited for. Keep this worksheet within easy reach and fill it out as you go through your day's activities. You may have everyday skills, interests, and personal qualities that could be enhanced and utilized for business purposes. Do you have a mechanical ability? You might consider a repair service. Are you interested in arts and crafts? You can turn what has been a hobby into a full-scale business. Do you enjoy working with other people? If so, you could consider tutoring or teaching.

When you have completed the first three columns of the worksheet, you are ready to tackle the fourth column, **business possibilities**. This column is filled out by evaluating and combining the other three. For example, if one of your interests is dining out and you have writing skills, you could write and publish a local dining guide. If you are interested in collecting music boxes, skilled in mechanical repairs, and proficient at working with the public, you can provide a music box service combining repairs and sales. Extra emphasis should be placed on the area of "interest." You will be spending a great deal of time in your business pursuit, and you might as well enjoy it. The ability to do well at your business may prove to be rewarding while the business is new, but if you do not like your work, it soon becomes a drudgery. Instead of looking forward to beginning your business day, you will be searching for ways to escape to more interesting diversions.

EVALUATING YOUR STRENGTHS AND WEAKNESSES

Analysis of your skills may have indicated areas where you lack an appropriate skill. You don't have to be an expert to start a business, but you must have a realistic understanding of your **strengths** and **weaknesses**. No business owner knows everything! The **Personal Assessment Worksheet 2** on page 8 has been provided to help you with this analysis.

If you identify an area in which you will need help, remember expertise can be learned or bought. You can compensate for weaknesses by taking classes, hiring staff, or using consultants. When you have an idea for a type of business, take classes to learn all that you can about your chosen field. Find a job in your field of interest and get hands-on experience. Community colleges, the Small Business Administration, and Small Business Development Centers in your area will offer or can direct you to workshops and classes on business topics such as recordkeeping, marketing, financing, and business planning.

Just as you looked at your strengths and weaknesses as a business owner, you must look at the strengths and weaknesses of your business idea. Do this before you quit your job, invest your money, or spend your time in starting the new business. When you have decided on a business, answer the following questions:

- Do you have the skills needed to run this business?

- Do you know what help you will need and where you will find that help?

- Do you have the time required to learn what you need to know?

- Can you afford the money needed to hire staff or pay consultants?

- Are you genuinely interested in this particular business?

- Are you committed to the business' success?

- Are you willing to devote the time needed to develop a successful business?

- Does this business fill an unmet need?

- Is there a sufficient consumer demand to support your business?

- Can you effectively compete in the marketplace?

- Will you be able to understand your business financial statements such as cash flow, profit and loss, and balance sheet?

- Are you developing a business plan that you can use throughout the life of your business?

To be the owner of a successful business venture, you must be able to answer "yes" to all of these questions. Research business ideas and see how they fit with your personality and background. Use the worksheets at the end of this chapter. Look at your skills, interests, and personal qualities in an objective manner. Then look at your strengths and weaknesses. Plan ways of overcoming your weaknesses. If this involves taking classes or hiring consultants or employees, calculate both the cost and time involved. The costs incurred must be included in your **Cash to Be Paid Out Worksheet** in Chapter 17. You may wish to delay the start of your business until you have gained the knowledge and help you need.

Stepping Along

Now that you have identified a type of business you would like to develop, let's look at the various alternatives available to you. Chapter 2 will help you look at the advantages and disadvantages of starting up a new business, buying an existing business, and buying into a franchise. Once you have a business idea and your start-up format, Chapter 3 provides information on evaluating the profitability or feasibility of the potential business.

Personal Monthly Expense Worksheet

Regular Monthly Payments	Column 1	Personal Expenses	Column 2
Rent/mortgage payments		Clothing/shoes	
Property taxes		Cleaning/laundry	
Insurance: Homeowners		Education/training	
Renters		Subscriptions/books	
Life		Medical/dental care	
Health		Prescriptions	
Vehicle		Eating out	
Other		Travel	
Credit card payments		Entertainment	
Groceries		Gifts/contributions/donations	
Childcare		Other	
Car expenses (gas, oil, etc.)			
Car payments			
Other loan payments		**Savings/Investments**	
Other payments			
Household Operating Expenses		**Column 2 Total**	
Telephone			
Gas		**Total Monthly Expenses (A):** **(total columns 1 + 2)**	
Electricity		**Total Monthly Outside Income (B):(non-business)**	
Water and sewer		**A – B = Minimum income needed from the business**	
Household maintenance/repair			
Household supplies			
Other			
Column 1 Total			

Personal Assessment Worksheet 1

Skills	Interests	Personal Qualities	Business Ideas
Organized	Sports	Enjoy meeting people	Sporting goods store
Can use computer	Fly-fishing	Independent	Teach classes
Writing skills	Reading	Self-confident	Conduct travel tours
Public speaking	Outdoor activities	Good work ethic	
Good phone skills		Enjoy learning	Write sports column
Communication skills		Decision maker	

Personal Assessment Worksheet 2

Strengths	Weaknesses	Action Plan	Cost	Time
Retail store experience	Lack of knowledge of business finances	Take basic accounting at community college	$150.00	6 weeks 4 hours per week
Managerial experience		Purchase Keeping the Books by Linda Pinson	$22.95	
Worked as customer service rep				
Well known in community as an athlete	Don't enjoy financial work	Use an accountant	$75 per month	2 hours per month
Worked as a tour guide		Attend SBA workshops "Business Start-Up"	$30.00	4-hour class
		Contact local SBDC		
Teaching experience				
	Lack of knowledge of marketing procedures	Attend marketing class at community college	$85.00	8-hour workshop
	Lack of knowledge of writing a business plan	Work with a counselor from SCORE	Free	2 hours per week
		Purchase Anatomy of a Business Plan by Linda Pinson	$21.95	
		Take Business Planning workshop from SBA	$40.00	8-hour workshop

CHAPTER

2

FINDING A BUSINESS

Starting and growing a business involves a great deal of decision making. In Chapter 1, you made a decision on the type of business you want to start. Now you are faced with three alternatives: start up a brand new business, buy an existing business, or buy a franchise. Each has benefits and drawbacks. Some of the differences in these choices are required investment capital, chance of survival, and expected profit. Examine the advantages and disadvantages of each option before taking the entrepreneurial leap.

• • • • •

DEVELOPING YOUR OWN BUSINESS

There are advantages to developing your own business. Generally, it costs less up front to start a business than to buy one, and you can make use of your creative talents in developing something unique. You can address unexplored markets. You are free to choose your own location and develop your own management style and policies, and you will not be buying the problems and flaws of an existing business.

Most people who start their own businesses are good at what they do. They have used their talents and creativity to develop something unique. They manufacture, provide, or sell a good product or provide a good service. But a successful entrepreneur has to provide a good product or service and understand how a business works.

There are certain inherent risks in developing your own business. You have to start from scratch. You are responsible for choosing a legal structure, location, and recordkeeping system. You must get licenses and permits. You develop your customer base, management and organizational systems, and marketing plan. At times, this can seem overwhelming. The purpose of this book is to take the mystery out of business start-up. You will see that a business starts and develops in a logical order. Understanding how a business works is one way to increase your chances for success.

BUYING AN EXISTING BUSINESS

There are some advantages to buying an existing business. It may be the only way to get a good location in the area where you want to do business. You can save some of the time, work, and money that go into the start-up phase of business development. Often, you are able to make use of the seller's invested capital. Many sellers will finance a large part of the sale for a lower interest rate than a lending institution would offer. An existing business already has an organizational plan and operating system in place. The customer base is already established. Often, the seller will consult with the buyer on the management of the company.

There are a number of ways to find businesses for sale. Trade associations and neighborhood business groups are usually the first to know a business that is for sale and about the business' performance and reputation. Business brokers are a good professional resource for information on available properties, locations, markets, and financing. They can represent sellers or buyers and are paid a percentage of the sale price. The "Business Opportunity" advertising section of a newspaper will have local listings. Bankers, the chamber of commerce, and other professional people within the community often know people who are selling or about to sell a business.

When you find a business you are interested in, determine why it is for sale. There may be serious business problems such as new competition, relocation of the primary customer base, obsolescence of a product line, or cash flow problems that have prompted the sale. Study the business and research its market carefully. Study the trends of the specific business. Learn about the competition, surrounding neighborhood, local business community, and current customer base.

An experienced and independent accountant can help you analyze the seller's financial statements and tax records in order to determine profitability and purchase price. Do not take the word of the seller's accountant. Evaluate the seller's projections for future growth and performance. In an eagerness to sell, the owner might make claims that are overinflated. If you have difficulty getting the financial information you need, it might be wise to move on to another opportunity.

When you buy a business, you purchase a number of tangible and intangible assets. You want to know what you will be purchasing and its current value before you set a price and close a sale. You want to know if any of the company's assets have been pledged as collateral for outstanding debt. It is wise to hire an appraiser to determine the value of the assets (or liabilities) being purchased. These items may include the following:

- Accounts payable and other liabilities

- Accounts receivable

- Building

- Business name

- Business clientele and customer list

- Consulting agreement with seller

- Covenant not to compete

- Credit relationships

- Equipment

- Furniture and fixtures

- Inventory

- Lease agreements

- Liabilities and liens

- Personnel

- Trademark, copyright, patent

- Unpaid taxes

A **Buying a Business Worksheet** has been included on page 14 to help you evaluate a company. Researching a business to buy takes time and focuses on discovering the truth about the enterprise being considered.

TECH TIP 2
BUYING AN EXISTING BUSINESS

The Web site, <www.business-to-buy.com> was put together to assist the entrepreneur in making an educated decision regarding the purchase of an existing business. It contains a free, comprehensive library of articles that cover Choosing a Business, Due Diligence, Legal Considerations, and Business Valuation. Another Web site with useful information and articles is <www.bizbuysell.com>.

BUYING A FRANCHISE

Many small business owners have minimized their risks by investing in a franchise. Franchising is a plan of distribution where an individually owned business is operated as a part of a large chain. The products and services offered are standardized. The company (franchisor) gives the individual dealer (franchisee) the right to market the franchisor's product or service and use the franchisor's trade name, trademarks, reputation, and way of doing business. The franchise agreement usually gives the franchisee the exclusive right to sell in a specified area.

In return, the franchisee agrees to pay to the franchisor a fee and/or a percentage of gross sales.

You may wish to explore the advantages of this means of business ownership. You will be able to start your business under a name and trademark that is already accepted by the public. You may be able to receive training and management assistance from people who are experienced in your type of business. You may also be able to obtain financial assistance from the franchisor. Often, equipment and supplies must be purchased from the franchisor. You could receive savings through the franchisor's quantity purchasing of products, equipment, supplies, and advertising materials. Some franchisors will guide you in day-to-day operations until you are proficient. Often, the franchisor provides management consulting on a continuing basis. This usually includes help with recordkeeping. National and regional promotions by the franchisor will help your business. The immediate identification many franchise operations enjoy can bring presold customers to your door.

You should also look at some of the disadvantages. Because of the required standardized operations, you cannot make all of the rules. You often lose the freedom to be your own boss and to make most of the decisions. The franchisor usually charges a royalty on a percentage of gross sales and that royalty fee must ultimately come out of your profits. On the other hand, the franchisor does not usually share your losses. You may be restricted in establishing selling prices, introducing new products or services, and dropping unprofitable ones, thus limiting your ability to be competitive. Franchisors require specific reports, and you may consider the time and effort spent in preparing them to be burdensome. A **Buying a Franchise Worksheet** has been included on pages 15 and 16 to help you evaluate this type of business.

Making the decision to franchise is not a matter to take lightly. Before entering into a franchise contract do the following:

- *Examine your interests and abilities.* What do you like to do? What are you good at?

- *Consult a directory of franchise opportunities.* A number of organizations publish information that includes descriptions of franchisor companies and the qualifications and capital that a franchisee needs.

- *Narrow your options.* Write to the companies that interest you and ask them to give you the names of franchisees you can contact.

- *Talk to franchisees.* Other franchisees have firsthand experience at operating the type of business that interests you.

- *Contact the Federal Trade Commission.* The FTC can provide free information on the FTC Franchise Rule, which requires franchisors to disclose certain information before a potential franchisee invests any money in the opportunity. For an information packet, write to the FTC at CRC-240, Washington, DC 20580, call 877-382-4357, or access the agency's Web site at <www.ftc.gov>.

- *Consult a lawyer and an accountant before signing a franchise contract.* Make sure you understand all of the details and ramifications of the contract. Their terms usually last 10 to 20 years.

You can prepare yourself to be successful by identifying all of the activities necessary for the development of your business. Then plan for each task to be handled properly. You can increase your chances of success by developing a business plan. A business plan serves as the foundation for any new business. It is the blueprint for your business start-up, operation, and growth. Whether you are starting your own business, buying an existing business, or buying a franchise, a business plan will help you make sound decisions for getting your business running and keeping it on track. Chapter 20 deals with this subject. For more comprehensive information, refer to *Anatomy of a Business Plan* (Linda Pinson, Dearborn Trade) and developed companion software, Automate Your Business Plan.

TECH TIP 3
BUYING A FRANCHISE

The Web site <www.franchise.com> provides buyer information on average franchise costs and access to the Web sites of individual franchises by category.

The Federal Trade Commission has put together a Web site to address the pitfalls of becoming involved in a "business opportunity." Access their site at <www.ftc.gov/bizop> for a list of articles, links to state agencies, and information on federal and state laws regarding key disclosures.

Stepping Along

Now that you have decided on a type of business and a method for start-up, it is time to take the next step: researching your business idea to determine its profit potential. We do this by identifying and analyzing a **target market**. This refers to your customers or clients, the entities that will be paying their hard-earned money for your products and services. The mission of Chapter 3 is to show you how to determine how much your target market spends on your type of product or service, how much of that revenue has been captured by your competition, and what portion of that revenue will be yours.

Buying a Business Worksheet

Name of business: _The Baseball Sports Shop_

Type of business: _Retail store: Baseball equipment, uniforms, trading cards_

Address: _786 Cherry Lane, Blair, NY 18760_

Contact person: _Sam and Alice Brockton, 555-0601_

Why is this business for sale? _Owner is retiring._

What is the history of this business? _Started in October 1976. Expanded and moved to present location in June 1986._

Has this business been profitable? _2002 net profit = $86,000_

2003 net profit = $110,000

Profit increase due to addition of school uniform accounts.

What will I be buying? _____

Accounts payable/liabilities: _$54,000_

Accounts receivable: _$21,000 (age of receivables)_

Business name: _Name limits business to sale of baseball-focused items. Not an asset—will have to be changed._

Customer list: _12,000 names—active customer list_

Fixed assets: _$128,000 (Itemize balance sheet and note age and condition.)_

Inventory: _$87,000_

Lease: _Two years remaining on existing lease. Rent = $1,000/month_

Personnel: _Must agree to keep current employees. Three full-time sales clerks ($8/hr each). One bookkeeper ($25/hr). Six part-time employees ($7/hr)._

Proprietary rights (copyright, patent, trademark): _Trademark — logo. High school and university baseball uniform account = $70,000/yr. income._

Unpaid taxes: _Accrued $10,000_

What is the selling price of this business? _$240,000_

How will I finance this purchase? _Present owner will assist in financing. $80,000 down payment. $160,000 financed at 8% over 25 years._

Buying a Franchise Worksheet

Name of franchise: American Sports and Trophies

Type of business: Retail store featuring full line of baseball, football, tennis equipment, footwear, clothing, and trophy and engraving sales.

Address: 762 Industrial Parkway, Atlanta, GA 30601

Contact person: Al Casey (401) 555-6250

What is the reputation of the franchisor?   Well-established (1984)

Good response from other franchisees interviewed.

Is the company involved in litigation?   None

What is the reputation of the individual business?

Name recognition and public awareness are good.

What training and start-up assistance is offered by the franchisor?

Six weeks management training in Atlanta—cost included in franchise fee.

What continuing assistance is offered by the franchisor?

Location assistance, inventory control system, bookkeeping system, promotion and advertising assistance.

What is the management structure of the organization?

Regional manager—Tom Anderson

District manager—Ann Johnstone

Are the location and territory protected?

Six-mile radius protected

Buying a Franchise Worksheet, continued

What are the operating practices of the franchise? _____

_____ Product line selected by franchisor. _____

_____ Pricing structure determined by franchisor. _____

What are the operating control policies? _____

_____ Quarterly financial reports _____

_____ Co-op advertising costs _____

What are the franchise costs? _____ $280,000 _____

_____

_____

Initial license fee: _____ $100,000 _____

_____

_____

Continuing royalty fees: _____ 2% of gross sales annually _____

_____

_____

Other fees: _____ Equipment—$60,000 _____

_____ Opening inventory—$120,000 (must be purchased from company). _____

_____

How will the sale be financed? _____ Through franchisor _____

_____

_____

Do I have the right to sell the franchise? _____ Must be sold through franchisor. ____

_____

_____

What are the terms of renewal and termination? _____ Contract written from year to year.

_____ "Escape clause" favors franchisor. _____

_____ 1. Nonrenewal by franchisor if sales do not reach projections in agreement. _____

_____

_____ "Buyback clause" _____

_____ 1. Franchisor can repurchase franchise at will. _____

DETERMINING BUSINESS FEASIBILITY

Before officially starting a business, it is prudent to conduct a feasibility study. The word feasible is defined as that which is able to be done, that which is practical. In business, this is synonymous with profitable. Are there customers out there who are interested in what you are going to provide? Will they buy enough to support your financial obligations? Will your business idea cover your personal expenses as well as business expenses with enough revenue left over to allow for growth? The only way to determine this is to get the answers to a few simple questions and then analyze how these answers apply to your business idea.

• • • • •

Your product or service may be in demand and your pricing competitive. You may have found the lowest prices for your raw materials and secured adequate financing for your business. All of this will be of no use if you have not taken the time to identify your customers and found the means to get your product or service to them. The key word here is **time**. It takes time to research a business idea, but it is time well spent. It may mean the difference between success and failure. Find out now if there is a need for your product or service **before** you commit a great deal of time and money to the project.

GENERATING A VIABLE BUSINESS IDEA

If you haven't yet decided on a business idea, you should reflect on your past experiences. Is there a particular hobby you enjoy? Do you have a unique knowledge? Has some experience such as travel or sports given you an expert perspective on a subject? Do you have a passion for something—perhaps children, the elderly, reading, a social or political cause? Have you spent a number of years in a certain industry or doing a specific job function? Do you have a special skill or talent?

Sometimes it is helpful to get feedback from people who know you well. Ask them about your strengths and weaknesses. Brainstorm business ideas that seem to fit with your background and interests. It's important that your business idea be something you will know and enjoy. After all, you will be spending an awful lot of time researching your potential competitors, getting to know your customers, writing a business plan, and running your business. You had better well enjoy it!

RESEARCHING YOUR MARKET

Market research involves finding out what a customer wants and needs and determining how your business can satisfy those wants and needs. You will need to examine your competition's abilities and successes in the marketplace. Based on your research, you will project revenue—the amount of money that will flow into your business—and expenses—the amount of money you will spend. Try to be objective and think like a customer.

There is a wealth of information available that will help you decide if your idea is viable. Begin by collecting data that applies to your business. There are two types of information you will need to collect. Start by observing the general environment and analyzing trends. This is often referred to as secondary data. Once you have examined the general environment, you will want to solidify this research by getting personal feedback, or primary data. At this stage you will talk directly with people who have the characteristics of your secondary data.

There are professional firms and individual consultants who can conduct market research for you. They conduct research on the general environment, produce market surveys, compile data, and make recommendations. This may be too costly for a small start-up business. You may choose to do your own work. The advantage of doing your own market research is that you will have firsthand knowledge of your industry and customers.

You will also want to examine trends that are prevalent in the marketplace you intend to serve. This may be global through e-commerce, regional in the form of transportable services such as mobile accounting agencies, or local as with corporate-sponsored, on-site childcare.

Some current marketplace trends are:

- *Technology.* Recent technological innovations allow us to reach markets faster and easier than ever. E-commerce allows us to purchase products and services over the Internet. Pagers and cell phones provide instant communication. Office equipment such as fax machines, copiers, and voice-mail systems are commonplace. Teleconferencing allows us to conduct meetings without leaving our respective offices. All of these new techniques need explanation, and this new equipment needs service and repair.

- *Fast action*. Because of recent technological advances, we have gotten used to getting what we want in a very short amount of time. We can drive through fast-food establishments; businesses are becoming mobile to bring their services directly to the consumer;

and movies pack a lifetime of action into two hours. Will this change the way you deliver your product or service to your customers?

- **International commerce**. Travel and language are no longer barriers to commerce. International trade has opened up wonderful opportunities for small business.

- **Aging boomers**. Currently in their late 30s to mid-50s, boomers are in their peak earning years. They comprise one-third of the country's consumers and account for 50 percent of total consumer spending. As a group, boomers will have more money to spend and invest. Are there ways in which you can tap into this market?

- **Growing youth market**. Census projections indicate that by 2008 the number of babies born each year in the United States will reach 4.3 million and that by 2020 the number will be 5 million. These numbers surpass the record high set at the peak of the baby boom. Spending will go up dramatically in the children's markets. Your business may be able to serve this growing market.

What is the climate for the business you want to start? Look for specific trends in your industry. Contact trade and professional associations in your field to determine the demand for the product or service you are considering. These entities can provide information on current acceptable pricing levels and average revenue by category.

For example, if you are interested in developing a hobby into a business, you will want to contact the Hobby Industry Association (HIA) at <www.hobby.org>. HIA conducts a biannual industry survey and can provide specific information regarding household spending patterns and average expenditures by craft category.

The Small Business Administration (SBA) estimates that more than 50 percent of all homes contain an office. The home-based business sector is growing in importance, driven by the advancement of information technology. Perhaps you have a background in computer technology and love mechanical and assembly type work. You want to cash in on this growing market. Your local Business License Department can tell you how many home-based business licenses have been issued in your geographical area. What percentage of the population does the number represent? Has this number increased over the past five years? Your chamber of commerce or Economic Development Department can provide population projections for your area.

If your business idea looks like it has possibilities at this point, look at the customer base for your business. Who is going to buy your product, who will use your service, how much are they going to spend, and how often do they make a purchase?

FINDING YOUR TARGET MARKET

The goal of market research is to find your best customers. Target markets are those individuals or groups most likely to become your customers. They have common characteristics and needs that your business will be able to satisfy. Your goal is to develop a profile of your customers. Gather this information through the study of demographics and psychographics.

The word **demographics** refers to statistical information such as age, sex, ethnic background, education, occupation, income, family status, and geographic location.

- *Population distribution* is one of several factors you will use to help you determine the size and location of the market. Studies show trends such as the shift of more affluent city dwellers to suburban communities.

- *Age distribution* dictates trends. The number of people age 65 and over is increasing, leading to a growing senior market.

- *Sex* is an obvious basis for consumer market analysis. Many traditional buying patterns are changing. The business example, Ace Sporting Goods, must not assume only men will be interested in fly-fishing!

- *Ethnic origin* may indicate product preferences, age distribution, population shifts, and language differences.

- *Family status* has changed in the past decade. Two distinct and new groups have emerged: single people living alone and unmarried people living together. If you are developing a take-out food business, look closely at the family status in your area. Will you be providing family-style meals or individual servings?

- *Education level, occupation, and income* are other demographics to be considered. Education level often points to changes in product preference. People with higher levels of education may have more specialized tastes and higher incomes. Occupation must also be considered as a meaningful criterion for analyzing the market.

Markets are also defined in terms of **psychographics**. These are psychological characteristics of your market and are as important as demographics. In fact, they often give insight into why people buy certain products or use certain services. The study of psychographics looks at lifestyle, personal behavior, self-concept, and buying style.

- *Lifestyle* refers to a person's manner of living. It is a broad category and involves personality characteristics. Lifestyle relates to a customer's activities, interests, and opinions. It reflects how leisure time is spent.

- *Personal behavior* is tied to personal values. The degree of community involvement, political activity, and neighborhood participation reflects the psychological makeup of a person. The degree of cautiousness, skepticism, and ambition reflects on buying patterns.

- *Self-concept* refers to how we see ourselves and hope to be seen by others. The demographics of family size, location, occupation, and income level may indicate an individual would purchase a mini-van, but the psychographics of self-image show that the individual would buy a sports car.

- *Buying style* of your market is critical. How often do they make a purchase? Was there a specific reason for the purchase, or was it an impulse buy? New products are first purchased by individuals who perceive themselves as adventuresome and open-minded.

COLLECTING GENERAL (OR SECONDARY) DATA

Marketing information comes to us from many sources. Depending on the type of information you are seeking, you can access reports published by federal, state, and local governments,

TECH TIP 4

USING THE INTERNET TO RESEARCH YOUR MARKET

You will do yourself a great service by using the Internet to conduct your research. It doesn't matter whether or not you own a computer, have Internet access, or are comfortable delving into this new, worldwide territory. You need to learn, and there are ways to get help. Much of the information you will need can be found in your public or college library, and many libraries are now online. If a library in your area offers Internet access, set up an appointment to sit down at the terminal with a library staff member familiar with business reference sites who will help you find what you need. Another option is to visit your nearest SBA Business Information Center (BIC). There are centers located around the country that provide publications, use of computers, and often, Internet access. The SBA BIC Web address is <www.sba.gov.bi/bics/>.

A few Internet resources to get you started:

- The Bureau of Labor Statistics Consumer Expenditure Survey (CEX) program consists of two surveys—the quarterly interview survey and the Diary survey—that provide information on the buying habits of American consumers, including data on their expenditures, income, and consumer unit (families and single consumers) characteristics. The information can be accessed at <www.bls.gov>.

- Trade and professional associations exist for every type of enterprise. Many have Web sites that detail their services and usually include "how to start a..." information. Gateway to Associations Online is a clearinghouse of hundreds of associations. To run a search, access their site at <www.asaenet.org/gateway/online assocslist.html>. Use <www.businesstown.com> and click on "Associations" for access to listings of trade and professional associations by business category.

- Search engines provide useful ways to obtain information. They send out "spiders" to bring back information containing the words and terms that you provide. Before beginning your research, you will need to develop key words, words that will make it easier for the spiders. For example, if you're interested in starting a fast-food restaurant and want to know current trends, you would use the search terms "fast food restaurant" and "trends." You will also need to be aware of the search format used by the site. Each site has "help" or "how to search" information. Some of the most effective search engines are: <www.google.com> and <www.metasearch.com>.

business directories, independent market research firms, associations, and the census. You might also consider media kits from radio, television, newspapers, and magazines, and articles in magazines and trade journals. The list goes on.

COMPETITION

Direct competition will be a business offering the same product or service to the same market through the same sales channels. **Indirect competition** is a company with the same product or service delivered to the market through different sales channels. For example, an independent bookstore will find direct competition from other bookstores in the geographical area they serve. They will find indirect competition from e-commerce entities such as Amazon.com, eBay, half.com, catalogs specializing in books, nontraditional booksellers such as grocery stores, and gift shops. Keep your eyes and ears open when identifying who your competitors are and where they come from.

Competition can be identified in a number of ways. Look through the business listings in your telephone directory to get an idea of the scope and location of the competition. The chamber of commerce and Economic Development Centers can provide information on business in general and your business area in particular for the region you wish to investigate. Your questionnaires and surveys may have indicated what companies your target market is currently using. Check to see if they belong to trade and professional associations.

Make a list of your competitors and a list of questions you want answered. Plan to visit each competitor and gather your data. Look at their pricing structure. Figure out their share of the total market. You may develop your own evaluation form or make copies of the **Competition Evaluation Form** on page 30. Complete one for each competitor.

When you analyze your evaluations, look for strengths and weaknesses in your competition. You will bring the strengths of the competition to your business and learn from their weaknesses. The weaknesses are your inroads to success. They point the way toward what will be **unique** about your business. They will help you identify what will **benefit your customer**. This information helps you capture your share of the market and may help you take some of the market away from your competitors.

COLLECTING PERSONAL (OR PRIMARY) DATA

After you have developed your idea, examined the trends for your business, and researched the competition and the general market environment, you will want to look more closely at how this information relates to the profitability of your business. Study the nature of the demand. Are your products or services seasonal? Are the products you provide and the services you offer a fad? Is there room for growth? Can you think of related products or services to round out your line?

You will want to talk to people firsthand about how your product or service solves a problem for them. Remember—this is essentially what your business will do for your customer. Now that you have researched your market, you will have a good idea of where to find customers.

If your secondary research indicates that your target market is people in home-based businesses, is there an association representing home-based businesses where you can meet with owners, survey them, and determine their needs? At local office supply and furniture stores, have you noticed an increase in floor space devoted to modular, build-it-yourself computer consoles, and office furniture? Ask the manager how this market is changing. Do buyers need assistance in assembling these kits and setting up their computers? Does the store provide this service and, if so, how much do they charge? How often are they called on to assemble office furniture? Do they set up computers in home offices? Observation and questioning can give you facts regarding demand for and interest in what you are proposing.

You may consider attending a trade show or conference that attracts your potential customers. Your attendance at trade shows will also introduce you to new products and services, give you indications of consumer demand, and allow you to meet with suppliers and vendors. Suppliers and vendors are also a rich source of information.

You might consider test marketing some samples of your product or providing your service free in exchange for a critique and a possible testimonial letter. Don't use friends or relatives; their opinions generally aren't objective! Perhaps you could contact the chamber of commerce or another civic group to see if you could present samples at one of their meetings.

USE OF QUESTIONNAIRES

The most-used and most cost-effective method of gathering information on your target market is through the use of questionnaires. Surveys are an excellent means of determining the response to what you have to offer, and a questionnaire is the most common means of collecting data. Contact the business departments of colleges and universities in your area. Students majoring in marketing may be required to conduct a market study, and your business could fill that need. Your questionnaire results can form a basis for zeroing in on your customers. They can give you feedback regarding the demographics and psychographics of your study group. Be sure you include questions that will generate the information you need.

Reach your market by giving the questionnaire to valid, potential customers, not family and friends. Your questionnaire should be circulated to people who meet the general characteristics you discovered in your secondary research. Surveying people who already have an interest in your product or service will greatly increase the validity of your survey. For example, Ace Sporting Goods is thinking of offering fly-fishing classes and fishing trips. It would be best to distribute the questionnaire in areas where people may have that interest, such as parks and preserves, sporting goods shows, sport associations, and outdoor clubs.

Your market can be contacted through the mail, by telephone, via e-mail, or through focus groups. You may rent a mailing list, use a geographical phone directory, or conduct interviews through clubs and organizations. Display tables at community events are also a good way to make contact with the buying public and gather information.

Plan your strategy for evaluation while you are developing your questionnaire. Use an **address code** on all of your mailings. For example, if your mailing address is 216 Main Street, code your return address by adding Suite 206 or Dept. 304. Suite 206 could be the code for mailings sent to a specific area. If the questionnaires are returned unsigned, you will still be able to have an idea of the geographical area responding. Department 304 could refer to a mailing sent in March of the year 2004. You also can color code your mailings. Print your questionnaires on different colors or different types of paper. Again, you will have a clear picture of the response from a geographical area.

A questionnaire begins with an introductory paragraph that must capture the reader's interest. "I am interested in offering fly-fishing classes and fishing trips and want to be sure that I meet your needs." Get the reader to buy into your business concept; make them feel like a "partner" in this endeavor. They are much more likely to continue reading and complete and return the survey if they feel their input will be valued.

A well-designed questionnaire can gather data covering four main areas:

1. *Interest in your product or service*. Include questions aimed at determining a need for your product or service. Would you be interested in home delivery of gourmet meals? How often would you use this service? How much do you spend in a month on take-out food?

2. *Demographics.* Questions can be structured to show you what kind of people your prospects are. These questions gather the demographic and psychographic information on your market. What is your age range? Do you work away from your home city? Do you shop where you work? Do you shop where you live? What price would you expect to pay for this product? What would you expect to pay for this service?

3. *The means for reaching your market*. Questions can be included that will show you how to reach your customers. What newspapers do you read? What radio stations do you listen to? What TV programs do you watch? Do you use discount coupons? Do you order through catalogs? Do you have an e-mail address? Do you shop over the Internet? Where would you expect to buy this product?

4. *The competition*. Questions about the competition can show you ways in which your company can be unique and can benefit the customer. What company do you currently use? What do you like about their product or service? How can the product or service be improved?

To illustrate how specific data can be gathered, a **Questionnaire Format Worksheet** for Ace Sporting Goods has been included on page 26. The business owner is interested in offering fly-fishing classes and guided fishing trips. Note the questions dealing with potential revenue: Would you be interested in classes on fly-fishing? Would you be interested in fishing trips? How much would you expect to pay for a ten-hour, guided fishing trip? The owner wants to know if the perceived target market is interested, how often they would use the service, and how much they would pay.

To help you develop your own survey, a **Sample Questionnaire for a Product** and a **Sample Questionnaire for a Service** have been included on pages 27 and 28.

To help you with your evaluation, we have included a **Questionnaire Coding Log** on page 29. Note the interest shown by Ace Sporting Goods' target market by groups, dates, and locations. Questionnaires can gather great information about where your market is located and how to reach them.

Identification of the total market and how much it spends is not enough. What percent of the total market has been already been captured by the competition?

PUTTING IT TOGETHER

The key to market research is gathering useful information, information that is timely and reliable. It is an orderly, objective way of learning about the people who will buy your product or use your service. A **Target Market Worksheet** has been included on pages 31 and 32 for your use in defining your market. Notice how Ace Sporting Goods has condensed the information gathered through use of questionnaires, interviews, and mailing lists to get a composite of the customer base.

A **Market Research Worksheet** has been included on page 33 to show you how you can translate the results of your research into a plan for action. Analysis of the findings in terms of potential revenue is included at the bottom of the example.

Remember that marketing is a dynamic process. Customers move, lifestyles change, and income levels vary. To work effectively, market research must occur continuously throughout the lifetime of your business. Always be alert for new competition, new products and services, population shifts, and new trends.

Stepping Along

As you work your way through the next chapters, keep track of your expenses for the worksheets in Appendix B. Chapters 16 and 17 will explain where amounts should be entered and how to arrive at the totals.

Questionnaire Format Worksheet for Ace Sporting Goods

Date: _____ Location: _____

(Demographic and psychographic information)

Please circle answers:

Sex/status: Male   Female   Single   Married   Other

Age: 18 to 25   26 to 35   36 to 45   46 and over

Your occupation/profession: _____

Do you enjoy outdoor activities? Yes_____ No_____

Do you enjoy fishing? Yes_____ No_____

(Information to determine interest and to learn about the competition)

Have you ever been fly-fishing? Yes_____ No_____

If yes:

    a) What did you think of the experience? _____

    b) Where did you go? _____

    c) Were instructors/guides present? _____

    d) Would you be interested in classes on fly-fishing? _____

    e) Would you be interested in fishing trips? _____

    f) How much would you expect to pay for a ten-hour, guided fishing trip? _____

If no:

    a) Would you be interested in fishing lessons? _____

    b) Would you be interested in rental equipment? _____

    c) Would you be interested in free viewing of instructional sports videos in our store? _____

(Information on reaching the potential market)

Do you use discount coupons? Yes_____ No_____

What newspapers do you read? _____

What radio station do you listen to? _____

Have you heard of Ace Sporting Goods? Yes_____ No_____

Thank you for your response. The following information is helpful to my study but is optional:

Name: _____

Address: _____

City/State/Zip: _____

Phone: _____

Sample Questionnaire: Product

I am developing a new product and am contacting a few people in your neighborhood for an important and quick survey. I hope you will take a moment to tell me how you feel about board games.

1. Do you play any board games? Yes_____ No_____ (If no, please go to #7)

2. What is your favorite board game?

   Backgammon ____   Checkers ____   Pictionary® ____   Life® ____

   Clue® ____   Monopoly® ____   Sorry® ____   Other ____

3. On the average, how often do you play board games?

   Less than once per month ____Once per month ____

   Twice per month ____   Once per week ____   More than once per week ____

4. Would you consider playing a new board game about the stock market?

   Yes_____   No_____   Maybe_____   I don't know_____

5. How much would you pay for a board game about the stock market?

   $6.00 to $10.00 ____ $10.01 to $15.00 ____ $15.01 to $20.00 ____   Over $20.00 ____

6. What is the first word that comes to mind when you think of the stock market? _____

   _____

7. On the average, how many hours of television do you watch per week?

   Less than one hour ____   1 to 3 hours ____   3 to 6 hours ____

   6 to 9 hours ____   9 hours or more ____

8. Do you clip coupons from the newspaper? Yes_____ No_____

9. What radio station do you listen to most often? _____

10. What is your age group?

    18 to 24 years ____   25 to 34 years ____   35 to 44 years ____

    45 to 54 years ____   Over 55 years ____

11. What is your average household income?

    Under $25,000 ___ $25,000 to $45,000 ___ $45,000 to $60,000 ___   Over $60,000 ___

   Thank you for your response. The following information is helpful to my study but is optional:

Name: _____

Address: _____

City/State/Zip: _____

Phone: _____

Sample Questionnaire: Service

I am developing a new product and contacting a few people in your neighborhood for an important and quick survey. I hope you will take a moment to tell me how you feel about take-out food.

1. Do you order take-out food? Yes_____ No_____

2. What is your favorite take-out food?

   Pizza _____   Deli food _____   Mexican food _____

   Burgers _____   Chinese food _____   Other _____

3. On the average, how often do you order take-out food?

   Less than once a month _____   Once a month _____

   Twice a month _____   Once a week _____   More than once a week _____

4. Would you consider full-course take-out meals?   Yes_____   No_____

5. Would you consider home-delivered meals?   Yes_____   No_____

6. How much would you be willing to pay for a full-course, home-delivered meal?

   $10.00 _____ $15.00 _____ $17.50 _____ $20.00 _____

7. What is the first word that comes to mind when you think of full-course, home-delivered meals? _____

8. On a scale of one to five, with five signifying very important, please rank the following items as they relate to your feelings about take-out food: (please circle)

Containers	1	2	3	4	5
Combinations of foods offered	1	2	3	4	5
Temperature when delivered	1	2	3	4	5
Taste	1	2	3	4	5
Delivery time	1	2	3	4	5

9. Do you clip coupons from the newspaper? Yes_____ No_____

10. What newspaper do you read? _____

11. What is your age group?

    18 to 24 years _____   25 to 34 years _____   35 to 44 years _____

    45 to 54 years _____   Over 55 years _____

12. What is your average household income?

    Under $25,000 ___ $25,000 to $45,000 ___ $45,000 to $60,000 ___   Over $60,000 ___

Thank you for your response. The following information is helpful to my study but is optional:

Name: _____

Address: _____

City/State/Zip: _____

Phone: _____

Questionnaire Coding Log for Ace Sporting Goods

Code	Date	Number Sent	Destination/ Recipient	Response Rate	Evaluation
Blue paper	2/04	500	Wed. 10 AM to 1 PM Shoppers at Fisherman's Wharf Mall	20 interviews 36 returned by mail	6 follow-up for classes/trips 30 follow-up
Yellow paper	2/07	500	Sat. 10 AM to 1 PM Shoppers at Fisherman's Wharf Mall	52 interviews 160 returned by mail	20 follow-up for classes/ trips 52 follow-up
Dept. 204	2/04	1,000	Mailing list #132 18-35 yrs. Live in 10-mile radius $35,000 average income	3/04 120 returned	26 follow-up for classes/ trips
Suite 204	2/04	500	Mailing list—local university students	3/04 287 returned	158 follow-up for classes/ trips
Dept 304	3/04	1,000	Mailing list #132 repeat rental	4/04 261 returned	57 follow-up for classes/ trips

By analyzing the questionnaire results, the owner of Ace Sporting Goods can determine that the Saturday shoppers at the Fisherman's Wharf Mall are more responsive. The questionnaire can be analyzed to get a composite of demographic information. The mailing to university students got a good response, and this group will likely form a good part of the target market. The response to the 2/04 and 3/04 mailings indicates the value of repeat mailings to the same group. Through the mailings, the business owner has developed his own mailing list of names of 349 individuals interested in fishing trips and classes.

Competition Evaluation Form

1. Competitor: _Smith Sporting Goods_

2. Location: _724 University Drive, Blair, NY 07682_

3. Products or services offered: _Full line of sports equipment with emphasis on golf_

4. Methods of distribution: _Retail sales, catalog_

5. Image: _Blue and white colors used in decor and uniforms_

   Packaging: _Plastic sales bags with logo_

   Promotional materials: _Baseball caps and T-shirts with name and logo_

   Methods of advertising: _KLXY radio ads, flyers-mail, Sunday supplement-newspaper_

   Quality of product or service: _Major brands, excellent sales staff_

6. Pricing structure: _100% mark-up on golf items, 75% mark-up on other merchandise_

7. Business history and current performance: _In current location for five years_

8. Market share (number, types, and location of customers): _One of two sporting goods stores in town, has high school and university trade_

9. Strengths (the strengths of the competition become your strengths): _Knowledgeable sales staff, established contacts with local golf courses and associations_

10. Weaknesses (looking at the weaknesses of the competition can help you find ways of being unique and benefiting the customer):

    - Does not offer classes or sports clinics

    - Closed Sundays

    - Does not stock fishing gear

    - Does not sponsor a youth team

Note: A Competition Evaluation Worksheet should be made for each competitor. Keep these records and update them. It pays to continue to rate your competition throughout the lifetime of your business.

Target Market Worksheet for Ace Sporting Goods

1. Who are my customers?

   Profile: _Results from questionnaires, interviews, mailing lists_

   _____

   Economic level: _52% college graduates   25% management_

   29% professionals   79% own or are buying homes

   Psychological make-up (lifestyle): _Value reliability of merchandise (guarantee)_

   Outgoing, athletic, like to travel

   Age range: _Average age = 32_

   Sex: _Male = 57%   Female = 43%_

   Income level: _Average household income = $58,000_

   69% income from two wage earners

   Buying habits: _Use coupons. Quality and reliability more important than cost._

   _____

2. Where are my customers located?

   Where do they live: _Within city limits of Blair, NY_

   _____

   Where do they work: _62% commute 20 to 35 miles, one way   24% work in Blair_

   14% retired

   Where do they shop: _32% of the commuters shop where they work and arrive home_

   after 6 PM

3. Projected size of the market:

   Target group represents 20% of total population within city limits.

   Total population = 52,000; 20% = 10,400

   _____

   Projections indicate that I can serve 10% of the targeted group for a

   customer base of 1,040.

   _____

Target Market Worksheet for Ace Sporting Goods, continued

4. What are the customers needs?

    a. Sports instruction. Opportunity to "try" equipment prior to purchase.

    b. Have interest in fishing, especially fly-fishing. Currently no store stocks a full product line of fishing gear.

    c. Due to commute time and number of two-income families, store should be open at times convenient to the consumer.

    d. Business commitment to the community.

    e. Knowledgeable staff.

    f. Reliability of merchandise.

5. How can I meet those needs?

    a. Offer rental equipment. Offer sports clinics and classes. Offer "how-to" sports videos for in-store viewing. If demand is present, will add videos to product line.

    b. Stock full line of fishing gear. Provide in-store demonstration.

    c. Will open on Sunday. Will stay open until 9 PM on Thursday and Friday.

    d. Sponsor youth sports team.

    e. Training program for employees: sales techniques, customer service, sports knowledge.

    f. Offer in-store guarantee on all merchandise.

6. What is unique about my business?

    Only sporting goods store in the county to stock and specialize in fishing equipment.

    Only store to provide an area for viewing sport instructional videos.

    In-store guarantee on all equipment.

Market Research Worksheet for Ace Sporting Goods

Questions	Information Source	Results	Effect on Plan
Would you be interested in fly-fishing lessons?	Mail list—27% response Questionnaire: Mall—Wednesday Mall—Saturday	241 interested 36 72	Expect 10% commitment or 35 class registrations. Offer one class Sat. 10 AM One class Wed. 10 AM
Would you be interested in guided fishing trips?	Mail list—27% response Questionnaire: Mall—Wednesday Mall—Saturday	241 interested 36 72	Expect 5% commitment or 17 class registrations. Offer one Sat. fishing trip limited to ten people.
How much would you expect to pay for a ten-hour fishing trip to the mountains?	Mail list—27% response Questionnaire: Mall—Wednesday Mall—Saturday	Average $65 (241 responded) avg. $45 avg. $55	Provide ten-hr. guided trip to Carson River for $55/person. (average of all responses)
What is your age group?	Mail list response Questionnaire: Mall—Wednesday Mall—Saturday	majority 25–34 35–44 35–44	Most responses fall within 25–34 range—average age is 32. Will use this factor in future mail list rental.

The results of direct mail, telemarketing, questionnaires, and networking can be translated and put into action on the Market Research Worksheet. For example, 349 people indicated an interest in guided fishing trips. It is realistic to expect 5 percent or 17 people to actually register for the trip. The results indicate that $55 is the average amount registrants would expect to pay for a ten-hour guided fishing trip to the mountains. After considering salaries for two guides, rental of a 12-person van, insurance, fishing permits, and equipment, financial projections may indicate that the trip would have to include ten people at a charge of $60 per person in order to break even. If Ace Sporting Goods wants to make a profit, more people could be included, and costs may be cut. The market has already indicated they will not pay much over $55. The store may consider breaking even with the hope of generating future equipment sales. One trip could be scheduled to test the response. The Market Research Worksheet helps you to put into perspective the information you have gathered on your customers.

CHAPTER 4

CHOOSING A BUSINESS NAME

Now that you have decided what your business will be, you must choose your business name. If you purchase a franchise, that decision will be made for you. If you purchase an existing business, you may want to keep the same name or change to a new one. If you develop your own business, you will also have to develop a business name.

• • • • •

The name you select explains who you are, identifies what sets you apart in the marketplace, and determines how you are perceived. This is an extremely important decision that takes careful consideration and research. Your business name is not something you will want to change; it will be your identification for many years. A name change can also be expensive; office supplies, marketing materials, signage, directory listings, and memberships are a few of the items that would have to be changed if you change your business name.

Before deciding on your business name, consider the following factors:

- ***Choose a name that has meaning for your target market***. Identify three to five personality traits or benefits that make your company special. These are the reasons for customers to decide to choose your business over that of the competition. Some examples are peace of mind, economy, friendliness, and innovation. Focus on the qualities your target customers appreciate. Make up a list of words or phrases that come to mind and are associated with the trait. Could this word be used as a business name? For example, the California high-tech company, Oracle, implies visionary power.

- *Avoid cute and clever names*. While unique names are usually easier to remember and may grab the attention of the consumer, the general rule is that they may not convey a business-like image. This would include names that play on words or have double meanings. Many wholesalers will not view the business as legitimate, even though you may be running a full-scale operation. Of course, there are exceptions to every rule. "Nice to Be Kneaded" is a good name for a massage center and "Franks for the Memory" is a memorable name for a snack bar featuring hot dogs! The bottom line is, will it attract buyers from your target market?

- *Use a descriptive name to advertise your product or service*. The consumer who sees your name will immediately associate it with the product or service you provide. For example, "Anderson's Financial Services," lets the consumer know the service being provided. "Anderson and Associates" does not. While conducting business, we all collect business cards. Later, when we look through the cards, we often haven't a clue as to the nature of a business if the name is not descriptive. Get some advertising mileage out of your business name.

- *Try not to have the name be restrictive*. Select a name that can become an umbrella for future products and services. If your business has been established to bring trendy products to the marketplace, avoid using a name that keys into a product with a short life span. It is better to give the business an umbrella name that covers a range of anticipated products and then choose clever names for the individual products. Don't make your business name so specific that you cannot expand your business without the name losing its descriptive quality. It is not always easy to anticipate the directions your company may take but try to project your future growth. It is difficult to change your business name once it is established. You risk losing the customer base and the goodwill you have built.

- *Think about how the name looks*. Sometimes a name becomes memorable because it can be paired with an effective visual image. For example, Apple Computer's logo is a rainbow apple with a bite taken out of it. Turtle Wax visually supports its name with the image of a hard-shelled turtle.

- *Plan for all uses of your business name*. Consider how your name could be abbreviated. Long names will not fit on computer generated mailing labels. If you are considering international trade, research the translation of your name into the languages of other countries.

- *Consider alphabetical listings in directories*. It is to your advantage to be listed closer to the A's than to the Z's. You have a captive audience through your directory listings. Consumers and clients do not look through business and professional directories unless they are trying to locate products or services. They generally look through the first few listings when deciding whom to call.

- *Check the white and yellow pages of area phone directories*. Study how other businesses use the words you may be considering. Usually, there will be many businesses with names starting with your city's name, the name of a regional landmark, and common terms such as "quality." When business names begin to look generic, potential customers tend to overlook or forget them.

- *Use your own name*. If you are already well-respected in your community or field of business, you may want to use your own personal name as part of your business name. It may give you a head start in the business world. If you use your full legal name, you may not have to file a DBA ("Doing Business As," see Chapter 11). Some states require you to register if only your last name is used in the business name. If you have a common name, you may still wish to file the DBA for protection of the name in reference to your business. For example, if your name were Jane Smith, you might register "Jane Smith Contracting" because Jane Smith is a common name.

Note: If you are thinking about using your own name, consider your long-range plan for the business. When you sell the company, you may also sell the business name…your name! The new owner may not conduct business in the same manner you do, and you may risk losing your good name.

TECH TIP 5
DOMAIN NAME CHOICE, USAGE, AND REGISTRATION

You can get extra mileage out of your business name when you also register it as your domain name. For example, when Sandy Stelter, a California-based professional organizer, was developing SOS-Strategic Organizing Solutions, she registered the domain name sos2day. Her e-mail address consists of her user name and domain name; <sandy@sos2day.com>. You can see how this has made it easy for clients to reach her and given added exposure to the business name.

Even though you may not be planning to develop a Web site as part of your marketing strategy, you will want to research the possiblity of using your company name or brand identity as part of your domain name. You can check name availability and registration at <www.networksolutions.com>.

InterNIC is a registered service mark of the U.S. Department of Commerce. It is licensed to the Internet Corporation for Assigned Names and Numbers (ICANN), the entity that operates the Web site <www.internic.com>. This site was established to provide the public with information regarding Internet domain name registration services and is updated frequently. The site provides a list of ICANN accredited registrars that are currently taking domain registrations.

NARROWING THE SEARCH

At this point, you will have narrowed your list of potential names. Let the list rest for a few days. Then review it and delete names that do not fit the image of your business. Think about how you would react to the various names if you were a prospective client or customer. Share the list with family, friends, and associates. Ask which name best communicates what your business is about. Usually one name rises to the surface. Take your top three choices and check their availability.

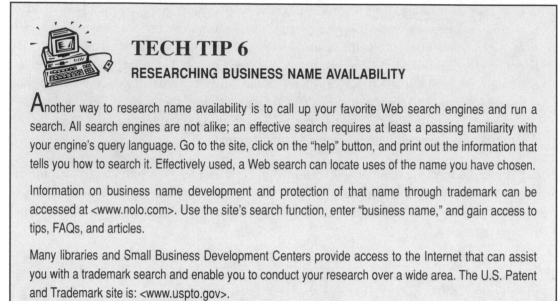

TECH TIP 6
RESEARCHING BUSINESS NAME AVAILABILITY

Another way to research name availability is to call up your favorite Web search engines and run a search. All search engines are not alike; an effective search requires at least a passing familiarity with your engine's query language. Go to the site, click on the "help" button, and print out the information that tells you how to search it. Effectively used, a Web search can locate uses of the name you have chosen.

Information on business name development and protection of that name through trademark can be accessed at <www.nolo.com>. Use the site's search function, enter "business name," and gain access to tips, FAQs, and articles.

Many libraries and Small Business Development Centers provide access to the Internet that can assist you with a trademark search and enable you to conduct your research over a wide area. The U.S. Patent and Trademark site is: <www.uspto.gov>.

NAME AVAILABILITY

Be sure the name you are considering for your business is available for use. There are a few horror stories about businesses who did not check their name's availability and later discovered the name legally belonged to someone else. To the best of your ability, determine that the name is not already in use. Check through the telephone directories in the public library. City and county business licensing offices can help you check for local use.

Trademarked names can be found in the Trademark Directories in state and federal depositories and at many county and university libraries.

Each state has an office responsible for the registration of names of businesses incorporated within that state, out-of-state corporations qualified to do business in the state, and names that have been registered or reserved by other corporations. Generally this office falls under the jurisdiction of the Secretary of State. Even if you are not considering forming a corporation as your legal structure, it is to your advantage to use this resource in researching the availability of your business name. If you choose to incorporate later, you will want to use your current name as your corporate name since it will be associated with your product or service. Most often, name infringement does not become a problem until you become visible in the marketplace and create a threat to the business that feels it has prior claim to the name. The time you spend in researching name availability can end up being very cost-effective.

Note: Do not use the word "corporation" in your business name unless you have chosen and registered that form of legal structure. Smith Corporation may sound larger and more established than Smith Company, but unless the company is a legitimate corporation, the use of the term will be illegal.

Choosing a business name is a very personal decision and not one to be rushed into. Take time to choose a name that projects the image you desire for your company. Choose one that is memorable, available, and allows your company to grow.

CHAPTER 5

CHOOSING A BUSINESS LOCATION

Your choice of location should be made early on in your plans to start a business. The first thing to consider is whether the location you choose is right for your type of business. What has your study of demographics and your market identification shown you? Base your decision on the type of products and services you provide and your target market rather than on your personal convenience. Your most important consideration in choosing a location is your ability to satisfy your target market. Retail stores and restaurants have to be located where customers can reach them easily and safely. Service businesses such as exterminators and landscapers who go to a client's site can be more flexible in location choice. Manufacturers may find locations remote from the customer base to be the most cost-effective because of availability of raw materials, availability of labor, taxes, regulations, and overhead costs. You may have discovered that your market expects to order via fax or over the Internet. Make sure the site you choose is appropriate for your market.

· · · · ·

LOCATION EVALUATION

One of the most effective ways to evaluate a location is to do a map analysis. Draw a map of the area where you wish to locate. Have a copy shop run off some duplicates and one transparency. On the transparency, indicate the location sites available within your target area and mark them with a colored pen or assign each of them a number. You will be coding information onto the duplicate maps. You will be able to place the transparency over the coded map in order to get a feeling for each site. For instance, take one of the duplicate maps to the police department. Ask about crime rates. Shade the high crime area on your map. When you place the transparency over the shaded duplicate, you will be able to see if any of your potential locations fall within high crime areas.

Market.   On another duplicate map, shade in the areas where your target market lives, shops, or works. Again use the transparency overlay to see if your customers will be able to reach you easily. Retail stores and restaurants have to be located near their customers. Is there freeway access, good traffic flow, and adequate parking? Customers are concerned about safety. Can they reach your place of business with a feeling of security? Your crime rate map will show if they have to pass through any high crime areas on the way to your establishment. Customers' trips to your business should be pleasant. Drive and walk the routes your customers will have to take and get a feeling for the neighborhood.

Competition.   Find out where your competition is located and try to determine their sales volume. Most businesses try to distance themselves from the competition. However, some types of businesses, such as restaurants and auto dealerships, seem to have great success when clustered together. Professional services tend to locate within an area around a main support facility such as doctors' offices near a hospital and attorneys' offices near the courthouse. The consumer expects to find such services in these areas.

Sources of supply.   Manufacturing companies may need to locate close to suppliers and will have to consider the transportation, labor and power costs, tax base, and zoning regulations of a site. If certain raw materials are crucial to the manufacture of your products, you may need to locate close to your suppliers in order to reduce freight costs and delivery times.

Labor force.   Another location consideration is the availability of employees. As your business grows, it becomes increasingly important to have a pool of qualified potential employees. Some areas do not have an adequate group of people to form a labor pool. The prevailing wage rate in the area may be out of line with competitors' rates in other areas. The local chamber of commerce will be able to give you wage and labor statistics for the location you are considering.

Cost.   Office space for minimal rent is not always the best reason for choosing a site. There usually is a reason why the rent is low. Find out why the space is available, how long it has been vacant, and the history of the previous tenants. If there has been a frequent turnover in occupancy, it may be considered a "bad location." The chamber of commerce can give you information on average square footage costs for your area. Check with the local zoning commission regarding any rezoning being planned for the surrounding area. Take a walk around the area. Does the location project the image that you have for your business?

Before beginning a search for the perfect location, outline your present requirements and project your future needs. If you plan to grow your business, will the location allow for that expansion? It is often difficult to relocate a successful business without losing some of your customer base. A **Location Analysis Worksheet** has been included on pages 44 and 45 to help you evaluate the locations you will be considering.

SHOPPING CENTER

You may consider locating your business in a minimall or shopping center. These sites are preplanned as merchandising units. On-site parking is available, which makes it easy for your customer to drive in, park, and shop. You can take advantage of the foot traffic that is drawn to the area by other stores.

There may be some disadvantages, however. You will be a part of a merchant team. You will be expected to pay your share of the site budget, which may include items such as building, landscaping, parking lot maintenance, co-op advertising, and promotional activities. You may have to keep regular store hours, maintain your windows and premises in a prescribed manner, and conform to established display guidelines. In larger shopping centers, you may be required to pay a percentage of your gross sales to the developers or mall owners in addition to the rent or lease payments.

Look carefully at the history and health of anchor tenants in a shopping center setting. Few small businesses are themselves "destination locations." They must count on anchor tenants to draw traffic, and the failure or relocation of the anchor tenant can have a serious impact on the small business.

BUSINESS INCUBATORS

Business incubators are especially suited to light manufacturing and service businesses that do not require large facilities. To reduce overhead costs for new businesses, the incubator program offers a number of services to tenants through a centralized resource station. Usually included in the tenant package are receptionist services, telephone response and conference call capability, Internet access, maintenance of building and grounds, conference room facilities that may have teleconferencing capability, and access to shipping and receiving services such as UPS and FedEx. Other services may include complete clerical services at a nominal charge. Incubator facilities are targeted toward new and smaller companies and offer lower overhead costs during the start-up stage. Many sites can be industry-specific such as software development incubators or light manufacturing/assembly facilities. Contact your chamber of commerce, Economic Development Department, or local SBDC to identify incubators in your area.

TECH TIP 7
BUSINESS INCUBATORS

The National Business Incubator Association maintains a Web site that provides a clearinghouse for information on the business incubator industry. Links are provided to an information resource center and topical articles. The site can be accessed at <www.nbia.org/>.

ENTERPRISE ZONES

We have been hearing a great deal about the advantages of locating in enterprise zones as communities work toward redeveloping depressed areas. Companies located in these zones can take advantage of significant tax incentives and marketing programs. Enterprise zone communities are committed to attracting new business investment and offer such incentives as reduction or elimination of local permit and construction-related fees and faster processing of plans and permits. Information on enterprise zones in your area can be obtained through the Department of Commerce, the SBA, and the local chamber of commerce.

LEASE PROVISIONS

A lease is a binding legal agreement between a landlord (the lessor) and a tenant (the lessee). It details the rights and obligations of each party. Signing a lease is a serious financial transaction; before signing any lease agreement, have the document reviewed by an attorney or a Service Corps of Retired Executives (SCORE) or SBDC consultant familiar with lease provisions. Following are some major considerations that must be understood and resolved to your satisfaction before a lease is signed:

Rent.   How much is the rent payment and how is it computed? Various methods can be used to determine the amount to be paid.

- Flat monthly payment that remains the same throughout the term of the lease.

- Set percentage of your gross sales. Note that percentage is based on gross sales without consideration for your expenses, draw, etc.

- Sliding percentage of your gross sales; the percentage varies at different increments of sales volume.

- Combination of set minimum payment and a percentage of your gross sales.

Term.   How long will the lease be in effect? Do you have the option to renew?

Sublet.   Do you have the right to rent out unused space to another party? This could be valuable if you find that you have leased too much space. You may have a dry-cleaning business and the addition of a tailor and/or an on-site shoe-repair facility would make you a one-stop-shop for your customers. Will your growth be limited by the terms of your lease?

Leasehold improvements.   Who is responsible for painting, remodeling, and other initial improvements? Who will pay for the improvements? Who will own the improvements, once made? Is the building up to code? For example, the Americans with Disabilities Act requires that commercial, nonresidential property in which public goods or services are provided be free of all architectural barriers. For more information contact <www.ada.gov>.

Insurance.   What insurance does the landlord provide? What coverage are you required to have? The landlord usually covers for accidents and damages that may occur in the common area. You may be required to have insurance to cover accidents, fire, theft, etc. in the leased area.

Security deposit.   Most landlords require a sum of money held during the term of the lease or occupancy to be used for any damage, lost rent, etc. This can be a sizable amount and must be included in your budget.

Termination.   Under what conditions does either party have a right to terminate the lease agreement?

Restrictions.   Are there any restrictions on the part of the landlord, the city, the zoning commission, or any agency regarding the use of the property?

Be sure you understand all of the provisions of the lease and that they fit with your plans for the site and your business. Be sure to transfer information regarding security deposit, lease-hold improvements, and rent to your cash flow statement.

TECH TIP 8
WEB-BASED INFORMATION FOR LOCATION AND LEASE CONSIDERATIONS

CCH Incorporated is a provider of business, legal, and tax information. The CCH Business Owner's Toolkit™, at <www.toolkit.cch.com>, contains a wealth of information covering all areas of business development and operation. Utilize the Google link to search "Location" and "Lease" via the CCHToolkit option. You will be able to access articles such as "Determining Your Facility Needs," "Leasing Office Space," "Lease Provisions," and "Should You Buy or Lease a Facility."

Another good resource is the Nolo Press site at <www.nolo.com>. Enter "Location" at the search function for access to articles and worksheets.

Before signing a lease, make sure that you understand all of its terms and provisions. It is a good idea to have a lease for business property reviewed by a professional. Phone the Legal Referral Service listed in the yellow pages of your phone directory or access the following Web sites to locate a professional in your area to review your lease:

Service Corps of Retired Executives (SCORE):   <www.score.org>

Small Business Development Center (SBDC):   <www.asbdc-us.org>

Location Analysis Worksheet for Ace Sporting Goods

1. Address: __271 Adams Street, Blair, NY 07682__

2. Name, address, phone number of realtor/contact person: __James Jones Century Realty,__
   __622 Mason Street, Blair, NY 07682, 555-7093__

3. Square footage/cost: __Retail shop space of 2,000 sq. ft. @$2.50/sq. ft., 50 ft. of__
   __window display area fronting on high foot traffic area. Classroom area in back__
   __of store.__

4. History of location: __Previous occupant: retail clothing outlet occupied site for seven__
   __years. Moved to larger store. Site vacant for two months.__

5. Location in relation to target market: __Primary retail and business sector for Blair. Draws__
   __customers from 20-mile radius.__

6. Traffic patterns for customers: __Bus stop—1/2 block; easy access from First Avenue__
   __and Main Street; traffic lights at crosswalks; customer merchandise pick-up area__
   __access in alley behind store.__

7. Traffic patterns for suppliers: __Alley access for deliveries.__

8. Availability of parking (include diagram): __Diagonal parking: 12 spaces in front of store;__
   __parking lot one block away.__

9. Crime rate for the area: __24-hour security in business sector; active neighborhood__
   __watch in surrounding residential area.__

10. Quality of public services (e.g., police, fire protection): __Police station: six blocks; fire station:__
    __two miles; fire alarm, sprinkler system, smoke alarms in place.__

11. Notes from walking tour of the area: __Homes well tended on north side; apartment__
    __house two blocks south—two abandoned cars; debris piled in vacant lot—three__
    __blocks east of site.__

Location Analysis Worksheet for Ace Sporting Goods, continued

12. Neighboring shops and local business climate: Dry cleaning/shoe repair; restaurant
    Good foot traffic; Association of Business Owners oversees the area.

13. Zoning regulations: Commercial

14. Adequacy of utilities (get information from utility company representatives):   Six phone lines into
    site; two bathrooms in store; city water, sewer, 220-wiring in place. No gas available.

15. Availability of raw materials/supplies: UPS, common carriers—daily delivery.

16. Availability of labor force: Temporary employment agency in business center.
    University five miles away; high school eight miles away.

17. Labor rate of pay for the area: $7.50/hr. average for store sales people; $12.00/hr. for
    store manager; $7.50/hr. for instructors/guides.

18. Housing availability for employees: Apartments and single family homes available in
    ten mile radius. Average rental for two bedroom = $600; average sale for two
    bedroom home = $125,000.

19. Tax rates (state, county, income, payroll, special assessments):   State income tax = 7%;
    state sales tax = 6.5%

20. Evaluation of site in relation to competition: Smith Sporting Goods: Smith Sporting Goods;
    six miles away, has better parking, located closer to university and high school.
    This location is housed in a minimall and offers more adjacent businesses, has a
    lower square footage cost and has more foot traffic than the location of Smith
    Sporting Goods.

CHAPTER 6

DEVELOPING A HOME-BASED BUSINESS

One of the fastest growing markets in the United States is the home-based business. It's interesting to note that one in four businesses located in an office or industrial area started in the home, including such well-known companies as Mary Kay, Hershey, Hewlett Packard, Lillian Vernon, Ford, and Apple.

It has been estimated that more than 32 million Americans are self-employed and working at home. This does not count those who are doing so on a part-time basis while holding a "regular" job. Part-time self-employed home workers number an additional 1,000,000+.

Home-based businesses span a wide range of occupations and industries. One multistate survey conducted by a team of university-based researchers found that the top five occupations were marketing/sales (24 percent), contracting (15 percent), mechanical/transportation (13 percent), services (12 percent), and professional/technical (12 percent). Other studies yield varying results, but all indicate that home businesses represent a wide range of occupations and industries.

The trend toward home-based business has occurred for several reasons. The advent of the electronic age with its computers, fax machines, copiers, and other office technology has made it possible for almost every family to start a business from home. Job insecurities and layoffs have forced white-collar workers to pile out of corporations. Many of these displaced middle-management people have taken their skills home and translated them into viable businesses run from their home offices. The trend toward home-based business has also been impacted by economic considerations such as eliminating rent for an outside business location and utilizing home-office deductions. As an additional bonus, having a home-based business has allowed parents to stay home with their families and addressed elder care and parental leave without added costs.

Home-based businesses can be very successful. They can also turn into disasters or, at the very least, unproductive semi-attempts at dabbling at business. In order to help you get off to a good start, we have devoted this chapter to some of the most important considerations that will contribute to the success of your home-based business.

HOW DOES A HOME-BASED BUSINESS DIFFER FROM OTHER BUSINESSES?

With the exception of the location, a home-based business is the same as any other business. All other issues including the need for a strong marketing plan and sufficient funding apply. The determining factor that favors operating out of your home will be that marketing your business will not be adversely affected by the physical location of your business. Some advantages are lower overhead and work flexibility, while some disadvantages are a sense of feeling isolated and the need for self-discipline.

DO YOU QUALIFY FOR A HOME-OFFICE DEDUCTION?

To qualify for a home-office deduction for the business use of your home, you must use that portion of your home *exclusively* and *regularly* for your trade or business, and it must be your *principal place of business*.

- *Exclusive use*. To qualify under the exclusive use test, you must use a specific area of your home *only* for your trade or business. The area used for business can be a room or other separately identifiable space. The space does not need to be marked off by a permanent partition. You do not meet the requirements of the exclusive use test if you use the area in question both for business and personal purposes. Exceptions apply if you use part of your home for the storage of inventory or product samples, or as a childcare facility.

- *Regular use*. To qualify under the regular use test, you must use a specific area of your home for business on a continuing basis. You do not meet the test if your business use of the area is only occasional or incidental, even if you do not use that area for any other purpose.

- *Trade or business use.* To qualify under the trade or business use test, you must use part of your home in connection with a trade or business. If you use your home for a profit-seeking activity that is not a trade or business, you cannot take a deduction for its business use.

- *Principal place of business.* You can have more than one business location, including your home, for a single trade or business. To qualify to deduct the expenses for the business use of your home, it must be your principal place of business for that trade or business.

Your home office will qualify as your principal place of business for deducting expenses for its use if

- you use it exclusively and regularly for administrative or management activities of your trade or business and

- you have no other fixed location where you conduct substantial administrative or management activities of your trade or business. Some of these activities are:
    - Billing customers, clients, or patients.
    - Keeping books and records.
    - Ordering supplies.
    - Setting up appointments.
    - Forwarding orders or writing reports.

The following administrative or management activities performed at other locations **will not disqualify** your home office as your principal place of business.

- You have others conduct your administrative or management activities at locations other than your home. (For example, another company does your billing from its place of business.)

- You conduct administrative or management activities at places that are not fixed locations of your business, such as in a car or hotel room.

- You occasionally conduct minimal administrative or management activities at a fixed location outside your home.

- You conduct substantial nonadministrative or nonmanagement business activities at a fixed location outside your home. (For example, you meet with or provide services to customers, clients, or patients at a fixed location of the business outside your home.)

- You have suitable space to conduct administrative or management activities outside your home, but choose to use your home office for those activities instead.

Other tests. The rules for *principal place of business* will not affect the other tests you must meet to claim the expenses for the business use of your home. You still must use the business part of your home both **exclusively** and **regularly** for your trade or business. If you are an employee, the business use of your home must be for **the convenience of your employer.** In addition, your deduction may be limited if your gross income from the business use of your home is less than your total business expenses.

Place to meet patients, clients, or customers. If you meet or deal with patients, clients, or customers in your home in the normal course of your business, even though you also carry on business at another location, you can deduct your expenses for the part of your home used exclusively and regularly for business if you meet the following tests:

- You physically meet with patients, clients, or customers on your premises. The part of your home you use exclusively and regularly for these meetings does not have to be your principal place of business.

- The use of your home is substantial and integral to the conduct of your business.

Note: Using your home for occasional meetings and telephone calls will not qualify you for a home-office deduction.

Separate structure. You can deduct expenses (subject to the deduction limit) for a separate free-standing structure, such as a studio, garage, or barn, if you use it exclusively and regularly for your business. The structure does not have to be your principal place of business or a place where you meet patients, clients, or customers.

CALCULATING YOUR DEDUCTION

Once you determine that you meet the tests that qualify you for a home-office deduction, it's possible to figure how much you can deduct. You will need to determine the percentage of your home used for business and the limit on the deduction.

Business Percentage

To determine the deduction for the business use of your home, you have to compare the size of the part of your home that you use for business to your whole house and find the percentage that is being used for business. The following are two commonly used methods for figuring the percentage:

- Divide the area (length multiplied by the width) used for business by the total area of your home.

- If the rooms in your home are all about the same size, you can divide the number of rooms used for business by the total number of rooms in your home.

For example, if your home measures 2,000 square feet and you are using 500 square feet for your home office, you will be able to deduct 25 percent of expenses such as rent, mortgage, interest, depreciation, taxes, insurance, utilities, repairs, etc. There are also other issues to be considered pertaining to the legalities of deductions. You will have to spend some time familiarizing yourself with them.

Part-Year Use

You cannot deduct expenses for the business use of your home incurred during any part of the year you did not use your home for business purposes. Consider only your expenses for the business use portion of the year.

Deduction Limit

If your gross income from the business use of your home equals or exceeds your total business expenses (including depreciation), you can deduct all of your business expenses related to the use of your home. If your gross income from the business use of your home is less than your total business expenses, your deduction of otherwise nondeductible expenses, such as insurance, utilities, and depreciation, allocatable to the business is limited. (See IRS Pub. 587 for thorough explanation.)

Deducting Expenses

If you qualify to deduct expenses for the business use of your home, you will also have to divide the expenses of operating your home between personal and business use. The part of your home operating expense you can use to figure your deduction depends on both of the following:

- Whether the expense is direct, indirect, or unrelated.

- The percentage of your home used for business.

TECH TIP 9
DOWNLOAD AND PRINT IRS PUBLICATION 587: BUSINESS USE OF YOUR HOME

The Internal Revenue Service has a 27-page publication that will give you more comprehensive information on issues pertaining to business use of your home. It addresses such things as: qualifying for a deduction, figuring deductions, deducting expenses, depreciating your home, day-care facilities, sale or exchange of your home, business furniture and equipment, recordkeeping, etc. It also contains worksheets and instructions that will help you figure your own deduction.

Publication 587, *Business Use of Your Home (Including Use by Day-Care Providers)*, can be downloaded via the Internet from <www.irs.ustreas.gov>.

Note. In order to read and/or print the publication, you will need *Acrobat Reader*, a software program that is available for free from Adobe at <www.adobe.com>. Download the publication, open Acrobat Reader, and then open the downloaded file.

IRS Warning: Home-Based Business Tax Avoidance Schemes

The Internal Revenue Service has issued consumer alerts regarding home-based business schemes that purport to offer tax "relief." In reality, they provide bad advice to unwary taxpayers that, if followed, results in improper tax avoidance.

Promoters of these schemes claim that individual taxpayers can deduct most, or all, of their personal expenses as business expenses by setting up a bogus home-based business. But the tax code firmly establishes that a clear business purpose and profit motive must exist in order to generate and claim allowable business expenses.

Some examples of personal expenses that are not deductible but are commonly claimed business expenses in home-based business tax avoidance schemes include:

- Deducting all or most of the cost and operation of a personal residence. For example, placing a calendar, desk, file cabinet, telephone, or other business-related item in each room does not increase the amount that can be deducted.

- Deducting a portion of the total house payment is not allowable if the business is not real.

- Paying children a salary for services, such as answering telephones, washing cars, or other tasks and then deducting these costs as a business expense is not real.

- Deducting education expenses from the salary wrongfully paid to children as employees is not allowed.

- Deducting excessive car and truck expenses for both business and personal use is not allowed.

- Deducting personal furniture, home entertainment equipment, children's toys, etc. is not allowed.

- Deducting personal travel, meals, and entertainment under the guise that "everyone is a potential client" is not allowed.

Any tax scheme that claims a person can deduct what would normally be personal expenses should be considered highly suspect. Taxpayers who have questions on this subject or wish to report possible schemes can call 866-775-7474. They can also contact the IRS by sending an e-mail to <irs.tax.shelter.hotline@irs.gov>.

IRS Form 8829: Expenses for Business Use of Your Home

For your convenience, we are including a copy of the worksheet used to figure the deduction for business use of your home on page 57.

INCREASING YOUR CHANCES FOR SUCCESS

If you are going to operate out of your home, there are several things you can do to ensure that you will be more successful. Home offices have long been under scrutiny by many who wish to question their credibility. In the following pages, we will discuss some of the issues that may make the difference between success and failure.

Organize Your Work Space

Setting aside your work space is not only an IRS requirement but a necessary element of any business. It is important to understand that a home-based business is the same as a business in a commercial location with the exception of some special tax considerations. That's exactly the way you should treat your business to maximize your chances for success.

Organize your work space in an efficient manner and eliminate nonwork items so that you will not be tempted to mix the two during working hours. If you are operating a lawn-mower repair shop out of your garage, don't use it to house your cars, bicycles, freezer, and old clothes. If you have an office in your family room, get rid of the TV, pool table, exercise machine, and ironing board. When a customer steps through the door into your office, it should feel like a business.

Take Care of Legal Responsibilities

A home business has the same legal requirements as any other business. You will still need a business license, DBA, and seller's permit. You should never mix your business finances with your personal finances. An effective recordkeeping system will have to be set up, and you will need to find an accounting professional who can help you maximize your tax benefits and prepare your final tax return. You will need a separate bank account and business telephone. You will need business insurance tailored to your products and services.

In other words, pretend that you have just opened business in a commercial location and do the same things you would have to do to get your business under way.

Set Business Hours

It will be important for you to establish regular business hours. Credibility is hard to come by, especially if you work out of your home. Your customers will take you more seriously if they see you are operating on a schedule. If you are not available when they call, you will soon find them looking elsewhere for the same service or product.

When you are required to be away from your business during normal working hours, be sure to provide a way to take a message and return your customer's call. Invest in a good answering machine and leave a new message telling when you will be back in your office and assuring the customer that you will return the call. I knew one business owner who continually left the message, "I am away from my office right now and will return in two hours." The problem was that the caller never knew what time the message was left or when the two hours would be up. A better message would have been, "I have an appointment with a client and will be back in my office at 2 PM." Also be sure to ask for a name and phone number and offer to return the call.

Protect Your Work Hours

Inform your family and friends that you are serious about your business and will need to work without interruption. For some reason, a home-based business is usually perceived as being a place where visitors are welcome to show up and stay for a friendly visit. They would never think of popping into a corporate office for a cup of coffee, but surely you would welcome a break in your working hours! We wish we had a nickel for all the times we have had to work late into the night because well-meaning friends decided we needed their company during the day.

Unfortunately, this is one of the most serious problems encountered in home-based businesses and one that is difficult to solve. It not only applies to family and friends, but to some of your customers who are anxious to establish a friendly relationship. We have used every trick in the book to get rid of unwanted visitors without offending them. We have resorted to proclaiming nonexistent appointments, calling each other from a telephone in the other room, walking the visitor slowly out the door, and any other means within our imaginations. When all else fails, tell the truth; it might just work.

Protect Your Free Hours

In addition to protecting your business hours, you will also have to decide what days and hours you wish to be closed and promise yourself to use them for nonbusiness pursuits. In fact, guard that free time with your life.

Be sure to inform your customers of your working hours. If they want to come during your off hours, tell them nicely but firmly that you are closed. Most will respect you and return during your regular business hours.

At the end of your working day, turn on your answering machine and shut the door to your business. Plan for activities with your family or friends and try not to overwhelm them with your business problems. The idea is to have fun and give yourself a break. You will soon feel overwhelmed and tired of your business if you never have the opportunity to get away from it.

It would be naive to pretend that a business owner will never have to work extra hours to make the business prosper. Do what you need to run your business, but don't let it run you—and don't let it cause you to burn out your enthusiasm and create problems with the people you care about. Remember, owning your own business is supposed to be a plus in your life.

Be Self-Disciplined

Owning your own business requires a great deal of time and effort. We have heard potential business owners exclaim that they are going to quit working eight hours a day for a company and be free to set their own hours. It is true that you can decide on your hours. However, working for yourself will probably be equivalent to holding down two jobs, at least for the first three or four years until the business is functioning smoothly. For this reason, you will need to develop a high degree of self-discipline.

Be willing to work long hours when it is necessary. If an extra effort is needed to get a job done, you will have to do it. Decide what hours you are willing to work and stick to your schedule. Don't fall into the trap of thinking you are free. You are your own boss and must treat yourself as you would an employee.

Dress for Success

Just because you are working at home, don't use it as an excuse to be a slob. Every trade has an acceptable mode of dress that should be adhered to. A home business is the perfect target for a 24-hour a day onslaught by customers. They will call on the telephone and ring the doorbell seven days a week from dawn to dark—and that includes holidays. No one can see what you look like on the other end of the phone, but if you are going to answer the door, look like a business person. If your customer is going to have confidence in your products or services, he or she must first have confidence in you. You are your best advertisement.

Be Totally Credible

Home-based business has come to represent a large segment of today's workforce and a powerful force in the economy. In fact, due in large part to modern technology, almost every kind of business imaginable is being run out of a home office somewhere. Unfortunately, those same home businesses are often regarded as "little hobbies." Both of us were in home-based businesses long before we started teaching business classes and writing and publishing business books. It would probably be impossible to count the times we were told what wonderful hobbies we had. We liked our businesses but can assure you that our reasons for being in business were measured in dollars as well as fun.

The truth is that a home-based business owner will have to expend extra effort to prove credibility and attract customers. Many professional business organizations, including chambers of commerce, are forming focus groups to help overcome this stigma. Meanwhile, professionalism is the only weapon that can be effectively used to overcome misconceptions about the seriousness of this major economic force.

Summary

- Understand the IRS tax regulations pertaining to the business use of your home.

- Check your zoning laws to be sure you can operate your business out of your home.

- Ensure that you have the technological support and furnishings without going overboard (fax, separate phone line, copier, computer, professional answering machine, etc.).

- Make sure your business is compatible with your homeowners policy—look at commercial coverage as an option.

- Keep efficient records.

- Never combine home and business accounts.

- Set up a network to avoid isolation.

- Be self-disciplined and don't allow distractions.

- Set fixed hours and an environment of professionalism.

- Have dedicated space for your business.

- Dress for work.

- Have a good relationship with your neighbors and be sensitive to deliveries, customer parking, etc.

- Have a supportive family network.

Can You Deduct Business Use of the Home Expenses?

source: IRS Publication 587, Business Use of Your Home

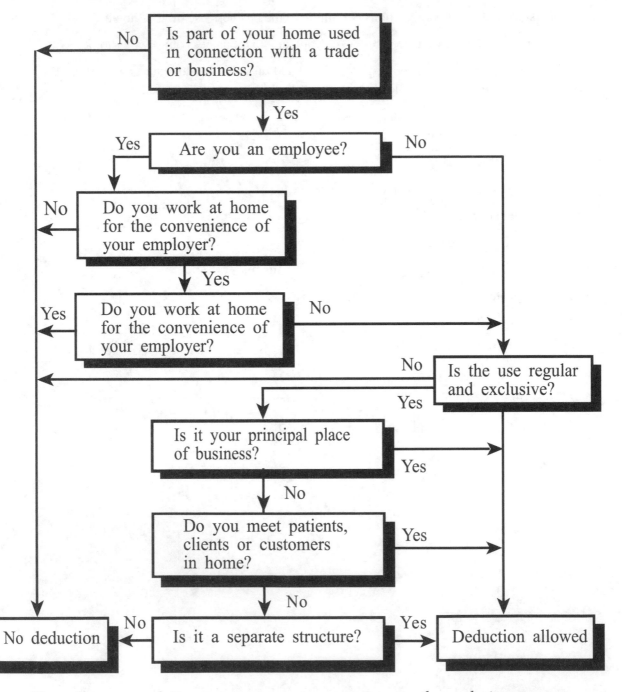

Note: Daycare and inventory storage are exceptions to the exclusive use test.

IRA Form 8829 Expenses for Business Use of Your Home

Figure B

Form **8829**	**Expenses for Business Use of Your Home**	OMB No. 1545-1266
Department of the Treasury Internal Revenue Service	▶ File only with Schedule C (Form 1040). Use a separate Form 8829 for each home you used for business during the year. ▶ See separate instructions.	**2002** Attachment Sequence No. **66**

Name(s) of proprietor(s) Mary Lake	Your social security number 412 : 00 : 1234

Part I   Part of Your Home Used for Business

1	Area used regularly and exclusively for business, regularly for day care, or for storage of inventory or product samples (see instructions)	1	1,600
2	Total area of home	2	3,200
3	Divide line 1 by line 2. Enter the result as a percentage	3	50 %

- For day-care facilities not used exclusively for business, also complete lines 4–6.
- All others, skip lines 4–6 and enter the amount from line 3 on line 7.

4	Multiply days used for day care during year by hours used per day	4	3,000 hr.		
5	Total hours available for use during the year (365 days × 24 hours) (see instructions)	5	8,760 hr.		
6	Divide line 4 by line 5. Enter the result as a decimal amount	6	.3425		
7	Business percentage. For day-care facilities not used exclusively for business, multiply line 6 by line 3 (enter the result as a percentage). All others, enter the amount from line 3 ▶	7			17.13 %

Part II   Figure Your Allowable Deduction

8	Enter the amount from Schedule C, line 29, **plus** any net gain or (loss) derived from the business use of your home and shown on Schedule D or Form 4797. If more than one place of business, see instructions	8	25,000

See instructions for columns (a) and (b) before completing lines 9–20.

			(a) Direct expenses	(b) Indirect expenses		
9	Casualty losses (see instructions)	9				
10	Deductible mortgage interest (see instructions)	10				
11	Real estate taxes (see instructions)	11				
12	Add lines 9, 10, and 11	12				
13	Multiply line 12, column (b) by line 7			13		
14	Add line 12, column (a) and line 13				14	-0-
15	Subtract line 14 from line 8. If zero or less, enter -0-				15	25,000
16	Excess mortgage interest (see instructions)	16				
17	Insurance	17				
18	Repairs and maintenance	18	171			
19	Utilities	19		850		
20	Other expenses (see instructions)	20		8,400		
21	Add lines 16 through 20	21	171	9,250		
22	Multiply line 21, column (b) by line 7			22	1,585	
23	Carryover of operating expenses from 2001 Form 8829, line 41			23		
24	Add line 21 in column (a), line 22, and line 23				24	1,756
25	Allowable operating expenses. Enter the **smaller** of line 15 or line 24				25	1,756
26	Limit on excess casualty losses and depreciation. Subtract line 25 from line 15				26	23,244
27	Excess casualty losses (see instructions)			27		
28	Depreciation of your home from Part III below			28		
29	Carryover of excess casualty losses and depreciation from 2001 Form 8829, line 42			29		
30	Add lines 27 through 29				30	-0-
31	Allowable excess casualty losses and depreciation. Enter the **smaller** of line 26 or line 30				31	-0-
32	Add lines 14, 25, and 31				32	1,756
33	Casualty loss portion, if any, from lines 14 and 31. Carry amount to **Form 4684**, Section B				33	-0-
34	Allowable expenses for business use of your home. Subtract line 33 from line 32. Enter here and on Schedule C, line 30. If your home was used for more than one business, see instructions ▶				34	1,756

Part III   Depreciation of Your Home

35	Enter the **smaller** of your home's adjusted basis or its fair market value (see instructions)	35	
36	Value of land included on line 35	36	
37	Basis of building. Subtract line 36 from line 35	37	
38	Business basis of building. Multiply line 37 by line 7	38	
39	Depreciation percentage (see instructions)	39	%
40	Depreciation allowable (see instructions). Multiply line 38 by line 39. Enter here and on line 28 above	40	

Part IV   Carryover of Unallowed Expenses to 2003

41	Operating expenses. Subtract line 25 from line 24. If less than zero, enter -0-	41	
42	Excess casualty losses and depreciation. Subtract line 31 from line 30. If less than zero, enter -0-	42	

For Paperwork Reduction Act Notice, see page 4 of separate instructions.   Cat. No. 13232M   Form **8829** (2002)

✸ *Printed on recycled paper*

CHOOSING A LEGAL STRUCTURE

One of the most important decisions you will make is how to legally structure your business. There are advantages and disadvantages to each form of organization. The type of legal format you choose will depend on the following factors:

- Your need for capital

- Your type of business

- When you want to start your business

- Your ability to finance your business

- The number of people involved in the business

- The liabilities and risks you are willing to assume

- Your personal tax situation

- Your plan for taking money out of the business

- Your plan for continuing the business if something should happen to you

- Your long-range business plan

· · · · ·

There are four different ways to organize your business: the sole proprietorship, the partnership, the corporation, and the limited liability company. The legal structure you choose will determine how much paperwork you will have to do, how much personal liability you will incur, how you will be able to raise money, and how your business will be taxed.

SOLE PROPRIETORSHIP

This is the easiest, least expensive, and least regulated business legal structure. A sole proprietorship is owned and operated by one person although it may have employees.

Advantages

- *Ease of formation.* There are fewer legal restrictions associated with forming a sole proprietorship.

- *Sole owner of the profits.* All profits go to you, the owner, as do the losses!

- *Least expensive to establish.* Costs vary according to the city in which the business is formed but usually include a license fee and may include a business tax. This information can be obtained by calling the business license bureau of the city government. If you live in an unincorporated area, contact the county offices.

- *Fewer records are needed with a minimum of regulations.* While regulations vary by state, a sole proprietorship can generally be established by registering the company's name (filing a DBA) and obtaining a business license.

- *Taxed as an individual.* As the sole owner, your business profit and loss is recorded on Federal Tax Form 1040, Schedule C, and the bottom line amount is transferred to your personal tax form. You will also file Schedule SE, which is your contribution to Social Security.

- *Total control.* The business is owned and operated by one person. All decision making is vested in you as the owner. You have total responsibility and control.

Disadvantages

- *Unlimited personal liability.* You will be responsible for the full amount of business debt, which may exceed the investment. This liability extends to all assets such as your home and vehicle.

- *Less available capital.* Funding must come from the proprietor, and obtaining long-term financing may be difficult. Loans are based on the strengths of the individual.

- *Limited growth potential.* The future of the company is dependent upon your capabilities in terms of knowledge, drive, and financial potential.

- *Heavy responsibility.* You are the only person responsible for the business. There will be no requisitions to central supply when you run out of envelopes. You will be responsible for evaluating office equipment and making the buying decisions. You have the ultimate responsibility for the purchase of supplies, equipment, advertising, and insurance. You will also handle employees, marketing, bill paying, and customer relations.

- *Death, illness, or injury can endanger the business.* The business ceases to exist as a legal entity upon the death of the owner.

The sole proprietorship is best suited for a single owner business where taxes or product liability are not a concern. Because the entity is inseparable from the owner, the main disadvantages of this structure are unlimited liability, no tax benefits, and dissolution upon the death of the owner. The owner is responsible for taxes and files a Schedule C with Form 1040. The sole proprietorship is the most common form of business and comprises 70 percent of all American business entities. Many who are just starting a business choose this form until it becomes practical to enter into a partnership or incorporate.

PARTNERSHIP

A partnership is a legal business relationship in which two or more people agree to share ownership and management of a business. Often a partner is chosen for the skills or expertise you may lack. Sharing ownership of a business may be a way to gain more start-up money. Evaluate the advantages and disadvantages of this legal structure before making a decision.

Advantages

- *Ease of formation.* The legal requirements and expenses are fewer than those involved with forming a corporation. While regulations vary by state, a partnership can generally be established by registering the company's name (filing a DBA) and obtaining a business license.

- *Shared responsibility.* Two or more heads are better than one! By sharing in the profits, partners are motivated to succeed. This form of legal structure allows for distribution of the workload and sharing of ideas, skills, and responsibilities.

- *Increased growth potential.* A partnership makes it possible to obtain more capital and tap into more skills.

- *Ease of operation.* The partnership has more freedom from government control and special taxation than the corporation.

Disadvantages

- *Unlimited personal liability.* Owners are personally responsible for the business debt. A partnership is not a separate legal entity, even though its income is reported on a separate informational tax return (Form 1065). Profits must be included on each partner's individual tax return according to their percentage of interest in the business.

- *Lack of continuity.* Like the sole proprietorship, the partnership terminates upon the death or the withdrawal of a general partner unless the partnership agreement provides otherwise. Death, withdrawal, or bankruptcy of one partner endangers the entire business.

- *Relative difficulty in obtaining large sums of capital.* While the opportunity for getting long-term financing is greater in a partnership, it is still dependent on review of each individual partner's assets.

- *Difficulty in disposing of the partnership interest.* The buying out of a partnership or sale to another party must be spelled out in the partnership agreement.

- *Distribution of responsibility in bankruptcy.* In case of bankruptcy, the partner with more personal assets will lose more.

- *Partner's responsibility.* Each general partner can act on behalf of the company in conducting business. Each partner represents the company and can individually hire employees, borrow money, and operate the business. Choose someone you trust; you will be bound by each other's decisions.

- *Profits.* Profits are shared among the partners according to the terms set out in the partnership agreement.

A partnership is best suited for a business with two or more owners where taxes and product liability are not a concern. The entity is inseparable from the owners but can have property and debt in its name. There are no tax benefits, and the partnership legally dissolves on change or death of a partner. Partners are responsible for filing taxes and use Form 1065.

There are different types of partnerships dependent on how active a role partners play in the business. **General partners** share equally in the responsibility for managing and financing the business. They also share equally in the liability. **Limited partners** risk only their investment in the business and are not subject to the same liabilities as a general partner as long as they do not participate in the management and control of the enterprise.

This business structure is used as a way of raising capital to run the business. General partners can take on limited partners as a means of raising cash without involving outside investors in the management of the business. The general partners remain liable for the business' debt. A limited partnership is more expensive to create, involves extensive paperwork, and is used mainly for companies that invest in real estate or speculative ventures.

Care should be taken when choosing a partner. This is a close working relationship, and you must look carefully at the work style, character, personality, financial situation, skill, and expertise of your potential partner.

PARTNERSHIP AGREEMENTS

Do not underestimate the need for a partnership agreement. Many friendships and good working relationships have ended over business disagreements. When financial considerations enter the picture, friendships are often put aside. Take some time and carefully prepare a partnership agreement and have it notarized. It will serve as the guideline for your working relationship with your partners. It will outline the financial, managerial, and material contributions by the partners into the business and delineate the roles of the partners in the business relationship.

The following are some subjects often covered in a partnership agreement:

- The purpose of the partnership business

- The terms of the partnership

- The goals of the partners and the partnership

- The financial contributions made by each partner for start-up and during the lifetime of the business

- The distribution of profits and losses

- The withdrawal of contributed assets or capital by a partner

- The management powers and work responsibilities of each partner

- The provisions for admitting new partners

- The provisions for expelling a partner

- The provisions for continuing the business in the event of a partner's death, illness, disability, or desire to leave

- The provision for determining the value of a departing partner's interest and method of payment of that interest

- The methods of settling disputes through mediation or arbitration

- The duration of the agreement and the terms of dissolution of the business

A partnership agreement is a contract that states how you want your business relationship to work. The Uniform Partnership Act (UPA) is a body of law that establishes the most basic legal rules applicable to partnerships. It has been adopted in all states except Louisiana. However, these rules can be changed by statements in your partnership agreement. Unless the agreement itself specifies a different date, a written agreement is effective when it is signed.

CORPORATION

The corporation is the most complex of the business structures. A corporation is a distinct legal entity, separate from the individuals who own it. It is formed by the authority of the state government, with approval from the secretary of state. If business is conducted in more than one state, you must comply with the federal laws regarding interstate commerce. Federal and state laws may vary considerably.

Advantages

- *Ownership is readily transferable.* The corporation does not cease to exist with the death of an owner.

- *Increased options for growth and fundraising.* A corporation has access to numerous investors and can raise substantial capital through the sale of stock.

- *The corporation is a separate legal entity.* It is responsible and liable for all debts. The shareholders are liable only for the amount they have invested. A corporation has an existence apart from the people who own it.

- *Authority can be delegated.* The corporation has the ability to draw on the expertise and skills of more than one individual.

Disadvantages

- *Extensive government regulations.* Corporations are complex to manage and highly regulated. Burdensome local, state, and federal reports must be filed, and regular stockholder meetings must be held.

- *Expensive to form and maintain.* The fees for setting up a corporate structure, the costs of stockholders' meetings, and the expense for legal fees and paperwork are some of the costs unique to the corporation.

- *Increased tax load.* Income tax is paid on the corporate net income (profit) and individual salaries and dividends.

Because of the complexity of the corporation, you may wish to consult an attorney regarding its formation. Whether you choose to form the corporation on your own or with legal help, you will have to consider the following items in order to be knowledgeable and prepared.

Certificate of Incorporation

The preparation of a **certificate of incorporation** is generally the first step to incorporating. Many states have a standard certificate of incorporation form that may be used by small businesses. Copies may be obtained from the state official who grants charters or from larger stationers or office suppliers. The following information is usually required:

- *Corporate name of the company.* The name chosen must not be similar to any other corporation authorized to do business in the state. The name must not be deceptive so as to mislead the public. To be certain that the name you select is suitable, check its availability through the designated state official in each state where you intend to do business before drawing up the certificate of incorporation.

- *Purposes of the corporation.* Purposes should be broad enough to allow for expansion and specific enough to give a clear idea of the business to be performed. Reference books and certificates of existing corporations are available at your local library and can provide examples of such clauses.

- *Length of time the corporation will exist.* The term may cover a number of years or be "perpetual."

- *Names and addresses of incorporators.* In some areas, at least one or more of the incorporators is required to be a resident of the state in which the corporation is being organized.

- *Location of the registered office of the corporation in the state of incorporation.* If you decide to obtain your charter from another state, you will be required to have an office there. You may appoint an agent in that state to act for you.

- *Proposed capital structure.* State the maximum amount and type of capital stock your corporation wishes authorization to issue. State the amount of capital required at the time of incorporation.

- *Management.* State the provisions for the regulation of the internal affairs of the corporation.

- *Director.* Provide the name and address of the person who will serve as the director until the first meeting of the stockholders.

The charter will be issued when and if the designated state official determines that the name is available, the certificate has been completely and properly executed, and there has been no violation of state law.

In order to complete the incorporation process, the stockholders must meet. They must elect a board of directors and adopt bylaws. The board of directors will in turn elect the officers who will actually have charge of operating the corporation. Usually, the officers include a president, a secretary, and a treasurer. In small corporations, the members of the board of directors are frequently elected as officers of the corporation.

Bylaws

The bylaws of the corporation may repeat some of the provisions of the charter and usually cover such items as the following:

- The location of the principal office and other offices

- The time, location, and notice of stockholder meetings

- Number of directors, their compensation, terms of office, method of election, and the filling of vacancies

- The time and location of directors' meetings

- Quorum and voting methods

- Insurance and form of stock certificates

- Methods of selecting officers and designating their titles, duties, terms of office, and salaries

- Method of paying dividends

- Decisions regarding the fiscal year

- Procedure for amending the bylaws

In general, the cost and complexity of the corporate legal structure make it an unrealistic option for many small businesses.

S CORPORATION

A few years ago, the S corporation was the only legal structure that would provide the business owner with the limited liability of corporate shareholders and allow the payment of income taxes on the same basis as a sole proprietor or partner. Although their popularity has declined since the creation of the LLC structure, S corporations are appropriate for some businesses. There are specific conditions for making and maintaining an S corporation election.

- Each shareholder must be a U.S. citizen or resident.

- S corporation profits and losses are allocated in proportion to each shareholder's interest in the business.

- An S corporation shareholder may not deduct corporate losses that exceed the amount of the investment in the company plus or minus a few adjustments.

- S corporations may not deduct the cost of fringe benefits provided to employee shareholders who own more than 2 percent of the corporation.

- The corporation must have 75 or fewer shareholders, all of whom are individuals or estates.

- The corporation must have issued only one class of stock.

- No more than 25 percent of the corporation's gross income can be derived from passive investment activities.

You can also accomplish the goals of limited liability and pass-through taxation by creating a limited liability company (LLC). Forming an LLC is often a better choice: it offers its owners greater flexibility in allocating profits and losses and is not subject to the many restrictions of an S corporation. Talk to your attorney or accountant to determine if the S corporation is the right form of legal structure for the business.

LIMITED LIABILITY COMPANY (LLC)

A limited liability company is a legal structure that fits between the corporation and the partnership or sole proprietorship. LLC owners report business profits or losses on their personal income tax returns. The LLC itself is not a separate taxable entity. Like a corporation, the owners are protected from personal liability for business claims or debts. This means that in the event of a lawsuit, only the assets of the business are at risk: creditors can't reach the personal assets of the LLC owners. An LLC is a state entity.

However, there are some exceptions. An LLC owner can be held personally liable if he or she:

- personally and directly injures someone

- personally guarantees a bank loan or a business debt on which the LLC defaults

- fails to deposit taxes withheld from employees' wages

- intentionally does something fraudulent or illegal that causes harm to the company or someone else

- treats the LLC as an extension of personal affairs rather than as a separate legal entity

Advantages

- *More liberal loss deductions.* The owners of an LLC do not assume liability for the business's debt, and any losses can be used as tax deductions against active income. Loss deductions are more limited under an S Corporation than under an LLC.

- *More stock options.* LLCs can offer several different classes of stock with different rights.

- *Less restriction on participation.* An LLC can be formed with just one person in every state except Massachusetts, which requires two owners. There is no maximum number of owners that an LLC can have.

Disadvantages

- *Difficulty in business expansion out of state.* If a company doing business in a state that allows LLCs decides to do business in another state without similar legislation, there is no provision for it to legally register to conduct business in the second state.

- *Transferability restriction test.* Ownership interests cannot be transferred to other parties without some restrictions.

- *Lack of uniform code.* In some states, the business is dissolved on the death, retirement, resignation, or expulsion of an owner.

To set up an LLC, you follow a path similar to the formation of a corporation. You must submit an article of organization and the appropriate filing fees to the secretary of state in the state where your business is organized. Because states differ in the information required, it is wise to consult your attorney or accountant if you think the limited liability company form of legal structure is right for your business.

GENERAL CONSIDERATIONS

In choosing your particular legal structure, you will want to give careful consideration to all of the options available and base your decision on a personal evaluation of the following items:

- *The size of risk.* Look at the amount of the owner's liability for debts and taxes under each structure. How much liability are you willing to assume? How would you want your earnings to be taxed?

- *The continuity of the business.* If something should unexpectedly happen to you, what would happen to your business?

- *Your access to capital.* How much money will you need to develop and run your business? Where will you get this money?

- *Your management skills.* What is your business experience? What are the skills and abilities you bring to the company?

- *Your purpose for starting a business.* What is your ultimate goal? What are the possibilities for business growth?

Keep in mind that your initial choice of a business form doesn't have to be permanent. You can start out as a sole proprietor. As your business develops, you may wish to take on partners. As the risks of personal liability increase, you may wish to form a corporation. If you change the structure of an existing business, you must notify the Internal Revenue Service and your state tax agency. A sole proprietorship or partnership must change legal form through the business license bureau, while corporations register with the office of the secretary of state. The SBA publishes material covering each type of legal structure. If you are unsure about which type of structure is best for your business, you may wish to consult an attorney who is knowledgeable about the various types of business organization.

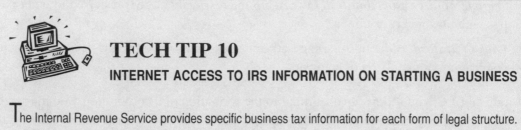

TECH TIP 10
INTERNET ACCESS TO IRS INFORMATION ON STARTING A BUSINESS

The Internal Revenue Service provides specific business tax information for each form of legal structure. The IRS Web site is <www.irs.gov>. Open this site and click on "businesses" under "contents." You will be able to access information on tax considerations by legal structure, take part in online small business workshops, and download tax worksheets and forms.

CHAPTER 8

PRESENTING YOUR BUSINESS

A company's image is based primarily on its paper correspondence. Such identity materials as stationery, business cards, and envelopes convey a company's image.

From the first day you begin business, it will be necessary for you to have certain materials that represent your business, not only to your customers but also to suppliers and other business owners. When you are organizing your venture, you will be approaching suppliers, dealers, and other people in related businesses. It is important they perceive your business as having a base of stability. Otherwise, they may choose to ignore your requests. It is almost impossible to do the background work that needs to be done to develop a business without having cards and letterhead. You may also need a brochure of some type to begin advertising your business. The marketing and advertising of a business is covered in more detail in Chapter 19. In this chapter, we will discuss developing your graphic identity through your printed materials.

• • • • •

GRAPHIC IDENTITY

First impressions are lasting, and often the first impression made by a business is through what is called "graphic identity." Graphic identity refers to the visual representation of your company. It includes the design of your logo and style of your promotional materials.

A company's graphic or visual identity usually includes a logo, logotype (type style), and company colors. The combinations you choose will create your identity and make your promotional and packaging materials recognizable. In today's highly competitive world, it is important to be recognized, remembered, and viewed as an established business.

TECH TIP 11
USE TECHNOLOGY TO TEST YOUR LOGO

Technology provides you with many marketing opportunities; it is important that you view the appearance and acceptability of your logo, logotype, and color choices in these different formats. If your marketing materials are multicolored, will they be expensive to reproduce? Will the design lose its impact when faxed and received as a black and white transmission? Photocopy your materials and see how the design holds up. Will it reproduce well in different sizes? Will the logo on your brochure be just as effective on your letterhead and business card? If your logo is produced by an out-of-house graphic designer, be sure to get the logo in an electronic format that can be pasted into documents and put on the Web. View the design on the Web. How does it look on the screen? If it is very detailed and colorful, it may increase download time for your potential customers. Try to anticipate all future uses of your marketing materials and determine how they will stand up to electronic and telecommunication mediums.

A **logo** is a symbol that represents the company. It may be a monogram of the company's initials or a design. A logo is a quick way of getting people to notice and remember your business. When designing your logo, you want to be sure that it is appropriate to your business and that the art work is timely. You can design your own, select from standard logos available from a printer, hire a professional artist, or work with a high school or college art student. Be sure to consider registering your logo with the Copyright Office or the Patent and Trademark Office in Washington, DC. Refer to Chapter 9 regarding these protections. The addresses of these agencies are listed in Appendix A.

Logotype refers to the type style used in the writing of your business name. The type size, placement, and style can communicate a great deal about your company. There are hundreds of type styles and sizes available and, within each type family, there are plain, italic, and bold versions.

Often a company will wish to adopt **company colors**. Most often two colors are used. Just as with type style, the colors you choose can set the tone for your marketing materials. Make sure the colors fit your company and the "feel" you wish to project.

You may be a small company competing with larger companies or a new company entering an existing market. You need to look competent and established. A carefully planned and implemented graphic identity can give you the edge you need and should last for many years.

BUSINESS CARDS

Business cards are one of the most universally used marketing tools. Not only do they give your business credibility, they serve as a visual reminder of you and your business. Be sure to have business cards printed as soon as possible. Whenever you attempt to deal with another business or individual, you should give them your card. This not only gives your business credibility, but the recipient now has a reminder of you and your business.

Begin to gather cards as you network in the business community, deal with suppliers, and evaluate competitors. When you have collected 30 to 40 of them, arrange them on a tabletop. Now scan the cards and see which ones catch your eye. Then evaluate the cards that caught your attention in terms of the following questions:

- What is it about this card that first draws your attention?

- Is the logo appropriate and descriptive?

- Is the company name legible?

- Is the contact person's name and phone number included?

- Does the card tell what product and/or service is offered?

- Does the card tell the location of the business?

- Is the overall appearance pleasing?

- Is the card one you will remember?

A business card is like a minibillboard. It should tell the what, why, who, how, when, and where of your business.

Do not buy your first cards in large quantity. Even though the purchase of a large quantity of business cards will save you money on a per unit basis, 5,000 cards will do you no good if the information on them is no longer valid. They will just have to be discarded, and the money you saved will be lost. In a very short time, you may want to change your card for any number of reasons: change of address, addition of a logo, inclusion of a fax or cell-phone number, adding an e-mail address, or addition of new products or services. The evolution of the business cards for the company, Ace Sporting Goods, is demonstrated on the **Business Card Development** example on page 74. As the location and nature of the business changed, the business card changed. All businesses change as they grow. By purchasing your cards in reasonable amounts, you can avoid having to discard ones that no longer apply to your situation.

PROMOTIONAL MATERIALS

A business card, the letterhead, and a brochure are the primary promotional materials of all businesses. Following is a listing of printed materials your company can use for business promotion and graphic identity presentation:

Brochures	Invoices
Building signs	Letterhead
Business cards	Mailing labels
Business reply envelopes	Name badges
Checks	Presentation folders

Contracts/agreements	Promotional give-aways
Display signs	Purchase orders
Envelopes	Uniforms
Flyers	Vehicle signs

We have already discussed the business card. The other printed material you will need is a **letterhead**. Your letterhead is your business stationery. It should be used for all business correspondence. It also lends credibility to your business. The color, type, and quality of the paper you use will reflect on your company. Expand the information formatted for your business card and develop a "look" that appears on all your promotional materials and carries over to your package design. Duplicate the format, type style, and colors used on your business card for continuity. When you have your letterhead printed, purchase a smaller quantity of second sheets. When writing a business letter, the letterhead is used only for the first page.

Brochures are essential for any business where the prospective customer needs detailed information about the qualifications and expertise of the owner and the services and products offered. More information can be supplied in a brochure than would be practical for a classified ad. Brochures can be mailed, distributed door to door, or given out at community events and trade shows. A **Guidelines for Developing a Brochure** worksheet has been included on page 75 to help you develop your own brochure.

The above-mentioned are the main presentation materials used for a small business. As your business grows, you may want to develop other materials. If you are a retailer, you may have a catalog printed and mailed to your customers. Signs may be needed for a display, your building, or a vehicle. To create a "total look" for your business, you can expand your graphic identity to include your business checks, mailing labels, purchase order forms, and invoices. For the small business just getting started, business cards, letterhead, a basic brochure, and an order form are enough to begin with. **Guidelines for Developing an Order Form** is included on page 76.

CHOOSING A PRINTER

Two of the major considerations in choosing a printer are quality of work and price. Sometimes the lowest bid is not the most cost effective. If the workmanship on the project and quality of materials are poor, your business image will suffer. After all, the presentation materials you use often determine how your customers, suppliers, and competitors will perceive your business.

Quality and price vary among printers. You will want to visit three or four printers in your area. Get a price list and view samples of their work. You may have your cards and letterhead done at one shop and your brochures printed at another shop that specializes in that type of printed matter.

In order to save money, much of your printing can be done from a disc or electronic files. This means you take the printer a finished product on a disc or send it electronically to be produced.

Your layout should look professional and businesslike. Desktop publishing companies can help you with this work.

Before having your printing done, be sure to get an estimate in writing. A colleague was given a verbal quotation for printing booklets and boxes for a novelty item. Upon delivery, she paid the bill in full. A month later, she was surprised to receive another bill for setup charges. The printer's claim was that the setup charges covered setting up and inking the printing press and were separate. The business owner consulted an attorney, but the outcome was that she was legally responsible for the additional charges. Because there was no written agreement, she was unable to prove her claim.

Business Card Development

The following examples illustrate how business cards can change as a business grows. Remember the lessons on developing a graphic identity presented at the first of this chapter: be consistent with colors, logo design, and logotype style. Once established, these items remained the same.

The initial card was used in the early stages of business development and start-up. Ace Sporting Goods began as a general sporting goods store. The market research initially conducted showed an interest within the target market for fishing. The company used this information and grew to become the area specialist in providing fly fishing gear and trips. An 800 number was added for the convenience of out-of-state buyers and travelers interested in the fishing trips as well as sporting gear. Team sponsorship and the selling of team equipment and uniforms were included to inform buyers and to publicize community involvement. A Web site was developed and the site address added to the business card.

In order to keep your market informed, these changes must be reflected on that "mini-billboard" called the business card. Use judgment in quantity purchase of promotional materials.

Guidelines for Developing a Brochure

A brochure is a general term for a promotional piece that contains the following information about your business:

1. Company name: _____

   _____

2. Company address: _Be sure to include the full address and zip code._____

   _____

   _____

   _____

3. Telephone, fax, cell phone, voice mail, pager, and e-mail: _Be sure to include the area code. Also_

   _include your Web site if you have one_____

   _____

4. Key people: _Clients and customers want to know the background and expertise of the_

   people with whom they will be doing business and feel more comfortable if they can

   ask for a contact person by name. You may wish to include short biographies of

   key people within your business. You may want to include photos.

5. Features: _Features are characteristics or attributes of your product or service._

   _Features "tell" about your business._____

   _____

   _____

6. Benefits: _Benefits "sell" your business. They describe the advantages of purchasing_

   _and using your product or service._____

   _____

   _____

7. Statement of purpose: _Including the mission statement of your business can convey_

   _your business philosophy and goals to the customer._____

   _____

8. Testimonials from satisfied customers: _____

   _____

   _____

   _____

Guidelines for Developing an Order Form

Most product and some service businesses will need an order form that tells a customer the terms of a sale. The following should serve as a guideline.

1. Business name: _____

2. Business address: _Be sure to include the full address and zip code._____
   _____
   _____

3. Telephone, fax, cell phone, voice mail, pager, and e-mail: _Be sure to include the area code. Also_
   _include your Web site if you have one._____

4. Name of contact person: _Customers prefer to ask for an individual when they call._____
   _____

5. Photos or drawings of your product or a representation of your service: _____
   _____

6. Description of your product or service: _____
   _____

7. Price list: _Indicate whether price is wholesale or retail. Indicate any quantity_
   _discounts._____

8. Terms of payment: _____
   _a. Net 30: Invoice must be paid in full within 30 days._____
   b. Net 30, 2%/10: Invoice to be paid in full in 30 days. If paid within 10 days, a 2%
   _discount can be taken on the bill excluding the shipping charges._____
   c. COD (cash on delivery): Invoice is to be paid to the delivery agent on receipt of goods.
   _d. Proforma: Goods will be shipped after receipt of full payment._____

9. Return policy: _You may wish to include a statement as follows: "Returns and/or adjustments_
   must be made within 14 days of receipt of goods." Use a time frame of your choice.

10. Shipping terms: _FOB origin would mean that the customer pays shipping charges and_
    assumes the responsibility for the goods from the time they leave your business.
    _Example: FOB Tustin, CA._____

11. Minimum order policy: _Can be a dollar or unit amount._____
    _____

12. Warranty and/or guarantee: _____
    _____

PROTECTING YOUR BUSINESS

We all have great ideas for new products or services and usually keep these ideas stashed away in the back of our minds. We think they are silly, or we are afraid that if we do disclose them, the idea will be stolen. Don't let the fear of having your idea stolen keep you from the marketplace. In order to develop and sell ideas, you have to disclose them.

When you are developing your business, you want to make certain you are not infringing on the rights of others. You also want to get protection for your own work.

• • • • •

DISCLOSURE LETTER

One way of protecting your idea is through the use of a disclosure letter. This is a letter outlining your idea for your new product or service, detailing the research and work you have done to date, and citing the people you have contacted while doing your research. Date the letter and have it notarized. The purpose of the disclosure letter is to verify the date on which the idea was yours. Place the letter in a sealed envelope and file it in a safe place.

JOURNAL

Establishing a date by means of a disclosure letter is not enough. You must be able to demonstrate that you are involved in an active business as opposed to a passive business activity. An active business is able to show continuous work and progress in developing the idea into a viable product or service. This may be done by keeping a **log** or **journal**. This is a diary in which you verify ongoing work through daily entries. To be considered a legal document, the journal must be a bound book (not loose-leaf), have consecutively numbered pages, be written in ink, and contain no erasures. If you make an error, line through it, initial it and make the correction. Do not use correction fluid. Include information regarding the people to whom you have spoken about your idea and the dates and locations of the meetings. The journal and the disclosure letter give you the security you need to begin your market research. You may be able to get further protection through a copyright, trademark, or patent. A **Sample Journal Page** with entries has been included at the end of this chapter.

COPYRIGHT

A **copyright** is a legal protection provided to the authors of "original works of authorship that are fixed in a tangible form of expression." The fixation does not need to be directly perceptible, so long as it may be communicated with the aid of a machine or device. Copyrightable works include the following categories:

- Literary works

- Musical works, including any accompanying words

- Dramatic works, including any accompanying music

- Pantomimes and choreographic works

- Pictorial, graphic, and sculptural works

- Motion pictures and other audiovisual works

- Sound recordings

- Architectural works

- Electronic media

These are broad categories. Contact the Copyright Office for clarification (see Appendix A).

Under present law, copyright protection starts from the time the work is created in fixed form. The copyright in the work of authorship immediately becomes the property of the author who created the work. Only the author or those deriving their rights through the author can lawfully lay claim to the copyright.

An exception would be a "work made for hire." In this case the employer and not the employee is considered to be the author. The copyright law defines a "work made for hire" as

- a work prepared by an employee within the scope of his or her employment.

- a work specially ordered or commissioned for use as a:
  - contribution to a collective work
  - part of a motion picture or other audiovisual work
  - translation

- supplementary work
- compilation
- instructional text
- text
- answer material for a test
- atlas

The employer and all contributors must agree in a written instrument signed by all concerned that the work shall be considered a work made for hire.

Use of the notice is recommended because it informs the public that the work is protected by copyright, identifies the copyright owner, and shows the year of the first publication. The notice for visually perceptible copies should contain all of the following three elements:

1. *The symbol* © (the letter c in a circle), or the word "copyright," or the abbreviation "copr."

2. *The year of first publication* of the work.

3. *The name of the owner of copyright* in the work, or an abbreviation by which the name can be recognized, or a generally known alternative designation of the owner.

Example: ©2004 Jane Doe

The "c in a circle" notice is used only on "visually perceptible copies." Certain types of works such as musical, dramatic, and literary may be fixed by means of sound in an audio recording.

Generally, no publication or registration in the Copyright Office is required to secure a copyright. There are, however, certain advantages to registration.

- Registration establishes a public record of the copyright claim.

- Before an infringement suit may be filed in court, registration is necessary for works of U.S. origin and foreign works not originating in a Berne Union Country.

- If made before or within five years of publication, registration will establish prima facie evidence in court of the validity of the copyright and the facts stated in the certificate.

- If registration is made within three months after publication of the work or prior to an infringement of the work, statutory damages and attorney's fees will be available to the copyright owner in court actions.

- Copyright registration allows the owner of the copyright to record the registration with the U.S. Customs Service for protection against the importation of infringing copies.

Registration may be made at any time within the life of the copyright.

To register a work, send the following three elements in the same envelope or package to the Copyright Office. The address is listed in Appendix A.

- A properly completed application form. (Free application forms are supplied by the Copyright Office.)

- A basic nonrefundable filing fee of $30 must be submitted with each application. Copyright fees are adjusted at intervals based on increases in the Consumer Price Index. Contact the Copyright Office for the current fee schedule.

- A nonreturnable deposit of the work being registered. The deposit requirements vary in particular situations and special deposit requirements exist for many types of works. If you are unsure of the deposit requirement for your work, write or call the Copyright Office and describe the work you wish to register.

A copyright registration is effective on the date the Copyright Office receives all of the required elements in the acceptable form, regardless of how long it then takes to process the application and mail the certificate of registration. The copyright protection is for the life of the author plus an additional 50 years after the author's death. The use of the copyright notice is the responsibility of the copyright owner and does not require advance permission or registration with the Copyright Office.

TECH TIP 12
COPYRIGHT, PATENT, AND TRADEMARK
INFORMATION VIA THE INTERNET

The Library of Congress Web site at <www.copyright.gov> provides access to copyright information circulars, fact sheets, and form letters. Browse through the information listings and view text to determine protection that may be available for your printed or graphic work. Through links from the home page, regulation requirements and registration forms can be printed. Information is available in Adobe Acrobat PDF format, which can be downloaded free from the site.

The U.S. Patent and Trademark Office Web site is located at <www.uspto.gov/>. The site's home page provides links to specific information on the trademark and patent processes. For example, clicking on "Patents" takes you to a page that allows you to search U.S. patent databases. Clicking on "Trademarks" takes you to a page that allows you to apply online or check on the status of a trademark application. A menu on the home page provides links to databases, search criteria, information on fee structures, and downloadable instructions and registration forms.

TRADEMARK

A **trademark** is a distinctive word, phrase, logo, Internet domain name, graphic symbol, slogan, or other device used to identify the source of a product and distinguish a manufacturer's or merchant's products from others. Product companies that have trademarked their names include Columbia™ Sportswear, Microsoft™ software, and Double Rainbow™ ice cream.

A **service mark** is essentially the same as a trademark but promotes services or events. As a general rule, when a business uses its name to market its goods or services in the yellow pages, on signs, or in advertising copy, the name qualifies as a service mark. Some familiar service marks are McDonald's (fast food service), ACLU (legal service), Blockbuster (video rental service), and the Olympic Games' interlocking circles (event).

A **certification mark** is a symbol, name, or device used by an organization to vouch for products and services provided by others. This type of mark may cover characteristics such as geographical origin (Napa Valley wines) and product quality (The Good Housekeeping Seal of Approval).

A **collective mark** is a symbol, label, word, phrase, or other mark used by members of a group or organization to identify goods, members, products, or services they render. The use of a collective mark is restricted to members of the group or organization that owns the mark. An example is the use of the Woolmark Gold Label on textiles; its usage certifies that the fabric contains top-quality Australian wool.

Consumers often make purchasing choices based on recognizable trademarks. The main focus of the trademark law is to make sure that the trademarks do not overlap in a manner that would cause consumers to become confused about the source of a product.

It is important to conduct a reasonably thorough trademark search. Penalties are severe if you attempt to use a trademark that has been federally registered by someone else. You can do your own search on the Internet by accessing the Patent and Trademark Office (PTO) Web site or visiting one of the Patent and Trademark Depository Libraries. These libraries house a combination of hardcover directories of federally registered marks and offer an online database of both registered and pending marks. Contact information for these resources is included in Appendix A.

Although there is no requirement to file, registration provides certain legal protection to trademark owners in the United States. Application and filing forms along with detailed instructions are available from the PTO. Registration requires three items:

1. A properly completed registration form.

2. An application for registration fee. **Note**: The current minimum filing fee for a trademark application is $325 per class of goods/services. Fees are adjusted at intervals; contact your PTO for the current fee schedule.

3. A physical representation of the mark.

There is a standard format for the use of the trademark symbol; the letters "TM" must be placed after every use, such as ™. The letters "SM" are used for a service mark (℠). Once the trademark registration has been completed and confirmed, the symbol "R" with a circle around it (®)will be placed after every use of the trademarked word or symbol.

These marks serve to identify and distinguish an owner's products, goods, or services from those of the competition. They can serve as good marketing tools provided the quality and reputation of the goods and services are maintained.

PATENT

A patent for an invention is the grant of a property right to the inventor. This right is granted by the PTO and prohibits others from making, using, selling, offering for sale, or importing the invention into the United States for a period of up to 20 years from the date of filing the application.

When you have an idea for a new invention or process, it is important to analyze that idea for originality and patentability. In order to be considered patentable, an invention must be

- *Novel.* The invention must be unique, new, and never before created.

- *Useful.* It must accomplish something and/or serve some purpose.

- *Nonobvious.* An invention is considered nonobvious if someone skilled in the particular field of interest would view it as an unexpected or surprising development.

The only way to be certain your idea satisfies these conditions is to conduct a patent search. Just as with a trademark, you can do your own search on the Internet by accessing the PTOs Web site or visiting one of the Patent and Trademark Depository Libraries. Contact information for these resources is included in Appendix A.

Once a thorough patent search has been completed and you can show that your invention is significantly different or unique, you can apply for the patent. The patent application is filed with the PTO, goes through a rigorous examination process, and is assigned to a patent examiner. The examiner is charged with verifying that the invention meets the requirements of patentability and that the application follows the required format.

There are two major parts to a patent application: the specification and the drawings. The specification is a written description of the invention; the drawings are a visual representation. The PTO has strict requirements for both claims and drawings. In addition, you will be required to submit a filing fee according to the fee schedule.

The preparation of an application for a patent and the conducting of the proceedings in the PTO to obtain that patent are undertakings that require a thorough knowledge of the scientific or technical matters involved in the particular invention as well as knowledge of the legal aspects of the patent process. Although inventors may prepare and file their own applications and conduct their own proceedings, they may get into considerable difficulty. The patent process can be tedious, complicated, and lengthy. Most inventors employ the services of registered patent attorneys or patent agents. However, it is to your advantage to be as knowledgeable as possible about the patenting process.

CONTRACTS

Another way to protect your business interests is through a contract. Businesses enter into various types of agreements and contracts with employees, vendors, customers, and partners. A contract is an agreement between two or more people, which creates an obligation to do or not to do something in exchange for money or some other consideration. Although an oral contract may be enforceable if its material terms can be proven, confusion can be avoided by creating a written document that provides evidence of the parties' agreements or nonagreements.

From a legal standpoint, many of the papers generated by a business are considered contracts. For example, a purchase order is a contract. In some cases, letters are considered contracts whose wording can be legally binding on a company. One of the most common forms of contract entered into by a new business is a lease. A lease is a contract between the owner of the building (lessor or landlord) and the occupant of the building (lessee or tenant). A lease sets forth the terms and conditions under which the tenant may occupy the building or space and the obligations of each of the parties. The subject of lease provisions has been covered in Chapter 5. Following are some other common situations requiring contracts:

- Bank or individual loans

- Sale or purchase of equity

- Sale or purchase of a business

- Sale or purchase of real estate

- Sale or purchase of products or services

- Insurance policies

- Long-term buying arrangements

- Long-term selling arrangements

- Partnership agreements

- Lease of property, or equipment

- Employee contracts

Develop a habit of keeping written records of important meetings and phone conversations. If anything is said in a conversation with a vendor, customer, or business contact, send a confirming letter documenting what has been said. If the need arises, you will have a permanent record you can refer to later.

HIRING AN ATTORNEY

Hiring an attorney is an expense that many business owners would like to avoid. However, saving on legal costs now may cost you more in the long run if a dispute, disagreement, or violation of a legal requirement occurs in the future. You will probably want to retain an attorney to prepare your partnership agreement or set up your corporation or LLC. You may also want to consult with an attorney to be sure you are obtaining the necessary licenses and permits for your type of business.

In most cases, the best way to find an attorney is through a referral from a banker, an accountant, or a business associate. The local bar association or legal referral service can also put you in touch with attorneys in your area.

Be sure the attorney you retain is qualified in the area of work you need done. Look for someone who is familiar with small business. If you need specialized assistance such as tax, labor, or patent law, ask an attorney for a referral to a specialist. Many trade and professional associations provide lists of attorneys that specialize in their areas of concern.

Once you find an attorney, get everything in writing. Fees and arrangements, the nature of the legal services to be provided, and attorney/client responsibilities must be understood to avoid problems.

Remember that the decisions you make about your business will be your own. An attorney can inform you regarding your options and the legal ramifications of those choices.

Sample Journal Page

Page 18

October 8, 2004: Adams Community College, Blair, NY: Took class in Basic Recordkeeping. Met with instructor, Linda Pinson, regarding consulting and setting up of my recordkeeping system.

October 11, 2004: Contacted Dan Jenkins at Adams Community College regarding teaching basic fly-fishing skills. We will jointly develop a questionnaire to be distributed to students in order to determine interest. 555-555-7642.

October 18, 2004: Arranged to speak to the chamber of commerce on the subject "Alternative Sports" on Thursday, December 12, 2004 at The Market Restaurant. Contact: Jane Morgan at 714-555-9734. Will distribute questionnaire to determine interest in sporting goods store in this community.

October 26, 2004: Taught class, "Basic Fly-Fishing," from 7 to 9 PM at Adams Community College, Blair. Twenty-seven students attended, ages ranged from 18 to 52, interest from five students regarding a fishing trip: Sam Johnson 463-9728; Glenn Smith 743-9652; Sarah Bennett 462-8931; Suzanne Kim 426-9276; and David Kelley 626-6201.

November 1, 2004: Exhibited at Community Days in the park on Beach Street. Approximately 10,000 attended event. Conducted questionnaire interviews with 462 people responding as follows:

1. Previous fishing experience = 36
   Where: river = 12   ocean = 24
   Did you enjoy:
   Yes = 16 (supervised, safety equipment, skilled leader)
   No = 20 (poorly planned, off schedule, canceled with no refund)

2. Interest in fly-fishing classes = 216
   Evenings = 113
   Weekday = 26
   Saturday = 186

3. Interest in fishing trips = 36

4. What would you expect to pay:
   Range $35 to $50 for four-hour class; $175 to $250 for two-day trip

5. Majority read Register (397), listen to KZLM radio (201), respond to coupons in Penny Saver (122).

November 8, 2004: Meeting scheduled for December 11 at 10:00 with Mr. Jim Anderson of SCORE to discuss developing a business plan.

CHAPTER 10

SECURING A BUSINESS LICENSE

Why do you need a business license? If your business is going to operate within the law, it will be necessary for you to obtain a license or permit in the city or county in which you will be doing business.

If that business is service-related and performs any portion of its work in other cities outside of its operational center, you may also be required to buy licenses in those cities. For example, if you have a repair service and make several calls to homes away from the city where your shop is located, you could be obligated to purchase business licenses in the cities you service. For occasional work in another city, you may only be required to obtain a permit for those days on which you perform the work.

Business licenses are serious matters in most cities. They provide a source of revenue for the city or county. Licensing is also a means of controlling the types of businesses that operate within their jurisdictions.

It is true that many businesses are currently operating without licenses. A crackdown in one major city showed that almost 50 percent of its businesses had failed to produce current business licenses. Fines were imposed and ultimatums issued that failure to secure licenses would result in shutdowns. A business license is inexpensive and lends credibility to your operation. Without one, you run the risk of being discovered and fined and/or barred from doing any business at all.

LOCATION CONSIDERATIONS

In Chapter 5, "Choosing a Business Location," you learned the basics of selecting the site of your business. Selecting your location and getting your business license is an interactive process. A business license is granted for a specific location, and the selection of the location must take into account licensing restrictions.

Contact the clerk's office in the city or county where you wish to locate your base of operation. They are an excellent source of information regarding police, fire, and health permits needed for your business. Because any business location must fall within the zoning regulations, you may obtain verification from the zoning commission to determine if your business is approved for the location you have chosen. The local business license bureau can also help you with your decision by giving you information on any special restrictions as to types of businesses allowed or disallowed at any location.

If you have decided to locate in a shopping center, industrial area, or other commercial location, call the chamber of commerce or city and ask for any publications that list available facilities and their square feet, price per square foot, and other pertinent information.

You may also contact the management of the commercial or industrial complex you are considering and request written information about that location and current availability of leasing space. You should be able to get detailed information as to lease terms, restrictions, traffic patterns, and other demographics. Be sure to read carefully and understand all the terms contained in a lease agreement. They vary and may well spell the difference between profit and loss for your business.

LICENSING A HOME-BASED BUSINESS

If you have elected to have a home-based business, restrictions may not permit you to get a business license to operate in your city. You may be forced to move your business outside the home or operate outside of the law. If your family happens to be moving and you are a seasoned entrepreneur, you may wish to select your home partly on the basis of whether or not that city's ordinances will allow you to operate your business—or any business—out of your home.

If you are thinking of living in a planned community, don't forget to check any restrictions the association may have that relate to business use of your home. Even if the city will allow you to operate your business, the association may preclude that option.

The passage of the Model Zoning Ordinance did much to help protect the legalities of working from home. However, different types of businesses may be subject to special restrictions by the city or county.

For instance, a mail-order business may be allowed in your home, but a direct-sales operation may be prohibited. Repair services may be allowed, but only if they do not involve the use of toxic chemicals. Food services will probably be disallowed, but the city may allow you to use your home as an administrative office for your business.

In most cities and planned communities, home-based businesses are not permitted to change the appearance of the neighborhood, and you may therefore be prohibited the use of advertising or equipment that can be viewed from the street. Very often, police or fire inspections will be conducted to see that your business does not violate any restrictions.

Doing some diligent groundwork ahead of time may eliminate the possibility of selecting a business location only to find later that it was not an appropriate and/or legal choice.

APPLYING FOR A BUSINESS LICENSE

Once you have determined that your business meets all the specific requirements for operation within the city or county you have chosen, you are ready for a trip to the Business License Bureau or the city or county clerk's office to legalize your business.

You will be asked to fill out an application. Call ahead to find out what information you will need. This will save you time and ensure that you have all of your information on hand.

The application is usually fairly simple and will require only general information. You will probably be required to supply such specifics as

- business name and address
- owner names and contact information
- organization information (manufacturing, wholesale, retail, service)
- type of legal structure
- nature of the business
- expected number of employees
- Federal employer ID (FEIN) and state sales tax no. (resale)
- expected gross
- other relevant information.

A typical fee for a business may be as little as $.10 per $1,000 of projected revenues. We have also seen specific license fees applied to certain kinds of business. For instance, in one eastern city, the charge for a home business license is $350.

You will probably be asked to submit your completed application together with one year's fee (frequently based on projected gross revenues). Your application will be reviewed by the proper agents, and a license will either be issued or refused within a few days.

Business licenses are renewed annually, subject to that city or county's codes and regulations. Your renewal notice will be sent to you, but it is your responsibility to see that you renew should you fail to hear from the licensing agency.

ALWAYS POST YOUR BUSINESS LICENSE

Having a business license is a way of assuring customers that yours is a legal business. Your license should be posted in a visible place at your business location. If you are exhibiting or

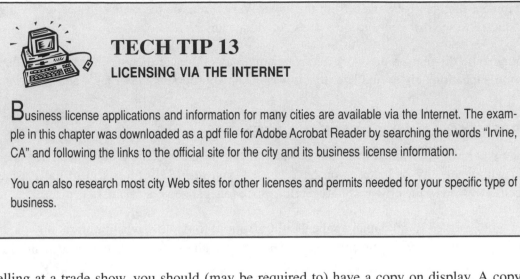

TECH TIP 13
LICENSING VIA THE INTERNET

Business license applications and information for many cities are available via the Internet. The example in this chapter was downloaded as a pdf file for Adobe Acrobat Reader by searching the words "Irvine, CA" and following the links to the official site for the city and its business license information.

You can also research most city Web sites for other licenses and permits needed for your specific type of business.

selling at a trade show, you should (may be required to) have a copy on display. A copy of your business license may also be requested to establish accounts with vendors or gain admission to trade and industry shows.

Example

To give you an idea of some of the types of information that may be requested, a sample of a business license application can be seen on the next two pages. Applications will vary according to your city or county.

City of Irvine Business License Application

- **CITY OF IRVINE**
- **BUSINESS LICENSE APPLICATION**

One Civic Center Plaza, PO. BOX 19575
Irvine, CA 92623-9575
(949) 724 6310   www.ci.irvine.ca.us

Date received

OFFICE USE ONLY

BUSINESS LICENSE NO.

Date Payment Posted

Important! Asterisk (*) Indicates Required Information If Applicable To This Business. Please Print Clearly. Be sure to complete and submit both sides of the application. Illegible, incomplete or applications without payment will be returned.

*1. Business Name Line 1:

*2. Business Name Line 2:

*3. Business Address:

Street (P.O. Box NOT acceptable)   Suite

City   State   Zip

4. Mailing Address:

Street   Suite

City   State   Zip

*5. Business Phone: *6. Fax Number:

7. Web Address: *8. E-Mail Address:

- **OWNER AND EMERGENCY CONTACT INFORMATION:**

*9. List residence, address, phone, title, and driver's license number of Owner, President, Partner, CEO, CFO, etc.
(Note: The name of the person listed here will be printed on the Business License Certificate; Attach a list of additional contacts)

Last Name,   First Name   Residence address   City   State   Zip

Title   Phone   Driver's License Number and State

*10. Please indicate whom the City should contact to secure the building in the event of an **emergency** such as fire:

Last Name,   First Name   Title   Phone

| - **IS YOUR OCCUPATION LICENSED BY THE STATE?** | - ☐ No | - ☐ Yes |

*11. State License Type: *12.: State License #   *13. Expiration:

Month/Day/Year

*14. Specify job location in Irvine:

*15. Does your business create, store, generate, or use hazardous substances or any products that are considered to be corrosive, reactive, ignitable, toxic, and/or ozone depleters?   ☐ No   ☐ Yes

- **ORGANIZATION INFORMATION: MUST BE COMPLETED**

*16. Is this business conducted from your home in Irvine?   ☐ No   ☐ Yes   (*If yes, complete the **Home Occupancy Form**)

| *17. Indicate type of business being conducted at Irvine location: Please check box(es) | ☐ Manufacturing: ☐ In Irvine?: | ☐ Wholesale: ☐ Durable and/or ☐ Non Durable Goods | ☐ Retail | ☐ Service |

*18. Type of Ownership: (check one of the following five options)

☐ Sole Proprietorship (Owner's Social Security No. _____)   ☐ Partnership (Complete Line 21)

☐ Corporation (Complete Line 21)   ☐ Limited Liability Co. (Complete Line 21)   ☐ Trust (Complete Line 21)

*19. **Please describe the exact nature of the business activity to be conducted** (i.e., Consultant, Physician, Painter, etc)

*20. Is your organization Tax Exempt?   ☐ No   ☐ Yes   If Yes, specify below & submit documentation with application [†] ☐ Non-Profit Organization   or   ☐ Organization paying in-lieu-of taxes to the state

*21. Federal Employer ID (FEIN):   22. State Employer ID (SEIN):

*23. State Sales Tax No. (RESALE):   *24. Date Business Started in Irvine:

Month/Day/Year

*25. Did you purchase this business?   ☐ No   ☐ Yes   (*If yes, enter date of purchase)

Form 22-05, Rev 4/02 Fax Library Document 200

City of Irvine Business License Application, continued

*26. How many people including owners, full & part time employees are working *in Irvine* for your business? _____

- **FOR BUSINESSES LOCATED IN THE CITY OF IRVINE ONLY**

*27. Do you manufacture/wholesale/sell taxable products or provide a taxable service such as renting products/equipment or fabrication labor from your location in Irvine? (Complete Line 23) ☐ No ☐ Yes   *If yes, what type of products are sold?

*28. Is this application made to move an existing business from another location? ☐ No ☐ Yes   *If yes, please list the former address

- **APPLICATION CANNOT BE ACCEPTED OR PROCESSED WITHOUT SIGNATURE AND PAYMENT**

It is the responsibility of the applicant/ licensee to ensure THEIR business complies with all applicable City of Irvine Codes and the City Zoning Ordinance. In the event it is determined the business does not comply, the business license may be revoked by the City. I hereby certify, under penalty of perjury, the information provided on this application is true and correct.

_____
*Projected Annual Gross Receipts (or Income)

_____
*Print Applicant's Name and Title

X
_____
*Applicant Signature

_____
*Date Signed

● 29 COMPUTATION OF FEES ‡§	
A. Annual Fee	$ 50.00
(If Projected Annual Gross Receipts (or Income) is less than $4,000 please call us to compute your fee)	
B. Prior Year Adjustment:	$
Choose the amount that applies from below:	
If the start date is:	
- Less than 60 days	0.00
- Greater than 60 days but less than 1 year	$ 50.00
- Greater than 1 year but less than 2 years	$ 150.00
- Greater than 2 years but less than 3 years	$ 250.00
- 3 years or greater	$ 300.00
Add Lines A and B. This is your Total Fee ●	$

- ‡ If your organization has multiple branch locations under the same Social Security Number or Federal Employer Identification Number, please indicate the business license certificate number(s) on the line provided below and omit payment.

- _____

§ For administrative, executive or similar functions that do not generate income, the annual fee is fixed at $50.00

Submit Original Application with Payment to:

City of Irvine Business Licenses, One Civic Center Plaza P.O. Box 19575, Irvine, CA 92623-9575

Please Allow Three Weeks To Receive a Business License Certificate

-

BUSINESS LICENSE REQUIREMENT The City of Irvine requires all organizations operating within the City to have a business license (Code of Ordinances Section 2-10-201). This requirement enables the City to maintain a database of businesses within the City that is used for police emergency response, disaster preparedness, estimating daytime population, and demographic studies. Certain public information is also beneficial in providing assistance to the business community for economic development purposes and coordinating business information with other governmental agencies.

ANNUALLY RENEWING YOUR BUSINESS LICENSE (RENEWALS) Much like an automobile or driver's license, it is your responsibility to ensure that you keep your license current by paying your annual business license fees on a timely basis. The City will mail courtesy renewal notices to the mailing address of record. However, if you do not receive a courtesy notice, you are not alleviated from this requirement. Penalties are imposed for late renewal applications.

†**NON-PROFIT BUSINESS LICENSE APPLICATION INSTRUCTIONS:** To qualify for a non-profit business license the City requires that the following documentation be submitted with your application: 1) Your IRS statement verifying non-profit status, 2) Incorporation statement from the Secretary of State, 3) Your corporation Bylaws and/or Charter, 4) A list of officers [be sure to include local representatives], 5) a letter describing your business activities and/or your method of solicitation, 6) a list of names, driver's license numbers and the state issuance, home address and telephone numbers of solicitors, volunteers or employees who will enter Irvine for business purposes. If your business activities include door-to-door solicitation each individual involved in the solicitation process must carry a valid employer/employee identification badge and a copy of your Business License. After review and approval of your business license application a Business License will be issued to your organization at no charge.

OBTAINING HELP COMPLETING THIS APPLICATION: For specific questions regarding any of the requirements on a New Application pertaining to business names beginning with A-K call 949-724-6481 for L-Z call 949-724-6312. For specific questions regarding Renewing Licenses (Renewals) call 949-724-6303. For general question please contact the Business License Section at business.permits@ci.irvine.ca.us or the information line at (949) 724-6310.

Form 22-05, Rev 4/02 Fax Library Document 200

CHAPTER 11

REGISTERING A FICTITIOUS NAME (FILING A "DBA")

What is a fictitious name (or DBA)? A fictitious name is commonly referred to as a DBA, which stands for "Doing Business As." A fictitious name is any business name that does not contain your own name as a part of it. In some states, that means your legal name (frequently first and last).

If you have not formed a corporation and plan to conduct business under a fictitious name, you must file a DBA. If you have formed a corporation, ownership of your name is ensured when you incorporate. Also, if your legal name is considered common, you may be required to file a DBA.

The following examples illustrate this point:

1. Ocean Adventures. DBA required

2. Glenn's Ocean Adventures. DBA required

3. Sullivan's Ocean Adventures. DBA probably required

4. Glenn Sullivan's Ocean Adventures. No DBA required

5. John Smith's Ocean Adventures. DBA may be required (common name)

6. Ocean Adventures, Inc. No DBA required (corporation)

Filing your DBA is one of the first tasks to undertake because every other piece of paperwork requires the business name. Your bank will also require a copy of your DBA before they will open a business account under that name. This is the only authorization they have for depositing or cashing checks made out to that business name or written against its account.

Your business name should be free of conflict with names already registered in your area. Find out if a corporation has staked a claim to your name by calling your state's office of name availability. You may also wish to check the DBA books at the county clerk's office. Finding out at a later date that your name is already legally registered to another business will result in your having to redo all of your paperwork.

Note: You may wish to refer back to Chapter 4, "Choosing a Business Name," for further information on how to research the name of your business.

IF YOU FAIL TO FILE

Registering a business name is important for your own protection as well as for compliance with the law. Registration of that name gives you exclusive rights to it. It also keeps others from filing the same or a similar name and capitalizing on the hard work and investments you have made in your business.

Unfortunately, there are individuals who lurk in the shadows waiting for just such an opportunity. About eight years ago, we had a business owner in one of our classes who had built a successful electronics firm. However, he failed to file a DBA. Someone else discovered his error, filed under his business name, and offered him the option of either paying to buy the name back or ceasing to do business under that name. The business owner refused to pay the blackmail and chose to reestablish under a new name. However the continuity of his business was set back, and he lost a large amount of business trying to reestablish under the new name.

The time and money required to file a DBA are small compared to the benefits you will derive from becoming the legal owner of your business name.

HOW TO FILE A DBA

Assuming you have chosen a fictitious name, it is time to register (or file) it with the city or county in which you are doing business. This is a two-part process: first you must publish your fictitious name through a general circulation newspaper; second you must file that name with the county clerk.

1. *Publishing your fictitious name.* Your fictitious name must be published in a general circulation newspaper in your area. It must appear in four consecutive editions. When your fictitious name is published, the newspaper will send you a copy of the publication and issue a publication certificate. The fee for this service may vary from $20 to $75.

2. *Filing with the county clerk.* The publication certificate has to be filed with the city or county clerk. They will send you proof that it has been recorded. Fees for filing your DBA vary, but most run from $15 to $50.

Some newspapers will collect your fees **and** file for you after publishing. This will save you a trip to the county clerk's office. Others only publish and require that you do your own filing. As you can see above, there is also a lot of variation in the fees they charge for this service.

Local newspapers frequently charge less and are easier to access. It would be wise for you to do some calling to various newspapers and ask the following questions:

- Do you publish new DBAs?

- What is your charge for the publication of a DBA?

- Do you (the newspaper) also file with the city or county clerk? If so, what are the fees for filing?

- What information do I need to bring with me in order to complete the fictitious name statement?

TECH TIP 14

DOWNLOADING FICTITIOUS BUSINESS NAME FORMS

Fictitious business name statement forms can be downloaded via the Internet in pdf format from most official county sites. The example at the end of the chapter was downloaded by searching the name "Orange County, CA" and following the links to the official Web site for the county and then choosing "forms to download."

RENEWAL OF YOUR DBA

You will be required to renew your DBA at certain intervals, such as every five years. You will be notified by the filing agency when it is time to renew. Again, it is your responsibility to know when it must be done and protect yourself by inquiring if you do not receive your renewal notification. Renewal does not require republishing, but will involve a fee to the city or county clerk.

Alert. There are companies that keep track of expiring DBAs and send you official-looking notices to refile. They also build in a hidden fee. Refiling is simple. Be sure your notice is the official one from the county clerk.

Sample Forms

The next two pages contain examples of a fictitious business name statement and a proof of publication that has been filed with the county clerk's office.

Fictitious Business Name Statement

TOM DALY
ORANGE COUNTY CLERK-RECORDER
12 CIVIC CENTER PLAZA, ROOM 106
POST OFFICE BOX 238
SANTA ANA, CA 92702-0238

FICTITIOUS BUSINESS NAME STATEMENT FILING INSTRUCTIONS
To ensure a prompt and accurate record of your filing, type or print in black ink only.
DO NOT ABBREVIATE.

THE FOLLOWING PERSON(S) IS (ARE) DOING BUSINESS AS:

1.	Fictitious Business Name(s) (optional) Business Phone No. (_____) _____
1A.	☐ New Statement ☐ Refile—List Previous No._____ ☐ Change
2.	Street Address, City & State of Principal place of Business City State Zip Code (Do **NOT** use a P.O. Box or P.M.B.)
3.	Full name of Registrant (If Corporation, enter corporation name) If Corporation/L.L.C. State of Incorporation or organization
	Res./Corp. Address (Do **NOT** use a P.O. Box or P.M.B.) City State Zip Code
	Full name of Registrant (If Corporation, enter corporation name) If Corporation/L.L.C. State of Incorporation or organization
	Res./Corp. Address (Do **NOT** use a P.O. Box or P.M.B.) City State Zip Code
	Full name of Registrant (If Corporation, enter corporation name) If Corporation/L.L.C. State of Incorporation or organization
	Res./Corp. Address (Do **NOT** use a P.O. Box or P.M.B.) City State Zip Code
4.	(CHECK ONE ONLY) This business is conducted by (○) an individual (○) a general partnership (○) a limited partnership (○) an unincorporated association other than a partnership (○) a corporation (○) a business trust (○) co-partners (○) husband and wife (○) joint venture (○) Limited Liability Co. (○) Other–Specify _____
5.	Have you started doing business yet? Yes ☐ Insert the date you started: _____ No ☐	NOTICE: THIS FICTITIOUS NAME STATEMENT EXPIRES FIVE YEARS FROM THE DATE IT WAS FILED IN THE OFFICE OF THE COUNTY CLERK-RECORDER. A NEW FICTITIOUS BUSINESS NAME STATEMENT MUST BE FILED BEFORE THAT DATE. THE FILING OF THIS STATEMENT DOES NOT OF ITSELF AUTHORIZE THE USE IN THIS STATE OF A FICTITIOUS BUSINESS NAME IN VIOLATION OF THE RIGHTS OF ANOTHER UNDER FEDERAL, STATE, OR COMMON LAW (SEE SECTION 14411 ET SEQ., BUSINESS AND PROFESSIONS CODE).
6.	If Registrant is NOT a corporation, sign below: (See instructions on the reverse side of this form.) Signature_____ _____ (Type or Print Name) I declare that all information in this statement is true and correct. (A registrant who declares as true information which he or she knows to be false is guilty of a crime.)	If Registrant is a corporation, an officer of the corporation signs below: If Registrant is a limited liability company, a manager or an officer signs below. _____ Limited Liability Company Name/Corporation Name _____ Signature and Title of Officer or Manager I declare that all information in this statement is true and correct. (A registrant who declares as true information which he or she knows to be false is guilty of a crime.) _____ Print or Type Officer's/Manager's Name and Title

(THIS FEE APPLIES AT THE TIME OF FILING)
FILING FEE $23.00 FOR ONE BUSINESS NAME.
$7.00 FOR EACH ADDITIONAL BUSINESS NAME.
$7.00 FOR EACH ADDITIONAL PARTNER AFTER FIRST TWO.
PROVIDE A SELF-ADDRESSED, STAMPED, RETURN ENVELOPE IF MAILED.
➡ F059-FictitiousBus.Stmt. (R12/02)

Publication Certificate Example

PROOF OF PUBLICATION
(2015.5c.c.p.)

STATE OF CALIFORNIA

COUNTY OF ORANGE

I am a citizen of the United States and a resident of the County aforesaid; I am over the age of eighteen years, and not a party to or interested in the above-entitled matter. I am the principal clerk of the printer of the Orange Big News, a newspaper of general circulation printed and published weekly in the City of Orangetown, County of Orange, and which newspaper has been adjudged a newspaper of general circulation by the Superior Court of the County of Orange, State of California, under the date of April 14, 1987, Case Number A-62222, that the notice of which the annexed is a printed copy (set in type not smaller than nonpareil), has been published in each regular and entire issue of said newspaper and not in any supplement thereof on the following dates, to wit:

.... 9/07 9/14 9/21 9/28 ....

all in the year 20 03.

I certify (or declare) under penalty of perjury that the foregoing is true and correct.

Dated at Orangetown, California, this......28th........day

of...September..............................., 20....03....

Arlene S. Herzog
....
Signature

ORANGE BIG NEWS
533 W Harper
Orangetown, California 92622

OCH FORM NO. 0023-6/78-621-2M

This space is for the County Clerk's Filing Stamp

FILED
SEP 28 2003
PETER M. JONES, County Clerk
By_____DEPUTY

Proof of Publication of

**FICTITIOUS
BUSINESS NAME
STATEMENT
F5987003**

The following person(s) are
doing business as:
Ace Sporting Goods
12345 Edwards St.
Anytown, CA 93456

1. JOHN R. SMITH
2345 Newstreet Drive
Anytown, CA 93456
This business is conducted
by an individual.
The registrant commenced
to transact business under the
fictitious business name or
names listed above on June 7,
2003.
Published: Orange Big News
September 7, 14, 21, 28, 2003

PROOF OF PUBLICATION

F-_____

OBTAINING A SELLER'S PERMIT

Anyone who purchases items for resale or provides a taxable service must obtain a seller's permit number. This number is required in all states where sales tax is collected.

APPLYING FOR A SELLER'S PERMIT

Information regarding sales tax and getting a seller's permit can be obtained through your state's Department of Revenue. Applications can be made through your local state offices. After filling out your application, you will be called in to interview. Following this interview and a review of your application, it will be determined whether or not you qualify for a seller's permit. For this reason, it is imperative that you understand exactly what you are requesting and the purpose for which you are requesting it. The wrong answer to a question can result in the denial of your certificate.

Note: An example application from the California State Board of Equalization is included in the last part of this chapter.

PURPOSE OF A SELLER'S PERMIT

A sales tax is imposed upon retailers for the privilege of selling tangible personal property at retail within a state. The retailer, not the customer, is the person liable and responsible for paying the sales tax. Consequently, every seller engaged in the business of selling a tangible product or providing a taxable service in a state where sales tax is collected is required to hold a seller's permit for the purpose of reporting and paying their sales and use tax liability. The seller's permit is more commonly referred to as a **resale tax number**.

Because of the complications involved in the sales tax process, it may be difficult to determine which of your products and services will be taxable. You may request information sheets from the State Department of Revenue or your local State Board of Equalization that will explain the sales tax regulations on your particular type of business. You may also request a ruling to determine whether or not your product or service is taxable under a particular circumstance. Later, you must be sure to keep abreast of any changes that are made regarding the taxing of sales for your particular industry.

Your request must be on the basis that your business will be selling taxable items to your customers or providing a taxable service. Any other reason for your request will be grounds for denial. For example, many food services are not taxable unless they are provided at an event that charges admission. Therefore, a resale tax number would not be warranted.

Warning. *Do not use the word "buy" when you are applying for a seller's permit. Even though you may gain some purchasing advantages by having a seller's permit, this is not a valid reason for getting one. In fact, the mention of your intent to use it for the purchase of goods may prejudice the interviewer against you.*

STATE LAWS VARY

The laws governing the collection of sales tax in any state can be complex. They also vary from state to state. There have been many attempts to come up with a uniform sales tax system that would be fair to the consumer and at the same time guarantee collection of tax on all applicable sales. Individual states are also working to ensure that out-of-state companies servicing their companies in state and selling their products through local outlets are collecting and reporting sales tax.

Some states (including California) have laws that require buyers of out-of-state goods to pay a use tax—a law that would increase state revenues significantly but is difficult to monitor or enforce.

Finally, there is the never-ending debate regarding the legalities of selling via the Internet without collecting or reporting sales tax. Brick and mortar businesses feel that selling tax-free via the Internet gives online sellers an unfair advantage. Internet sellers think they should not have to collect sales taxes. It remains to be seen how the issue will be resolved.

MISUSE OF YOUR SELLER'S PERMIT

Once you have been issued a resale tax number, it is imperative that you use it only for the purpose for which it was intended. Many tax numbers have been used to avoid paying sales tax on business-related purchases as well as tax on personal items. Purposeful misuse of a seller's permit has long been a laughing matter with many users. If you get caught, however, it may cease to be something to brag about. Most states are expanding their efforts to catch offenders. The penalties for misuse are serious and may involve a heavy fine and/or jail sentence.

The rule of thumb is: If you do not intend to resell your purchase through your business, do not use your resale number in order to buy it without paying sales tax.

At this point, it is only fair to say that there is some validity to using your resale number to purchase wholesale. Many wholesalers do ask you to file a resale card with them before they will sell to you at wholesale prices. However, this does not mean you are not required to pay sales tax if you are not purchasing for resale. It may only be a means of adding credibility as a business owner. In fact, if the seller does not collect from you at the time of the sale, you will be required to include the purchase in your periodic sales tax report and pay the sales tax at that time.

RESALE CERTIFICATE

If you are purchasing goods for resale, the supplier or manufacturer will ask you to fill out a resale certificate that may be kept on file to validate selling to you on a tax-free basis. By the same token, when you sell to another dealer, you must also have him or her fill out a resale card for your files. If the state later questions your nontaxable sales, you will have documentation as to why you did not collect tax on the sale. Pads of resale certificates may be purchased at almost any stationery supply store.

Note: An example of a **resale certificate** can be found in the final portion of this chapter.

REPORTING SALES TAX

As previously stated, the purpose of a seller's permit is to provide the state with a means of collecting sales tax. To accomplish this, the sales tax must be accounted for by the final seller and sent to the state along with a report of the sources of those taxes. For this reason, the seller must keep accurate records on the types of sales made and the amount of sales falling within each of the following categories:

- Gross sales
- Purchase price of property you bought without paying sales tax and that you used for purposes other than resale
- Sales to other retailers for purposes of resale
- Nontaxable sale of food products
- Nontaxable labor (repair and installation)
- Sales to the U.S. government
- Sales in interstate or foreign commerce to out-of-state consumers
- Bad debt losses on taxable sales
- Other exempt transactions

Note. Sales tax rates may vary from county to county. When you are selling out of your local area, you will collect sales tax based on the current rate in that area. You will also be required to keep an accurate record of those sales. In many cases a portion of your state's sales tax may be designated as belonging to a transit district, special assessment, etc. For instance, the State of California has many transit districts that are allocated one half of one percent to support their mass transportation systems. Therefore, a retailer from Los Angeles selling at a trade show in San Francisco will have to report the amount of those sales so the funds may be properly divided by the state agency.

The state will require you to file a quarterly report in which you summarize your sales for the period. If your taxable sales are unusually small, you may only have to report annually. If they are excessive, you may be required to place a bond and report monthly. The reporting form will be sent to you by the Department of Revenue or State Board of Equalization. You must complete the report and mail it to the state, along with your check in the amount of sales tax due, by a certain date (usually at the end of the month following the reporting period).

A note of caution about responsibility for reporting: If you do not receive a report form in the mail, it will be your responsibility to call the Department of Revenue and request that officials send you one.

When you receive this report, you will also receive a tax information sheet with featured articles on sales tax regulations and crackdowns. Take the time to read it carefully, especially the information that may pertain to your particular industry. Failure to properly report may result in loss of your resale privilege as well as the more serious penalties mentioned above.

Sample: A copy of a **California State Board of Equalization Report** form is included at the end of this chapter. The form for your state will probably be similar.

TECH TIP 15
KEEPING TRACK OF SALES FOR EASY SALES TAX REPORTING

Sales tax reporting can be a long and tedious process, or you can do it at the click of a mouse. The secret is to utilize your accounting software to generate the information you need for your report to your local sales tax authority.

In order to generate the right information, you will have to think in terms of sales tax reporting when you set up your chart of accounts. This means that revenue accounts will need to be divided not only by the types of products and services you sell but also according to their applicability to sales tax reporting responsibility.

Example. If you are in the business of selling two taxable products and your state requires sales information on taxable sales, out-of-state sales, sales to resellers, and sales tax payable, your chart of revenue accounts could be set up as follows:

Taxable Sales	Out-of State Sales	Reseller Sales
Product #1	Product #1	Product #1
Product #2	Product #2	Product #2

When sales revenue deposits are made, they are "split" deposits, and revenues are allocated among the appropriate accounts. Sales tax amounts will be automatically calculated on the taxable sales.

The benefit. At any given time, you will be able to generate a report that will give you the numbers you need for your state's sales tax report.

Sales Tax Flowchart

In the event that you are somewhat confused as to the progression of goods from the manufacturer to the consumer and final payment of taxes to the state by the seller, we have prepared a Sales Tax Flowchart for you. Examination of the flowchart should help to eliminate some of the confusion. The chart will cover sales that are made under five separate circumstances.

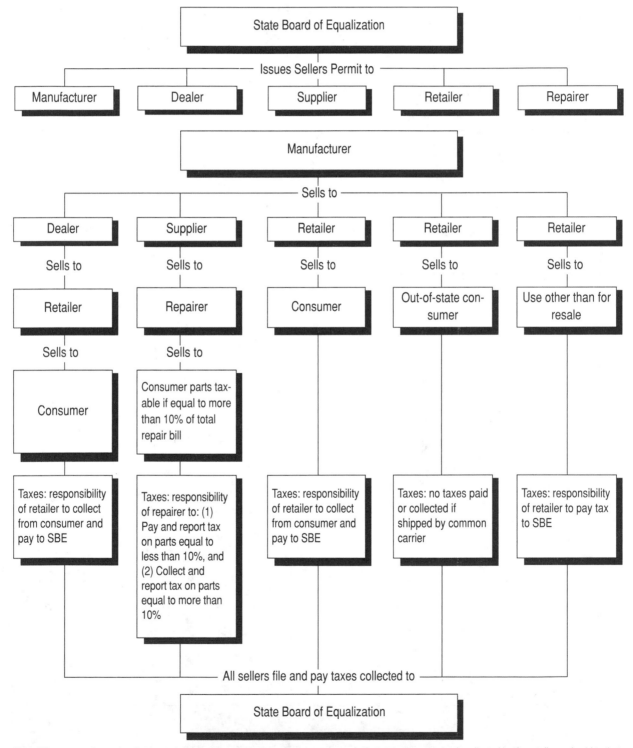

Note: When a manufacturer sells to out-of-state retailer who in turn sells to a consumer in that state, the sales tax is collected by the retailer and paid to that state. If mailed directly to consumer, no sales tax is paid.

Application for Seller's Permit

BOE-400-MIP (FRONT) REV. 18 (1-03)

**APPLICATION FOR SELLER'S PERMIT AND REGISTRATION
AS A RETAILER (INDIVIDUALS/PARTNERSHIPS)**

STATE OF CALIFORNIA
BOARD OF EQUALIZATION

Use additional sheet(s) to include information for more than two partners

SECTION I: OWNERSHIP INFORMATION	FOR BOARD USE ONLY			
1. PLEASE CHECK TYPE OF OWNERSHIP	TAX	IND	OFFICE	NUMBER
☐ Sole Owner ☐ Husband/Wife Co-ownership	**SR**			
☐ General Partnership ☐ Limited Partnership				
☐ Limited Liability Partnership *(registered to practice law, accounting or architecture)* Provide documents filed with Secretary of State.	BUSINESS CODE		AREA CODE	
Enter Federal Employer Identification Number (FEIN), if any	APPLICATION PROCESSED BY		VERIFICATION: ☐ DL ☐ Other	

OWNER OR PARTNER

2. PARTNERSHIP NAME *(if applicable)*

3. Did you include a copy of your partnership agreement? ☐ Yes ☐ No

4. FULL NAME *(first, middle, last)*

5. SOCIAL SECURITY NUMBER

6. DRIVER LICENSE NUMBER *(attach verification)*

7. RESIDENCE ADDRESS *(street, city, state, zip code)*

8. RESIDENCE TELEPHONE NUMBER
(   )

9. NAME, ADDRESS & TELEPHONE NUMBER OF A PERSONAL REFERENCE WHO DOES NOT LIVE WITH YOU

CO-OWNER OR PARTNER

10. FULL NAME *(first, middle, last)*

11. SOCIAL SECURITY NUMBER

12. DRIVER LICENSE NUMBER *(attach verification)*

13. RESIDENCE ADDRESS *(street, city, state, zip code)*

14. RESIDENCE TELEPHONE NUMBER
(   )

15. NAME, ADDRESS & TELEPHONE NUMBER OF A PERSONAL REFERENCE WHO DOES NOT LIVE WITH YOU

SECTION II: BUSINESS INFORMATION

16. BUSINESS NAME [DBA] *(complete if different than entity name)*

17. BUSINESS ADDRESS *(street, city, state, zip code) [do not list P.O. Box or mailing service]*

18. BUSINESS TELEPHONE NUMBER
(   )

19. MAILING ADDRESS *(street, city, state, zip code) [if different from business address]*

20. BUSINESS FAX NUMBER
(   )

21. DATE YOU WILL BEGIN BUSINESS ACTIVITIES *(month, day & year)*

22. TYPE OF ITEMS SOLD

23. NUMBER OF SELLING LOCATIONS *(if 2 or more, attach list of all locations)*

24. TYPE OF BUSINESS *(check one that best describes your business)*

☐ Retail ☐ Wholesale ☐ Mfg. ☐ Repair ☐ Service ☐ Construction Contractor

CHECK ONE
☐ Full Time ☐ Part Time

25. OWNERSHIP CHANGES

Are you buying an existing business? ☐ Yes ☐ No If yes, complete items 26 through 30 below.

Are you changing from one type of business organization to another (for example, from a sole owner to a general partnership or from a general partnership to a limited liability company, etc.)? ☐ Yes ☐ No If yes, complete items 28 and 29 below.

Other: _____

26. PURCHASE PRICE
$

27. VALUE OF FIXTURES & EQUIPMENT
$

28. FORMER OWNER'S NAME

29. SELLER'S PERMIT ACCOUNT NUMBER

30. IF AN ESCROW COMPANY IS REQUESTING A TAX CLEARANCE ON YOUR BEHALF, PLEASE LIST THEIR NAME, ADDRESS, TELEPHONE NUMBER AND THE ESCROW NUMBER

31. DO YOU MAKE INTERNET SALES?
☐ Yes ☐ No If yes, answer 32.

32. WEBSITE ADDRESS

Continued on Reverse

— tear at dotted line —

Application for Seller's Permit, continued

BOE-400-MIP (BACK) REV. 18 (1-03)

33. IF ALCOHOLIC BEVERAGES ARE SOLD, PLEASE LIST YOUR ALCOHOLIC BEVERAGE CONTROL LICENSE NO. AND TYPE

34. NAME, ADDRESS & TELEPHONE NUMBER OF BUSINESS LANDLORD

35. NAME, ADDRESS & TELEPHONE NUMBER OF PERSON MAINTAINING YOUR RECORDS

36. NAME & LOCATION OF BANK OR OTHER FINANCIAL INSTITUTION *(note whether business or personal)*	CHECKING ACCOUNT NUMBER(S)
	SAVINGS ACCOUNT NUMBER(S)
37. NAMES & ADDRESSES OF MAJOR SUPPLIERS	PRODUCTS PURCHASED

SECTION III: SALES AND EMPLOYER INFORMATION

38. PROJECTED MONTHLY SALES *(if unknown, enter an estimated amount)*

Total gross sales $ _____   Taxable sales $_____

39. INFORMATION CONCERNING EMPLOYMENT DEVELOPMENT DEPARTMENT *(EDD)*

Are you registered with EDD? .... ☐ Yes ☐ No

If no, will your payroll exceed $100 per quarter? .... ☐ Yes ☐ No

If yes, you must apply with EDD.

Number of employees _____ (See pamphlet DE 44, *California Employer's Guide*)

I received pamphlet DE 44, *California Employer's Guide*. .... ☐ Yes ☐ No

CERTIFICATION

All owners and partners must sign below.

I am duly authorized to sign the application and certify that the statements made are correct to the best of my knowledge and belief. I also represent and acknowledge that the applicant will be engaged in or conduct businesses as a seller of tangible personal property.

NAME *(typed or printed)*	SIGNATURE	DATE
NAME *(typed or printed)*	SIGNATURE	DATE
NAME *(typed or printed)*	SIGNATURE	DATE
NAME *(typed or printed)*	SIGNATURE	DATE

FOR BOARD USE ONLY
Furnished to Taxpayer

REPORTING BASIS	FORMS	PUBLICATIONS
SECURITY REVIEW	☐ BOE-8 ☐ BOE-400-Y	☐ PUB 73 ☐ PUB DE 44
☐ BOE-598 $_____	☐ BOE-467 ☐ BOE-519	
☐ BOE-1009	☐ BOE-1241-D	
BY		
APPROVED BY	REGULATIONS	RETURNS
REMOTE INPUT DATE	☐ REG. 1668 ☐ REG. 1698	
BY	☐ REG. 1700	
☐ Permit Issued Date _____		

CLEAR   PRINT

State Board of Equalization Report

BOE-401-A2 (S1) REV. 92 (10-02)

STATE, LOCAL and DISTRICT SALES and USE TAX RETURN

STATE OF CALIFORNIA
BOARD OF EQUALIZATION

BOARD USE ONLY		
RA-TT	LOC	REG
RA-BTR	AACS	REF

DUE ON OR BEFORE | **FOR** | PERIOD | YEAR

IMPORTANT:

Your account number and reporting period are required.

SELLER'S PERMIT ACCOUNT NUMBER

EFF

Mail To:
BOARD OF EQUALIZATION
PO BOX 942879
SACRAMENTO CA 94279-7072

NAME

BUSINESS ADDRESS

CITY | STATE | ZIP

READ SCHEDULE T AND RETURN INSTRUCTIONS 02-2 BEFORE PREPARING THIS RETURN

1. TOTAL *(gross)* SALES	1.	$	.00
2. PURCHASES SUBJECT TO USE TAX	2.		.00
3. TOTAL *(add lines 1 and 2)*	3.		.00

PLEASE COMPLETE LINES 4 THRU 10(f) ON THE **BACK PAGE** OF THIS RETURN.

11. TOTAL NONTAXABLE TRANSACTIONS REPORTED *(Enter total deductions from line 11 on the back page)*	11.	.00
12. TRANSACTIONS SUBJECT TO STATE TAX *(subtract line 11 from line 3)*	12.	.00
12.(a) ENTER AMOUNT FROM TAX ADJUSTMENT WORKSHEET LINE 12, COLUMN B	12.(a)	.00	
13. **STATE** TAX 6% *[multiply line 12 by .06* **OR** *enter line 13(c) amount from the Tax Adjustment Worksheet]*	13.	.00	<
14. (a) TRANSACTIONS SUBJECT TO COUNTY TAX *[add amount in box 61 (back) and line 12 above]*	14.(a)	.00	
(b) **COUNTY** TAX 1/4% *[multiply line 14(a) by .0025]*	14.(b)	.00	<
15. ADJUSTMENTS FOR LOCAL TAX *(see line 15 instructions)*	15.	.00	
16. TRANSACTIONS SUBJECT TO LOCAL TAX *[add or subtract line 15 to/from line 14(a)]*	16.	.00	
17. **LOCAL** TAX 1% *(multiply line 16 by .01)*	17.	.00	<
18. **DISTRICT** TAX *(from Schedule A, line A11)* YOU **MUST** COMPLETE FORM BOE-531-A, SCHEDULE A IF YOU ARE ENGAGED IN BUSINESS IN A TRANSACTIONS AND USE TAX DISTRICT	18.	.00	<
19. **TOTAL STATE, COUNTY, LOCAL AND DISTRICT TAX** *[add lines 13, 14(b), 17, & 18]*	19.	.00	
20. DEDUCT SALES OR USE TAX IMPOSED BY OTHER STATES AND PAID ON THE PURCHASE PRICE OF TANGIBLE PERSONAL PROPERTY. THE PURCHASE PRICE MUST BE INCLUDED IN LINE 2 ABOVE.	20.	.00	
21. **NET TAX** *(subtract line 20 from line 19)*	21.	.00	
22. LESS-TAX PREPAYMENTS 1st prepayment (Tax only) $ 2nd prepayment (Tax only) $	22.	.00	
23. REMAINING TAX *(subtract line 22 from line 21)*	23.	.00	
24. PENALTY of 10% *(.10)* is due if your tax payment is made, or your return is filed, after the due date shown above. *(see line 24 instructions)*	PENALTY 24.	.00	
25. INTEREST: One month's interest is due on tax for each month or fraction of a month that payment is delayed after the due date. The adjusted monthly interest rate is .0075 (9% divided by 12).	INTEREST 25.	.00	
26. **TOTAL AMOUNT DUE AND PAYABLE** *(add lines 23, 24, and 25)*	26.	$	.00

REC. NO

PM

RE

IF YOU PAID BY CREDIT CARD AS DESCRIBED ON PAGE 1 OF THE INSTRUCTIONS, CHECK HERE [   ].

I hereby certify that this return, including any accompanying schedules and statements, has been examined by me and to the best of my knowledge and belief is a true, correct and complete return.

YOUR SIGNATURE AND TITLE | TELEPHONE NUMBER ( ) | DATE

PAID PREPARER'S USE ONLY | PAID PREPARER'S NAME | PREPARER'S TELEPHONE NUMBER ( )

I/F

Make a copy for your records.

State Board of Equalization Report, continued

BOE-401-A2 (S2) REV. 92 (10-02)

STATE OF CALIFORNIA
BOARD OF EQUALIZATION

STATE, LOCAL and DISTRICT SALES and USE TAX RETURN

YOUR ACCOUNT NO.	REPORTING PERIOD

Deductions/Exemptions Schedule

4. SALES TO OTHER RETAILERS FOR PURPOSES OF RESALE	50	$ .00
5. NONTAXABLE SALES OF FOOD PRODUCTS	51	.00
6. NONTAXABLE LABOR *(repair and installation)*	52	.00
7. SALES TO THE UNITED STATES GOVERNMENT	53	.00
8. SALES IN INTERSTATE OR FOREIGN COMMERCE	54	.00
9. SALES TAX (if any) INCLUDED ON LINE 1 ON THE FRONT OF THE RETURN	55	.00
10. (a) (1) BAD DEBT LOSSES ON TAXABLE SALES	56	.00
(2) BAD DEBT LENDER LOSSES	62	.00
(b) COST OF TAX-PAID PURCHASES RESOLD PRIOR TO USE	57	.00
(c) RETURNED TAXABLE MERCHANDISE	58	.00
(d) CASH DISCOUNTS ON TAXABLE SALES	59	.00

(e) PARTIAL STATE TAX EXEMPTION - *YOU MUST COMPLETE THE PARTIAL STATE TAX EXEMPTION WORKSHEET AT THE BOTTOM OF BOE-531-T, SCHEDULE T BEFORE YOU CLAIM ANY OF THESE DEDUCTIONS.*

TOTAL PARTIAL STATE TAX EXEMPTIONS *(Enter amount from Partial State Tax Exemption Worksheet at the bottom of Schedule T, Column C, box 60)*	60	.00
(1) AMOUNT SUBJECT TO THE MANUFACTURER'S EQUIPMENT EXEMPTION *[Enter amount from Schedule T, Column C, line 10(e)(1)]*	63	.00
(2) AMOUNT SUBJECT TO THE TELEPRODUCTION EQUIPMENT EXEMPTION *[Enter amount from Schedule T, Column C, line 10(e)(2)]*	64	.00
(3) AMOUNT SUBJECT TO FARM EQUIPMENT EXEMPTION *[Enter amount from Schedule T, Column C, line 10(e)(3)]*	65	.00
(4) AMOUNT SUBJECT TO THE DIESEL FUEL USED IN FARMING AND FOOD PROCESSING EXEMPTION *[Enter amount from Schedule T, Column C, line 10(e)(4)]*	66	.00
(5) AMOUNT SUBJECT TO THE TIMBER HARVESTING EQUIPMENT AND MACHINERY EXEMPTION *[Enter amount from Schedule T, Column C, line 10(e)(5)]*	67	.00
(6) AMOUNT SUBJECT TO THE RACEHORSE BREEDING STOCK EXEMPTION *[Enter amount from Schedule T, Column C, line 10(e)(6)]*	68	.00
TOTAL ADJUSTED PARTIAL EXEMPTIONS - *(Enter the total from Column C, box 61 on your Partial State Tax Exemption Worksheet.)*	61	.00
(f) OTHER *(clearly explain)*	90	.00
11. **TOTAL NONTAXABLE TRANSACTIONS** *[Add lines 4 thru 10(d), box 61 and line 10(f), then enter here **and** on the front page line 11]*	11	$ .00

Sample Resale Certificate

APPENDIX A

California Resale Certificate

I HEREBY CERTIFY:

1. I hold valid seller's permit number:_____.

2. I am engaged in the business of selling the following type of tangible personal property:
   _____.

3. This certificate is for the purchase from _____ of the item(s) I have listed in paragraph 5 below.
   [Vendor's name]

4. I will resell the item(s) listed in paragraph 5, which I am purchasing under this resale certificate in the form of tangible personal property in the regular course of my business operations, and I will do so prior to making any use of the item(s) other than demonstration and display while holding the item(s) for sale in the regular course of my business. I understand that if I use the item(s) purchased under this certificate in any manner other than as just described, I will owe use tax based on each item's purchase price or as otherwise provided by law.

5. Description of property to be purchased for resale:
   _____.
   _____
   _____

6. I have read and understand the following:

For Your Information: A person may be guilty of a misdemeanor under Revenue and Taxation Code section 6094.5 if the purchaser knows at the time of purchase that he or she will not resell the purchased item prior to any use (other than retention, demonstration, or display while holding it for resale) and he or she furnishes a resale certificate to avoid payment to the seller of an amount as tax. Additionally, a person misusing a resale certificate for personal gain or to evade the payment of tax is liable, for each purchase, for the tax that would have been due, plus a penalty of 10 percent of the tax or $500, whichever is more.

Name of Purchaser	
Signature of Purchaser, Purchaser's Employee or Authorized Representative	
Printed Name of Person Signing	Title
Address of Purchaser	
Telephone Number	Date

SETTING UP A BANK ACCOUNT

The selection of the bank with which you will do business should be undertaken with a great deal of consideration. Banks vary greatly in the services they offer, as well as in the charges for those services. You will want to think about such factors as interest rate paid on accounts, holding periods on deposited funds, locality, hours of operation, loan policies, and merchant credit services.

The following will give you some basic information to think about when you are deciding which bank to select:

- *Have you already established a personal relationship with your banker?* If you already know the key management and personnel at your bank, you will have a head start when you need special consideration.

- *What kind of loan programs are available through the bank?* Does this bank make business loans, or does it confine itself to personal financing? Is the bank a participating SBA guaranteed lender? Does it participate in any other programs aimed at helping small business owners? Either now or sometime in the future you may need additional funds to operate or expand your business. It is easier to go to your own banker than to have to approach an unknown lender.

- *Does the bank have merchant credit card services?* You may find that your business will be more profitable if you can offer VISA and MasterCard or American Express services to your customers. We are living in an age in which buyers of products and services do not carry cash and expect to pay with a credit card. The merchant has the advantage of being able to instantly authorize the purchase and have funds deposited to the business account within 24 to 48 hours. The bank generally charges the merchant between 3 and 4 percent of the purchase amount for the service, but having the capability may significantly increase your sales.

Instant online credit card authorization has made selling over the Internet an important source of business income. If your bank offers online merchant accounts, you will need to be sure that your shopping cart system will work seamlessly with the bank's authorization and deposit system.

Warning! *If you are considering credit card services, do some careful planning before you commit your business to a program. You will get calls from lots of third-rate companies wanting to set you up with merchant services. Their salespeople are trained in the "fast sell." They thrive on signing up new small business owners. However, the costs to you can far outweigh the advantages of having the service. Ask for (and review in writing) all of the costs involved in setting up the service and monthly charges for maintaining it. Also determine the cost should you decide to discontinue services after a period of time.*

One company rented their "Brand-X" machine for $10 per month. However, if a client quit in six months, he or she would owe $1,750 for the machine. The irony was that the "Brand-X" machine cost only $200 to $300 to purchase from a reputable bank. Most banks will rent and update machines for a few dollars a month with no cost to you should you discontinue your merchant account. Watch for nonrefundable application fees and other miscellaneous charges, as well as restrictions on types of purchases you may accept (i.e., telephone orders, etc.).

- *What does the bank offer in the way of a business account?* Is there a holding period on your deposits? Can it be waived? What are the service charges? What is the policy regarding returned checks? Do they have overdraft protection? Is it an interest-bearing account? If so, do you have to maintain a minimum balance? What other kinds of accounts does the bank have that will allow you to divert temporary funds where they can earn more and still stay liquid?

- *Is the bank a federal depository bank?* If your business has employees and you are paying any of those employees more than a certain amount, you will have to deposit funds in a separate depository account on a regular basis. It will be more convenient if you can do all of your banking in the same place.

- *What additional services are available at the bank?* Do they have branches available in several locations? What hours are they open? Do they have 24-hour ATM services? Do they have safe deposit boxes? Do they have notary services? What other services does the bank have that might be required by your business?

- *Does the bank provide electronic banking services?* With the advances in computer technology, many banks now offer remote banking through online services. You can quickly access account information, transfer money, pay bills, and more—all from the convenience of your computer.

Note: It would be wise for you to spend some time telephoning banks to gather information. It can also be helpful to talk to other business people and see which banks they use and whether or not they would recommend them for your needs. You can also check out banks on the Internet.

SEPARATE BUSINESS AND PERSONAL FINANCES

Many times, a new business owner will be tempted to run business finances through personal accounts. **Do not mix** the two by trying to use the same checking account for your home and business. It is imperative that you keep your personal and business finances separate.

The IRS does not look kindly on businesses that "commingle" personal and business monies. The fate of more than one small business owner has been determined based on this issue during an audit—and not in the business's favor.

Mixing business and personal finances will also cause you many problems with your accounting and tax computations. The accounting process becomes complicated and creates a confusing paper trail when you use business funds for personal obligations and vice versa.

Business accounts are necessary for credibility when dealing with other businesses. Many of your vendors will not accept a check unless it is preprinted with your business name and address. It may also be difficult, if not impossible, to establish an open account with a supplier or wholesaler if you do not have a business bank account.

OPEN A CHECKING ACCOUNT

The first account you will need is a checking account. The following are some pointers that should help you to make needed decisions:

- *Your DBA is required.* If your business name is an assumed one, you cannot open a checking account under that name without first having filed a DBA as discussed in Chapter 11. The DBA is a means for giving the bank authority to deposit and cash checks under your fictitious name. It should be noted that banking policies at most financial institutions preclude offering interest-bearing checking accounts unless your name is part of the company name. If you have filed a DBA, be sure to take your receipt with you when you open your checking account. The bank will require a copy for their records.

- *Select a checkbook style.* When you open your checking account, you will be asked what style of checks you wish to order. You will have to decide between the book type and wallet type. The smaller one is easier to carry, but the book type is the better choice. It will allow you to record more information about your checking transactions—information that can be invaluable during accounting procedures. There is a personal desk type checkbook that is smaller than the business size and still adequate. You will have to ask about this particular style as it is not included under business checkbook selections.

- *How many checks should you order?* Be sure to think ahead as to your needs before deciding on the number of checks to order. Reordering of checks can be costly. Start with a minimum order. In most cases there will be some change that needs to be made before long. You may get a new telephone number or decide to add or subtract a name.

  At the same time you order, you may request that your checks be numbered beginning at a number other than 101. Frequently, this request will be denied on new accounts. However, if you are successful, the use of higher-numbered checks may keep the recipients of your checks from being tipped off that you are a new business. If all else fails, you can discard the first book or books of checks and start your business with a higher check number.

Note: You do not have to order your checks from your bank. There are now many computer check-writing software programs that allow you to design, generate, and print your own checks. You can also order checks from office supply companies such as NEBS. The bank is the easiest source, but others may be less expensive or suit you better.

- *Arrange for overdraft protection.* It is best if you always maintain a healthy checking account balance for your business. However, there may be times when you have to make an unexpected purchase or an arithmetic error causes your account to be overdrawn. Providing coverage for these instances can save you time and embarrassment.

- *Get an ATM card for your account.* This will allow you to deposit or withdraw funds during nonbanking hours. It will also allow you to access your funds at remote locations.

ADDITIONAL ACCOUNTS YOU MAY WISH TO CONSIDER

In addition to your checking account, you may also wish to consider other types of accounts such as savings, money market, and CDs. The interest rates are the lowest on regular savings accounts. They are usually higher on money market, CD, and other special accounts. Some have limits, and withdrawals before specified dates may impose penalties. Some are more liquid, and a limited number of checks can be drawn on the account without penalty as long as you maintain a minimum balance. The earnings are usually proportionate to the length of time for which your funds are committed.

In Conclusion

Keep in mind that all accounts need not be at the same financial institution. However, it only makes sense that the amount of business you do with any one bank will be directly proportional to the benefits you will derive from it. Be sure to look at the stability of the bank you are considering. You want to feel secure that tomorrow morning when you wake up your funds will still be available to you.

A good banking record, along with the establishment of rapport with management and personnel of your bank, may get you special concessions. For example, the hold on your deposits may be waived if the management so desires, or notary services may be extended for free as a courtesy. If you already have a bank with which you have been satisfied, you may wish to deal where you already have the advantage of being known by them as a valued customer.

Banking is serious business. Selection of the right bank and the right kinds of services will be a definite asset to your business.

Note: On the next page you will find a worksheet titled **Choosing a Bank**. It will help you to compare advantages and disadvantages of the financial institutions you are considering.

Choosing a Bank

	Name of Potential Financial Institution		
	A. City Bank	B. Home National Bank	C.
1. Have you already established a working relationship with a. the management? b. the personnel?	Manager: J. Smith personnel: great	Manager: L. Jones (service-oriented) tellers: friendly	
2. What kind of business bank accounts are available?	business checking + CDs, etc.	business checking + CDs, etc.	
3. Does this bank offer merchant credit card services?	no	yes	
4. Does the business participate in business loan programs?	real estate only	preferred SBA lender	
5. Is the bank a federal depository bank?	yes	yes	
6. Is the bank a stable financial institution?	27-year-old	22-year-old	
7. How many branches does the bank have?	7	103	
8. Is the location of the bank convenient for your business?	yes	yes	
9. What are the bank's hours of operation? Are they open on Saturdays?	9-3 Mon-Thurs. 9-6 F; 10-1 Sat	9-3 Mon-Thurs. 9-6 F; 10-3 Sat	
10. Will the bank place a holding period on your deposits?	3 days	waived except for 2nd party	
11. What will it cost you to have a business checking account?	free w/$500 min.	free w/$750 min.	
12. What other services does the bank have: a. electronic banking? b. safe deposit? c. notary public? d. electronic transfer? e. other?	a. no b. yes (free) c. no d. yes e. ATM	a. yes b. yes c. yes d. yes e. ATM; seminars	
13. What is your overall feeling about the bank?	nice bank, but does not fill need	seems to be stable and fills all needs	

SELECTING YOUR INSURANCE

At some point during the formation of a business, the question of insurance needs will necessarily arise. In fact, if you are writing a business plan, insurance will be one of the topics you cover in the organizational plan and interpret into costs in your financial documents.

Today's world of rapidly expanding technology goes hand-in-hand with a society steeped in lawsuits. The most innocent business owner can find himself or herself involved in legal actions against the business. In addition to liability, there are many other insurance considerations such as fire, flood, earthquake, theft, auto, workers' compensation, and health insurance that need to be addressed during the period of ownership.

The above are all concerns during the lifetime of the owner. What happens if the owner dies? There may be a need for life insurance and a buy-sell agreement to safeguard your beneficiaries.

SHOPPING FOR AN INSURANCE COMPANY

Shopping for an insurance company is like shopping for a bank. Careful research will help you determine what company can best serve your needs and provide you with affordable coverage.

Call your current insurance company and see what they have to offer in the way of business insurance. Check with several other independent agents you know or ones recommended by your business associates. Ask them to discuss your business with you and recommend an insurance package that will give you the best coverage for the least number of dollars.

If your insurance needs are unique because of your type of business, you can look through your trade journals. Many times, business insurance companies will advertise in those journals, especially if the type of insurance they are advertising is not available with major companies. For example, food industries have their own unique considerations. Coverage is expensive, and they must usually seek a specialized insurance company.

THE BASIC KINDS OF INSURANCE

As stated previously, there are many different kinds of insurance. In fact, there are so many kinds that most small business owners would go bankrupt if they were paying for the highest protection possible in all areas.

Most small businesses buy what is generally known as a business owner's policy (BOP). The policy generally includes property, liability, criminal coverage, and various specialty coverages needed by the business. The advantage of a business owner's policy is that it usually costs less than if each of the types of coverage were purchased separately.

In the following pages, we will address some of the most basic types of insurance that should be considered. There are two general categories under which all business insurance falls. They are property and liability insurance and life and health insurance.

PROPERTY AND LIABILITY INSURANCE

Property insurance covers buildings and their contents against losses due to such things as fire, theft, wind, earthquake, and flood. Some of those risks may be specifically excluded in your policy and may require the purchase of additional policies (earthquake, flood, groundwater, etc.).

Liability protects a business when it is sued for injury or property damage to third parties. This type of coverage pays damages related to bodily injury, property damage, and personal injury. These policies carry certain limits on the maximum that will be paid by an insurer for specific kinds of occurrences.

- *General liability*. Regular liability insurance pays for claims brought against your business because a customer or other person (the owner and employees are **not** covered) was injured on the business premises. It is wise to have this kind of liability insurance in force when you open your business. It is not uncommon for a customer to fall and file a lawsuit that will be difficult for you to pay. Regular liability insurance also generally includes coverage for damage to property that you do not own or rent for your business (such as a water leak from your property that damages property in an adjoining business).

- *Property damage liability.* This policy covers damage to property that you lease or rent and property that belongs to your customers.

- *Fire insurance.* Protects your premises, fixed assets, and inventory against fire. Fire liability covers fire damage to property you are leasing or renting.

- *Earthquake insurance and flood insurance.* If you live in an area that has a likelihood of being damaged by an earthquake or some other serious act of nature, you may be wise to obtain special insurance coverage. The premiums are usually high but well worth it if you are hit by a disaster.

- *Theft.* Protects against burglary and robbery at your place of business.

- *Fidelity bonds.* Protect a company against employee dishonesty.

- *Surety bonds.* Provide monetary compensation in the event a contractor fails to perform specific acts or complete work within the agreed-upon period of time.

- *Boiler and machinery coverage.* Protects against breakdowns of equipment that is essential to the business (computer and telephone systems, production equipment, etc).

- *Product liability.* Protects against claims filed by anyone using your product after it leaves your business. In most cases, you will be liable even if your product has not been used correctly. The cost of product liability is generally in proportion to the volume of sales and degree of hazard involved.

- *Workers' compensation.* Most states require an employer to provide insurance that covers all employees in case of disability or illness related to the workplace. You can call your insurance carrier to get workers' compensation or contact the state employment department for information on state-operated insurance. Although this is insurance that will cover employees, it is paid in full by the employer. The amount charged for workers' compensation varies according to the number of employees you have and the degree of risk involved. If you are in a high-risk industry, the premiums can be very high.

Workers' compensation is one of the most controversial issues today. Due to a high rate of fraud and the trend toward stress claims, many employers have literally been forced out of business because of their inability to pay increasing insurance costs. Many businesses have instituted safety-in-the-workplace and intervention programs to cut down on claims. There is also an emphasis being placed on fraud detection. To relieve stress-related claims, legislation is pending that will place a percentage value that must be attributable to those claims.

- *Business interruption insurance.* Coverage can generally be added to your regular policy that will pay you an amount approximately equal to what you would have earned in the event that you have to close your business while your premises are being rebuilt or repaired. You can also buy **overhead insurance** that will pay operating expenses during that time. There are additional types of coverage that can be purchased to cover business operations under separate circumstances such as hospitalization.

- *Vehicle insurance.* Most states require that you carry a certain amount of liability coverage if you are going to operate a vehicle. Your regular insurance carrier will probably be able to insure your business vehicle. If you use the vehicle for both personal and business purposes, you will need to see that a rider is attached that will cover the business use. If you have employees that will be driving your business vehicles, be sure you have coverage that will be in effect in case of an accident.

- *Umbrella insurance.* A liability policy that protects the business against catastrophic losses. It provides for extra protection for accidents involving a number of people. It also extends liability limits on auto policies (usually in increments of $1,000,000).

LIFE INSURANCE

One of the concerns of spouses and beneficiaries of a business owner is the question of what happens to that business if the owner dies. With the death of an owner comes responsibility for providing for the disposition of the business. You may need life insurance and some kind of a buy-sell agreement. If you die without having made necessary provisions, your beneficiaries may be forced to sell or dismantle the business to pay the estate taxes that might be due. However, if you have planned ahead and have an adequate life insurance policy, your beneficiaries can use the insurance proceeds to pay the estate taxes and allow the business to continue to operate. If they decide to sell the business, they will still be left with something to sell.

Life insurance can be an especially important consideration for a partnership. In many community-property states, if a partner dies, his or her spouse now owns that share of the business and has the authority to make that partner's decisions. This can create a situation that may be extremely unsatisfactory to either the surviving partner or the spouse. That is why it is important to have a partnership agreement that spells out what happens if one partner dies. A life insurance policy can be included as part of the partnership agreement with a provision designating that the policy payoff be used by the surviving partner to buy the deceased partner's share of the business.

The purchase of individual permanent life insurance by business owners can fund a deferred compensation program on a nontax-qualified basis allowing owners to set aside money for retirement or pay a death benefit to the surviving spouse. Key life insurance can also be purchased to cover key people whose death might affect the company's sales and profitability. A term policy would pay to help replace the loss of the person. A permanent key-person life insurance policy would also accumulate cash value to help fund that person's retirement plan.

HEALTH INSURANCE

Health insurance has long been the nemesis of the self-employed. The costs are often prohibitive and the coverage poor. Many group policies are available through trade associations and insurance companies specializing in small business, but most of the premiums are fairly high.

The best advice we can give is to tell you that you should explore every avenue and continue to get quotes on new coverage being made available. If you have the opportunity to keep purchasing health insurance from a previous company you worked for, that may be your best avenue.

EMPLOYEE BENEFITS

This is another issue requiring some important decisions if you are a small business owner. Your employees certainly need health insurance and are probably entitled to expect it. However, the prohibitive costs of group health plans have made it almost impossible for the small business owner to provide it for employees even if they wish to do so. According to statistics, it now costs an average of more than $4,000 per employee per year, and the costs are rising due to a number of factors such as complexity of treatment, unnecessary care, stress claims, and defensive medicine.

There is also much controversy about this area in the government sector. Regulatory legislation is pending that may require every business owner to provide health plans for all employees working more than a certain number of hours.

In order to get away from paying employee benefits, many companies, including major corporations, are hiring personnel through temporary agencies. There are both state and IRS rules that apply to non-employee (or contract) services. Be aware that these restrictions exist and be sure you are properly classifying your workers. Classifying an employee as contract services when he or she is actually an employee carries some heavy tax penalties.

OTHER CONSIDERATIONS

Insurance coverage is a complicated subject and cannot be covered adequately in the space allotted here. We are not in the insurance business and therefore do not wish to have you consider this as advice in regard to the insurance you should purchase or from whom you should purchase it.

The material covered in this chapter is for the purpose of acquainting you with some general information regarding types of insurance that you should consider.

See your insurance professional to determine what is available and what would be best for your business and you. It would also be wise to consult with your tax planner, especially in the area of life insurance.

After You Have Your Information

When you have received information from several insurance companies regarding coverage and costs, you will have some final decisions to make. You will have to look at your insurance needs in terms of immediate needs and long-term protection. Know what is required by the federal and state government, your lender, or the title holder of your vehicles, etc. Also decide what kinds of insurance you will need to protect your business. Divide your insurance needs into those that are required, necessary, and desirable. Decide what you can purchase now, what you will purchase when financing allows, and what you will put on hold until a future time.

To help you with your insurance shopping we have provided a worksheet on the next page that will help you when you are comparing insurance companies for coverage and costs.

Insurance Fact Sheet

I. Types of Business Insurance

Property and Liability
General liability
Property damage liability
Fire insurance
Earthquake/flood insurance
Theft
Fidelity bonds
Surety bonds
Boiler and machinery coverage
Product liability
Workers' compensation
Business interruption insurance
Vehicle insurance
Umbrella insurance

Life and Health
Life insurance
Disability insurance
Employee benefits
Group insurance
Retirement programs
Overhead expenses

II. Figure Out Your Insurance Priority Shopping List

Immediate protection that is:

1. Required _____
2. Necessary _____
3. Desirable _____

Long-term protection that is:

1. Required _____
2. Necessary _____
3. Desirable _____

III. Key Points

• Insurance is and should be a major factor to consider in forming a business.

• First-year property and liability premiums will sometimes be higher than other years due to frequency of misstatement by the insured and high risk to the insurance company.

• Choosing your insurance agent/broker (consultant and buyer) is one of the most important decisions you can make.

IV. Five Steps to Prevent Your Business from Failing Due to an "Insurable" Cause

• Recognize risks you will be facing

• Follow guidelines for covering them economically

• Have a plan in mind

• Get advice from experts

• Do it now!

CHAPTER 15

FINANCING YOUR BUSINESS

When you are planning to start a new business (or expand your current operation), four important questions arise relating to finance:

1. Will you need to borrow money?

2. If you need outside financing, how much do you need and when will you need it?

3. What are the sources of funding available to meet your needs?

4. How much will it cost?

In order to make an intelligent decision on a timely basis, you will need to address all four of these questions. If you fail to do so, the lack of sufficient and ready capital can quickly lead to business failure.

WILL YOU NEED TO BORROW MONEY?

The first step is to ask yourself some questions that will help you make the right decision—and understand your financial needs and keep you from making costly errors that may ultimately bankrupt a potentially viable business. To determine whether or not you will need outside financing, some of the questions you might ask yourself are:

- *Have I written a business plan* so that I can make financial decisions based on achieving the desired goals for my business? If you haven't written one, do so.

- *Would I be willing to risk my own money on my venture?* What are the risks? What are my own sources of available capital? If you are not willing to take a risk, don't expect someone else to.

- *Do I really need additional financing* or do I just need to manage my present cash flow more effectively?

- *What do I need the money for?* If I borrow, can I realistically project increased revenues? If so, when will those increased revenues justify the debt?

HOW MUCH DO YOU NEED AND WHEN DO YOU NEED IT?

If you have decided you need additional financing, you must carefully assess your needs and determine not only the amount required, but when you will need it. Many business owners overestimate or underestimate their capital requirements and/or do not time their financing to the best advantage. Either can lead to serious problems.

The first thing you need is a realistic **business plan**, one you intend to follow as closely as possible. (Does this sound repetitive?) The only way to look at every aspect of your business is through the planning process. It will force you to create an organizational plan and a marketing plan and quantify your concepts through the development of projected financial statements whose numbers can then be analyzed and used in the decision-making process. Those projections give you an educated estimate of your financial needs and tell you when they will most likely occur. Your business plan will answer such questions as:

- What are my most critical needs?

- If I need the money for immediate operating capital, how much must I have to operate my business until it becomes self-sustaining?

- If I need the money to buy fixed assets for my business, has my research shown that I can reach the target market that will justify the purchase of those assets? If not now, when would be the optimum time to add those assets?

- If I need the money for marketing, what are the most effective ways to reach my target market? How much will it cost to advertise? Will the increased marketing be reflected in even higher increases in revenues? According to my industry trends, what are the best selling periods, and when will I need financing in order to have the lead time to advertise for the best results?

WHAT ARE THE SOURCES AVAILABLE TO YOU?

We get calls almost every day asking for direction to sources of start-up capital. Sources of financing available to prospective and expanding businesses fall into two broad categories, which are discussed in the remainder of the chapter.

- Debt financing (dollars borrowed)

- Equity financing (ownership dollars injected into the business)

Debt Financing

Debt financing is generally obtained from one of two sources. It can come either from a non-professional source such as a friend, relative, customer, or colleague or from a traditional lending institution such as a bank, commercial finance company or, on special occasions, directly from the U.S. Small Business Administration (SBA).

- *Friends or Relatives.* Borrowing from a friend or relative is generally the most readily available source, especially when the capital requirements are smaller. This is frequently the least costly in terms of dollars, but may become the most costly in terms of personal relations if your repayment schedule is not timely or your venture does not work out. This avenue should be approached with great caution!

- *Angel programs.* For smaller business owners, women and minorities, there has been a growing trend toward the development of "Angel" programs through business organizations and companies specializing in small business. Individuals and small companies that want to invest smaller amounts in promising businesses are linked with those companies and the two decide whether or not the loan will be made. This avenue is still relatively new, but holds even more promise for the future.

TECH TIP 16
ANGEL INVESTORS

Several organizations exist that serve as an intermediary between angel investors and business owners. Business owners can submit their business plans, which will then be matched and submitted to prospective investors with funding interests in specific plans. For a list of intermediary networks and lists of angel investors, use the following key words in a search on the Internet: "angel investors."

- *Traditional Lending Institutions.* Banks, savings and loans, and commercial finance companies have long been the major sources of business financing, principally as short-term lenders offering demand loans, seasonal lines of credit, and single-purpose loans for fixed assets.

  You should be aware of the fact that almost all lending institutions are strict about collateral requirements and may reasonably require established businesses to provide one-third of the equity injection and start-ups up to 50 percent or more. Again, as a borrower, you will be required to have a business plan with adequate documentation demonstrating a projected operating cash flow that will enable you to repay (on time) the loan with interest.

- *SBA Guaranteed Loans.* The SBA guaranteed loan program is a secondary source of financing. This option comes into play after private lending options have been denied. The SBA offers a variety of loan programs to eligible small businesses that cannot borrow on reasonable terms from conventional lenders in the amount needed without governmental help. Most of the SBA's business loans are made by private lenders and then guaranteed by the agency. Though it may not necessarily be easier to be approved for an SBA guaranteed loan, the guaranty will allow you to obtain a loan with a longer maturity at better repayment terms and interest rates, thereby reducing your monthly payments and the initial loan burden.

– *7(a) Guaranteed Loan Program.* This is the SBA's primary loan program. You can use a 7(a) loan to: expand or renovate facilities; purchase machinery, equipment, fixtures, and leasehold improvements; finance receivables and augment working capital; refinance existing debt (with compelling reason); finance seasonal lines of credit; construct commercial buildings; and/or purchase land or buildings.

Loan amounts of $100,000 or less receive an SBA guaranty as high as 80 percent. All other loans receive a 75 percent SBA guaranty. Currently, the maximum amount for a loan guaranty is $750,000 (75 percent of $1 million). The average size loan is $175,000 with an eight-year maturity. The 7(a) loan program is available to businesses that operate for profit and qualify as small under SBA size-standard criteria.

You submit a loan application to a lender for initial review. If the lender approves the loan subject to an SBA guaranty, a copy of the application and a credit analysis are forwarded by the lender to the nearest SBA office.

The SBA looks for good character, management expertise, financial resources to operate the business, a feasible business plan, adequate equity or investment in the business, sufficient collateral, and the ability to repay the loan on time from the projected operating cash flow.

After SBA approval, the lending institution closes the loan and disburses the funds; you make monthly loan payments directly to the lender. As with any loan, you are responsible for repaying the full amount.

Generally, liens will be taken on assets financed by SBA proceeds, and the personal guarantee of the principal owners and/or the CEO is required. The borrower must pledge sufficient assets, to the extent that they are reasonably available, to adequately secure the loan. However, in most cases a loan will not be declined by SBA where insufficient collateral is the only unfavorable factor. The lender sets the rate of interest: loans under seven years, maximim prime +2.25 percent; seven years or more, maximum 2.75 percent over prime; under $50,000, rates may be slightly higher. The length of time for repayment depends on the use of proceeds and the ability of the business to repay: usually five to ten years for working capital and up to 25 years for fixed assets.

– *CAPLines.* Eligibility and interest rate rules are the same as for 7(a) guaranteed loans. It is for the financing of assets. The primary collateral will be the short-term assets financed by the loan. SBA will guarantee 75 percent up to $750,0000 (80 percent on loans of $100,000 or less). There are five short-term working-capital loan programs for small businesses under CAPLines: (1) Seasonal Line, (2) Contract Line, (c) Builders Line (d) Standard Asset-Based Line, and (5) Small Asset-Based Line. The asset-based lines must revolve.

– *International Trade Loan Program.* Applicants must establish either that the loan proceeds will significantly expand existing export markets or develop new ones, or that the applicant is adversely affected by import competition. SBA can guaranty 75 percent of an amount up to $1,250,000 in combined working-capital and fixed-asset loans. The lender must take a first-lien position on items financed. Only collateral located in the U.S., its territories, and possessions is acceptable as collateral under this program. Additional collateral may be required including personal guaranties, subordinate liens, or items that are not financed by the loan proceeds. The proceeds of the loan may not be used for debt repayment. Fees and interest rates are the same as for 7(a) loans.

– *Export Working Capital Program (EWCP).* This program is for exporters seeking short-term working capital. The SBA will guarantee 90 percent of the principal and interest, up to $750,000. When an EWCP loan is combined with an International Trade Loan, the SBA's exposure can go up to $1.25 million. The EWCP uses a one-page application form and streamlined documentation, and turnaround is usually within 10 days. You may also apply for a letter of prequalification from the SBA. Businesses must have operated for the past 12 months, not necessarily in exporting, prior to filing an application. Interest rates are not regulated by the SBA, and the lender is not limited to the rates specified for regular 7(a) loans.

– *Defense Loan and Technical Assistance Program (DELTA).* The DELTA Program is available to help defense-dependent small business concerns adversely affected by defense cuts to diversify into the commercial market. The program provides both financial and technical assistance. A joint effort of the SBA and the Department of Defense, DELTA offers about $1 billion in gross lending authority. At least 25 percent of the business' revenues from the immediate preceding year must have come from defense-related contracts, and the borrower must show he or she will create or retain one job per $35,000 of SBA assistance. Loan amounts are up to $1,250,000. The SBA processes, guarantees, and services DELTA loans through the regulations, forms, and operating criteria of the 7(a) program and the 504 Certified Development Company Program. Technical assistance is provided through SBDCs, SCORE, other federal agencies, and other technical and management assistance providers.

Streamlined Applications and Approvals

There are several options available to lenders that help streamline delivery of the SBA's loan guaranty.

• *LowDoc Loan Program.* LowDoc is one of the SBA's most popular programs. Once you have met your lender's requirements for credit, LowDoc offers a simple, one-page SBA application form and rapid turnaround for loans of $100,000 or less. SBA will guarantee up to 80 percent of the loan amount. The loans should be adequately secured. Business assets are usually pledged, and personal guarantees of the principals are required. The applicant completes the front of a one-page SBA application; the lender completes the back. The lender requires additional information. The same interest rate rules apply as in the 7(a) program. To be eligible, a business must have average annual sales for the past three years not exceeding $5 million and must have fewer than 100 employees. Business start-ups are also eligible for the LowDoc Loan Program.

• *FA$TRAK Loan Program.* This program makes capital available to businesses seeking loans of up to $100,000 without requiring the lender to use the SBA process. Lenders use their existing documentation and procedures to make and service loans. The SBA guarantees up to 50 percent of a FA$TRAK loan. Your local SBA office can provide you with a list of FA$TRAK lenders.

- *Certified and Preferred Lenders Program.* The most active and expert SBA lenders qualify for the SBA's Certified and Preferred Lenders Program. Participants are delegated partial or full authority to approve loans, which results in faster service. Certified lenders are those that have been heavily involved in regular SBA loan-guaranty processing and have met certain other criteria. Preferred lenders are chosen from among the SBAs best lenders and enjoy full delegation of lending authority. A list of participants in the Certified and Preferred Lenders Program may be obtained from your local SBA office.

- *7(M) MicroLoan Program.* The MicroLoan program provides small loans ranging from under $100 to $25,000. Under this program, the SBA makes funds available to nonprofit intermediaries; these, in turn, make the loans. The average loan size is $10,000. Completed applications usually are processed by an intermediary in less than one week. This is a pilot program available at a limited number of locations.

Microloans may be used to finance machinery, equipment, fixtures, and leasehold improvements. They may also be used to finance receivables and for working capital. They may not be used to pay existing debt. Depending on the earnings of your business, you may take up to six years to repay a microloan. Rates are pegged at no more than 4 percent over the prime rate. There is no guaranty fee. Each nonprofit lending organization will have its own collateral requirements but must take as collateral any assets purchased with the microloan. Generally the personal guaranties of the business owners are also required.

- *504 Certified Development Company.* CDCs are nonprofit corporations set up to contribute to the economic development of their communities or regions. They work with the SBA and private-sector lenders to provide financing to small businesses. The program is designed to enable small businesses to create and retain jobs; the CDC's portfolio must create or retain one job for every $35,000 of debenture proceeds provided by the SBA. They provide small businesses with 10- or 20-year financing for the acquisition of land and buildings, machinery, and equipment or for constructing, modernizing, renovating, or converting existing facilities. To be eligible, the business must operate for profit. Tangible net worth must not exceed $6 million, and average net income must not have exceeded $2 million for the past two years.

The maximum loan amount is generally $750,000. The amount may go up to $1 million if the project meets public policy goals (i.e., business district revitalization, expansion of export, expansion of minority business). Collateral may include a mortgage on the land and the building being financed. Personal guaranties of principals are required. SBA will take business assets as collateral. Interest is set at second TD rate based on the current market rate for five and ten year U.S. Treasury bonds and is generally below market rate.

Equity Financing

If your company has a high percentage of debt to equity (what you owe compared to what you own), you will find it difficult to get debt financing and probably need to seek equity investment

TECH TIP 17

INTEREST RATES APPLICABLE TO SBA LOANS

Interest rates are negotiated between the borrower and lender but are subject to SBA maximums, which are pegged to the prime rate. Interest rates may be fixed or variable. Fixed rate loans of $50,000 or more must not exceed prime plus 2.25 percent if the maturity is less than seven years, and prime plus 2.75 percent if the maturity is seven years or more.

Loans between $25,000 and $50,000. Maximum rates must not exceed prime plus 3.25 percent if the maturity is less than seven years, and prime plus 3.75 percent if the maturity is seven years or more.

Loans of $25,000 or less. Maximum interest rate must not exceed prime plus 4.25 percent if the maturity is less than seven years, and prime plus 4.75 percent if the maturity is seven years or more.

- For current prime rates, visit <www.bankrate.com>.
- For more information on SBA programs, visit <www.sba.gov/financing>.

for additional funds. This simply means you will trade a certain percentage of your company for a specific amount of money to be injected into the company.

Where does equity financing come from?   As with debt capital, this type of capital can come from friends and relatives, SBA-licensed investment companies, or professional investors known as **venture capitalists**.

- *Friends and relatives.* Again, be reminded that mixing your friends or relatives and business may not be a good idea.

- *SBA-licensed investment companies.* The SBA also licenses Small Business Investment Companies (SBICs). They make venture/risk investments by supplying equity capital and extending unsecured loans to small enterprises that meet their criteria. The SBIC program provides an alternative to bank financing, filling the gap between the availability of venture capital and the needs of small businesses that are either starting or growing. They use their own funds plus funds obtained at favorable rates with SBA guaranties and/or by selling their preferred stock to the SBA. SBICs are for-profit firms

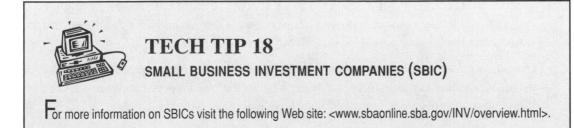

TECH TIP 18

SMALL BUSINESS INVESTMENT COMPANIES (SBIC)

For more information on SBICs visit the following Web site: <www.sbaonline.sba.gov/INV/overview.html>.

whose incentive is to share in the success of a small business. The program provides funding to all types of manufacturing and service industries.

- *Special considerations relating to venture capital.* The venture capitalist is a risk taker, usually specializing in related industries and preferring three- to five-year-old companies that have shown high growth potential and will offer higher-than-average profits to their shareholders. These investments are often arranged through venture capital firms that act as "matchmakers."

As risk takers, venture capitalists have a right to participate in the management of the business. If the company does not perform, they may become active in the decision-making process. The most frequent question we get asked is, *"What is the standard amount of equity you have to trade for financing?"* The trade of equity for capital is based on supply and demand. In other words, the deal is made according to who has the best bargaining power.

Venture capitalists also require the inclusion of an **exit strategy** in the company's business plan. The exit strategy lays out the future goals for the company and minimizes risk to the investor by providing a way out if there is a strong indicator that the business will fail to reach its profitability goals.

WHICH TYPE OF FINANCING COSTS THE MOST?

The cost of financing is usually related to the degree of risk involved. If the risk is high, so is the cost.

- *The least expensive money to use is your own.* The cost to you is whatever you would have made on your money by investing it in other sources (savings, money market accounts, bonds, retirement plans, real estate, etc.).

  Note: It's important to mention credit cards here. Many new business owners borrow heavily on their credit cards only to find themselves in hock up to their ears. Credit cards are one of the most expensive sources of cash and have paved the road to bankruptcy court more than once. Don't get caught in this trap!

- *Friends and relatives.* The next lowest in cost generally comes from friends and relatives who may charge you a lower interest rate. But don't forget that it may cost you in other ways.

- *Banks and other traditional lenders.* The third on the cost ladder is probably the traditional lender (banks, SBA, etc.). This lender will want to know what the capital will be used for and require that it be used for those specific needs. If the risk is too high, most conventional lenders cannot approve your loan because it would be a poor financial decision for the bank's investors. One default out of ten will undermine their whole program.

- *Outside lenders and venture capitalists.* Traditionally, the most expensive is the outside lender who charges a high interest rate because of the risk involved and the venture capitalist who requires a percentage of your business.

Calculating the Cost

Before you get a loan, take time to understand the terms under which the loan will be made. What is the interest rate? How long do you have to repay the loan? When will payments begin and how much will they be? What are you putting up as collateral? If you have venture capital injected into the business, what will be the overall price to you of the equity and control that you will forfeit?

Any source of financing can and should be calculated as to cost before the financing is finalized. This goes back to your business plan. Determine when the financing is needed, plug cash injection, repayment figures, and resulting income projections into your cash flow statement, and check out the result. Will the financing make you more profitable and enable you to repay the lender or distribute profits to the venture capitalist?

In Summary

Securing financing for your company must be planned well in advance. The more immediate your need, the less likely you are to get the best terms. Don't ask your banker to give you a loan yesterday . . . and don't expect a venture capitalist to jump on the bandwagon because you suddenly need money. Planning ahead for cash flow is one of the best means for determining if and when you will need a lender or investor. It will also help you to determine how much you need.

When you plan for financing, remember that you will not only have to show your industry has good potential for profit but also have to present a strong case for the ability to manage your company through the period of debt. Getting financing is serious business for both you and for the lender/investor. *Take time to plan carefully for your financial needs, and your company will prosper and grow accordingly.*

CHAPTER 16

KEEPING YOUR BOOKS

I t is not the purpose of this book to give you a course in small business accounting. However, we will attempt in the next few pages to acquaint you with the basic records that you will need to keep. For a more comprehensive guide, we have a book entitled *Keeping the Books: Basic Recordkeeping and Accounting for the Small Business* (Dearborn Trade). You can also take classes through most community colleges, and the IRS gives small business tax classes at various locations on a regular basis. We also urge an alliance with a reputable tax professional to help you work with your accounting.

THE IMPORTANCE OF GOOD RECORDKEEPING

Recordkeeping has two main functions:

1. To provide you with tax information that can be easily retrieved and verified. Poor accounting can cause you a multitude of problems and may result in audits, penalties, and even the termination of your business.

2. To provide you with information you can use to analyze your business. Accurate financial statements will help you to see trends and implement changes during the life of your business.

The keeping of accurate accounting records is imperative if your business is to succeed. To be the most effective, you should set up a system that is as simple as possible and yet complete enough to give you any information that will be helpful in your business. If you have an accurate set of records, it will be possible for you to tell at a glance what is happening with your business—which areas are productive and cost-effective and which will require change.

TECH TIP 19
ACCOUNTING SOFTWARE

If you have a computer (as most people now do), you will be able to effectively utilize it to do your small business accounting.

The use of accounting software is only beneficial if: (1) you first have a good working knowledge of accounting principles, and (2) you have developed reasonable skills when it comes to the operation of your computer. Even the most simple accounting software will require you to make decisions and adapt the setup to your own particular accounting needs.

QuickBooks Pro (not Quicken) by Intuit is one of the software programs that does a good job of tracking business finances. There are also some other well-known accounting packages such as One-Write Plus, MYOB (Mind Your Own Business), and Peach Tree. Most of these packages are reasonably-priced. The price may vary depending on how many modules are attached.

Once you set up the software for your business and develop a chart of accounts, the program will allow you to do as much or as little as you wish. For instance, you can choose whether or not to generate invoices and/or write checks from within the software. At any time, you can generate reports (P&Ls, balance sheet, customer accounts, etc.) for the time period of your choosing. This will enable you to look at your business at any time and utilize the reports as analysis tools upon which you can make decisions and implement changes. At the end of the year, if you have kept your bookkeeping up-to-date, it will also enable you to generate, at a click of your mouse, an annual profit and loss statement and balance sheet to take to your tax accountant.

Note: It would be wise to have the accounting professional who will handle your annual income tax returns help you do the initial setup of your software. The professional can recommend the software he or she believes will work best for you and get you started by helping you set up your business, develop a chart of accounts, and learn how to handle issues (such as sales tax) that may require more advanced understanding of the software.

SHOULD YOU HIRE AN ACCOUNTING PROFESSIONAL?

Involving yourself in your bookkeeping as much as possible will make you doubly aware of what is going on in your business. If your business is small, we suggest you set up a hands-on system and maintain most of your own general records throughout the year. If you are computer-literate (or brave enough to tackle the project), get one of the accounting software packages mentioned above.

Because few business owners are knowledgeable about all the fine points and changes in tax laws, it is best to delegate some jobs to an accounting professional. He or she can help you develop a chart of accounts and set up your books using coordinating software for easy transfer of information. Your tax professional can also maintain difficult records such as payroll and depreciation. You will want that same specialist to maximize your tax benefits by preparing your tax return at the end of the year.

Even if you feel more comfortable having an accounting professional do all of your bookkeeping, it's wise to educate yourself about the basics. Ask your accountant to prepare a balance sheet and profit and loss statement (P&L) at the close of every month and be sure you are able to read and understand them. The information on these two financial statements is essential to the effective running of your business.

WHEN DO YOU BEGIN?

If you are reading this book, you are thinking about going into business or have already begun your business. So now is the time to begin keeping records. All of the expenses you incur in start-up will be valid costs of doing business. Conversely, any revenues you generate must also be accounted for.

You can start by keeping a journal of your daily activities: where you go, who you see, what you spend. Keep track of business classes, mileage, supplies purchased, telephone calls, professional materials—everything that might relate to your business.

WHAT RECORDS DO YOU NEED TO KEEP?

Your accounting should be tailored to your individual needs. Because no two businesses have exactly the same concerns, it is best that you do not buy a ready-made set of books. Familiarize yourself with the information you will need and set up your records accordingly. As a business owner, you will be required to keep track of all of your income and expenses.

Again, simplicity is the key to small business accounting. There are many different types of general accounting records. Their purpose is to record each transaction that takes place in your business. The general records are then used to develop monthly and yearly financial statements to be used for tax reporting and financial analysis. You should set up only those general records you will need to document the information for your particular business. For instance, a car wash that does only cash business would not need "accounts receivable" records. Fewer records are easier to read and require less bookkeeping time.

General Records

Every business will require certain records to keep track of its daily transactions. These records are used to generate your monthly P&L statements and balance sheets. You should set up a bookkeeping schedule and keep your records current.

To acquaint you with the most common general records, we will define each one, provide you with a filled-in example at the back of the chapter, and give you a blank form in Appendix B for you to copy and use for your own business.

- *Revenue and Expense Journal.* This is the main general record used by a business. It's used to record individual transactions for which income is received or checks are written by your business. The transactions are recorded as revenues (monies for sales and interest earned) and expenses (checks written to pay for products and services received by you). At the end of the month, the columns in the revenue and expense journal are totaled. The totals are then transferred to that month's P&L statement. The new month begins with all revenue and expense categories at zero. See page 139 for an example of a Revenue and Expense Journal.

- *Petty Cash Record.* Petty cash refers to all of the purchases made with cash or personal checks when it is not convenient to pay with a business check. These transactions are recorded in a separate journal and paid by periodically writing a business check made out to "petty cash" that is recorded as an expense in the revenue and expense journal and as a deposit in the petty cash record. Petty cash transactions require careful recording. See page 140 for an example of a Petty Cash Record.

- *Inventory Records.* These are records that keep track of all products purchased or manufactured for resale. The IRS requires a beginning and ending inventory for each taxable year. Inventory control is a major factor contributing toward business success—or failure. Internal use of these records will greatly enhance your profits. See pages 141 and 142.

- *Fixed Assets Log.* This is a list of all assets (tangible and intangible) that will have to be capitalized (or depreciated over a specified number of years). They are items purchased for use in your business (not resale), usually at a cost of $100 or more and not debited to an expense account. They are depreciated over a period determined by tax regulations. Examples might be as follows: buildings, vehicles, office equipment, production equipment, office furniture. Land does not depreciate. Depreciation can be difficult to calculate because of the many IRS regulations that must be applied. It is best to let your tax preparer figure out your depreciation at the end of the year. See page 143 for an example.

- *Accounts Payable.* This is a record of debts owed by your company for goods purchased or services rendered to you in the pursuit of your business. You will need an efficient system for keeping track of what you owe and when it should be paid to get the best terms. If you are going to have a good credit record, the payment of these invoices must be timely. If you do not accumulate unpaid invoices, you may be able to dispense with this record. See page 144 for an Account Payable Record example.

- *Accounts Receivable.* This record is used to keep track of debts owed to you by your customers as a result of the sale of products or the rendering of services. Each client with an open account should have a separate page with account information. Statements of balances due are sent to your account holders at the close of each month. If you do not have open accounts, you will also be able to dispense with this record. See page 145.

- *Mileage, Entertainment, and Travel Records.* These are the records used to keep track of auto and transportation expenses, meals, and entertainment of clients, and travel out of your local area. Due to past abuse in these areas, the IRS requires careful documentation as proof that deductions claimed are in fact business-related expenses. We strongly suggest that you organize a travel log, trip records, and entertainment records so they can be carried with you. It is much easier to keep track of them at the time they occur than to try to remember them and find receipts after the fact. In addition, keep all of your receipts. You can read more about "Travel and Entertainment" in IRS Publication #334,

TECH TIP 20
DATABASE SOFTWARE

It is a common practice to set up database files using software such as Microsoft Access, Q&A, Paradox, or any of a variety offered today. The software will allow you to customize fields of information that can be accessed at the click of a mouse, generating targeted mailing lists, sales information, demographics, etc. You can also print mailing labels and customized letters. With the search functions, you can narrow any list down to only those customers who meet the requirements of your current focus. It is important to remember as you set up your database files and customize your fields, that the output will only be as good as the input.

Tax Guide for Small Business. There are also separate IRS publications containing more detailed information. See pages 146 through 148.

- *Payroll Records.* The IRS has strict regulations regarding withholding and payroll taxes and their reporting. Payroll records are not easy to keep, even with a payroll software program. Leave these records to a trained tax expert. You will be informed what checks to write, and these will be recorded in the Revenue and Expense Journal. The accounting professional will do all the tax reporting for you.

- *Business Checkbook.* Your checkbook is not only the means to pay your bills. It also serves as a record of who was paid, how much was paid, and what was purchased. Deposits are recorded, and a balance of cash available is always at your fingertips. It is best to use a desk-size checkbook with plenty of space for recording information. Always reconcile your checkbook with your monthly bank statement and record any service charges, check purchases, and interest earned. Your checkbook information will be transferred to your Revenue and Expense Journal when you do your bookkeeping.

- *Customer Records (or Databases).* These records are kept to help a business deal more effectively with its customers. The type you keep is purely subjective. The basic idea is that you keep the information that will enable you to sell more of your products or services to the customer, give the customer better service, and have the information you need regarding your transactions with them at your disposal. The database can be as simple or as complicated as you choose. A simple example of hand-generated customer files might be a set of 3" by 5" cards, one for each customer, with specialized information such as name, address, telephone number, services rendered, products sold, and any other information that will help you to better serve the customer. Customer records are especially effective in service industries or in small businesses dealing in specialty retail sales.

Financial Statements

Financial statements are developed from the general records discussed on the preceding two pages. These statements are used to provide information for preparing tax returns. Even more importantly, the use of these financial statements can help you see the financial condition of your business and identify its relative strengths and weaknesses. The business owner who takes the time to understand and evaluate his or her operation through financial statements will be far ahead of the entrepreneur who is concerned only with the product or service.

We will now introduce you to the two principal financial statements of any business: the Balance Sheet and the P&L Statement.

- *Balance sheet.* The balance sheet is a financial statement that shows the condition of your business as of a fixed date. It is most effectively done at the end of every accounting period. The closing balances from your general records will supply you with the information. (If you are using accounting software, a balance sheet can be easily generated at the close of the accounting period.)

  The balance sheet can be likened to a still photograph. It is the picture of your firm's financial condition at a given moment and shows whether your financial position is strong or weak. Examination of this statement will allow you to analyze your business and implement timely modifications.

  A balance sheet lists a business's assets, liabilities, and net worth (or capital). The assets are everything your business owns that has monetary value (cash, inventory, fixed assets, etc.). Liabilities are the debts owed by the business to any of its creditors. The net worth (or owner's equity) represents the cumulative profits and losses of the company plus or minus any equity deposits or withdrawals. The relationship between assets, liabilities, and net worth can be seen in the following well-known accounting formula:

  Assets – Liabilities = Net Worth

  If a business possesses more assets than it owes to its creditors (liabilities), then its net worth will be positive. If the business owes more than it possesses, its net worth will be a negative. See filled-in example on page 149.

- *Profit and loss statement (P&L or income statement).* This financial statement shows your business financial activity over a specific period of time. Unlike the balance sheet, a P&L statement can be likened to a moving picture. It shows where your money came from and where it was spent over a specific period of time. You will be able to pick out weaknesses in your operation and plan ways to run your business more effectively, thereby increasing your profits.

  A P&L statement should be prepared at the close of each month. The totals from your revenue and expense journal are transferred to the corresponding columns of the P&L statement. At the end of December (or your tax year), you will have a clear picture of your revenues and expenses for the 12-month period. (Accounting software is also set up to generate both monthly and annual P&L statements for your business.)

  Comparison of the P&L statements from several years will reveal such trends in your business as high revenue periods, effective advertising times, increases or decreases in profit margins, and a host of other valuable information. Do not underestimate the value of this important tool.

Just as the balance sheet has an accepted format, a P&L statement must contain certain categories in a particular order. A filled-in example of this financial statement can be found at the end of the chapter on page 150.

KEEPING THE BOOKS ON SCHEDULE

There is a specific order for keeping your books. It must be done in a timely manner if the records are to be effective. Since the two goals of accounting are the retrieval of tax information and the analysis of information for internal planning, your schedule will have to provide for these goals. The tasks are listed according to frequency: daily, weekly, monthly, and end of the year. Schedules for filing tax information are not included. See IRS Publication #334, *Tax Guide for Small Business* for that information.

Free IRS Publications

The IRS provides many free publications that will be helpful to you as a small business owner. Information on ordering all publications may be obtained by calling the IRS toll free at 1-800-TAX-FORM (1-800-829-3676). Start your tax publication file by asking for Publication #334, *Tax Guide for Small Business*. This publication provides a comprehensive overview on most tax topics. Other publications deal in more specific information relating to individual topics such as: business use of your car, legal structure, depreciation, etc. If you subscribe to an online service, you can download electronic print files of current tax forms, instructions, and taxpayer information publications over the Internet by going to the IRS Web site at <www.irs.gov>.

Note: The **General Recordkeeping Schedule**, located on the next page, will help you organize the various chores that need to be done. We suggest you make a copy and keep it close at hand. It should serve as a basic guide for the person who has no bookkeeping experience.

TECH TIP 21
ACCESS IRS INFORMATION BY COMPUTER AND MODEM

The IRS offers the ability to download and print out electronic print files of current tax forms, instructions, and taxpayer information publications (TIPs) in three different file formats. Internal Revenue Information Services (IRIS) is housed within FedWorld, known also as the Electronic Marketplace of U.S. Government information, a broadly accessible electronic bulletin board system. FedWorld offers direct dial-up access, as well as Internet connectivity, and provides "gateway" access to more than 140 different government bulletin boards.

IRIS at FedWorld can be reached by:
- Modem (dial-up) Internal Revenue Information Services bulletin board at 703-321-8020
- Telnet—<iris.irs.ustreas.gov>
- World Wide Web—<www.irs.gov>

General Recordkeeping Schedule

(Post for your convenience)

Daily

- Go through mail and sort according to action needed.
- Pay any invoices necessary to meet discount deadlines.
- Record current day's invoices in Accounts Receivable.*
- Unpack and shelve incoming inventory (product business).
- Record inventory information (product business).

  * **Accounting software users.** Invoices generated from within your software will be automatically posted to the proper accounts.

Weekly

- Prepare income deposit and make deposit in bank.
- Enter deposit in checkbook and Revenue and Expense Journal.*
- Enter sales information in Inventory Record (product business).
- Enter week's checking transactions in Revenue and Expense Journal.
- Record petty cash purchases in Petty Cash Record. File receipts.*
- Pay invoices due. Be aware of discount dates. File invoices.
- Record purchase of any depreciable purchases in your Fixed Asset Log. *

  * **Accounting software users.** Enter deposits, checks written, and petty cash expenditures for the week.

Monthly

- Balance checkbook and reconcile with bank statement.*
- Enter interest earned and bank charges in Revenue and Expense Journal and checkbook.
- Total and balance all Revenue & Expense Journal columns.*
- Check Accounts Receivable and send out statements to open accounts.
- Prepare monthly Profit & Loss Statement and Balance Sheet.*

  * **Accounting software users.** Perform bank reconciliation. P&L and Balance Sheets can be generated automatically using the software.

End of the Year

- Pay all invoices and other expenses that you wish to use as deductions for the current year.
- Transfer 12th month totals from the Revenue & Expense Journal to the P&L. *
- Prepare annual P&L. Total horizontal columns to get totals for each category. *
- Prepare an end-of-the-year Balance Sheet. *
- Prepare a Cash Flow Statement (budget) for the coming year using the P&L as an aid.
- Set up new records for the coming year.

  * **Accounting software users.** Annual P&L and Balance Sheets can be generated by the software. User selects date parameters for all reports (i.e., This Fiscal Year, This Month, Last Fiscal Year, *etc.*). Accounting is continuous and does not need to be set up.

Ace Sporting Goods Revenue and Expense Journal

July 2004, page 2

CHECK NO.	DATE	TRANSACTION	REVENUE	EXPENSE	SALES	SALES TAX	SERV-ICES	INV. PURCH	ADVERT	FREIGHT	OFF SUPP	MISC
		Balance forward----	1,826 00	835 00	1,218 00	98 00	510 00	295 00	245 00	150 00	83 50	61 50
234	7/13	J. J. Advertising		450 00					450 00			
235	7/13	T & E Products		380 00				380 00				
236	7/16	Regal Stationers		92 50							92 50	
***	7/17	Deposit:	1,232 00									
		1. Sales (taxable)			400 00	32 00						
		2. Sales (out of state)			165 00	O.S.						
		3. Sales (resale)			370 00	Resale						
		4. Services					265 00					
O.K. BANK	7/19	Bank charges		23 40								(bank chg) 23 40
237	7/19	Petty Cash deposit		100 00								(p/cash) 100 00
		TOTALS	3,058 00	1,880 90	2,153 00	130 00	775 00	675 00	695 00	150 00	176 00	184 90

Ace Sporting Goods Petty Cash Record

PETTY CASH - 2004					Page 6	
DATE	PAID TO WHOM	EXPENSE ACCOUNT DEBITED	DEPOSIT	AMOUNT OF EXPENSE	BALANCE	
	BALANCE FORWARD —				10	00
Jul. 19	✳✳ Deposit (Ck. 237)		100 00		110	00
20	ACE Hardware	Maintenance		12 36	97	64
23	Regal Stationers	Office Supplies		20 00	77	64
23	U.S. Postmaster	Postage		19 80	57	84
31	The Steak House	Meals		63 75	(5	91)
Aug 1	✳✳ Deposit (Ck. 267)		100 00		94	09

> Toward the end of the year, you can let the Petty Cash account run a minus balance. On December 31st, a check is written for the balance and the account is zeroed out.
>
> The amount of cash spent during the year will be exactly equal to the amount deposited into the Petty Cash Account from your checking account.

NOTE:
1. Save all receipts for cash purchases.
2. Exchange receipt for cash from petty cash drawer.
3. Use receipts to record expenses on petty cash form.
4. File receipts. You may need them for verification.
5. Be sure to record petty cash deposits.

Ace Sporting Goods Inventory Record—Nonidentifiable

DEPARTMENT/CATEGORY: _Ski Hats / Headwear_

PRODUCTION OR PURCHASE DATE	INVENTORY PURCHASED OR MANUFACTURED		NUMBER OF UNITS	UNIT COST		VALUE ON DATE OF INVENTORY (Unit Cost X Units on Hand)	
	Stock #	Description				Value	Date
2/05/02	07-43	Knitted Headbands	5,000	2	50	0	1/04
3/25/02	19-12	Face Masks	3,000	5	12	450.80	1/04
9/14/02	19-10	Hat/Mask Combo	1,200	7	00	3,514.00	1/04
4/18/03	19-09	Hats, Multi-Colored	10,500	4	00	5,440.00	1/04
8/31/03	19-07	Gortex (w/bill)	10,000	8	41	50,460.00	1/04
BEGIN 2004							
2/01/04	19-12	Face Masks	2,500	4	80		
2/28/04	19-09	Hats, Multi-Colored	10,300	4	00		

NOTE:

1. This record is used for inventory of like items that are manufactured or purchased in bulk. It is a good idea to divide your records by department, category, or by manufacturer.

2. Inventory of these items is done by a physical count or by computer records. A physical inventory is required at the close of your tax year.

3. Inventory is valued according to rules that apply for **FIFO** or **LIFO** (_first in first out_ or _last in first out_). The selected method must be used consistently. In order to understand and apply rules for inventory evaluation, refer to IRS Publication 334, _Tax Guide for Small Business_.

Ace Sporting Goods Inventory Record—Identifiable

| WHOLESALER: _Anderson Custom Designs_ | | | | | Page _1_ |

PURCH DATE	INVENTORY PURCHASED		PURCH. PRICE	DATE SOLD	SALE PRICE	NAME OF BUYER (Optional)
	Stock #	Description				
1/16/04	Blue M	Golf Design	16 00	2/24/04	32 00	J. Pearce
1/23/04	Red S	Tennis T-Shirts	12 00			
	Red M	Baseball T-Shirt	12 00			
	Blue L	Soccer T-Shirt	12 00	2/07/04	24 00	S. Wong
2/16/04	Wt. L	Golf T-Shirt	14 00	3/01/04	26 00	K. Lee
3/16/04	Wt. M	Soccer T-Shirt	14 00			
3/16/04	Gr. L	Tennis T-Shirt	14 00			
	Gr. M	Basketball T-Shirt	14 00			

NOTE: 1. Use this record for keeping track of identifiable goods purchased for resale. If your inventory is very large, it may be necessary to use some sort of **Point-of-Sale** inventory system.

2. Each page should deal with either: (1) purchases in one category, or (2) goods purchased from one wholesaler.

3. Use the name of the wholesaler or the category of the purchase as the heading.

Ace Sporting Goods Fixed Assets Log

COMPANY NAME: _Ace Sporting Goods_

ASSET PURCHASED	DATE PLACED IN SERVICE	COST OF ASSET	% USED FOR BUSINESS	RECOVERY PERIOD	METHOD OF DEPRECIATION	DEPRECIATION PREVIOUSLY ALLOWED	DATE SOLD	SALE PRICE
1998 Dodge Van	1/08/99	18,700 00	80%	5 yr.	200% DB	15,469 00	9/12/03	8,500 00
IBM Computer	7/15/00	6,450 00	100%	5 yr.	200% DB	3,620 00		
Ricoh Copier	12/29/00	3,000 00	100%	5 yr.	S/L-DB	1,469 00		
Climbing Simulator	6/17/03	4,500 00	100%	15 yr.	150% DB	—		
2003 Dodge Van	8/05/03	28,000 00	80%	5 yr.	200% DB	—		
Tennis ProString	3/15/04	1,500 00	100%	7 yr.	200% DB	—		

NOTE: See IRS Publication 334, _Tax Guide for Small Business_, for more detailed information on depreciation. Also see Publications 534, 544, and 551.

Ace Sporting Goods Accounts Payable Record

CREDITOR: _Johnson Mills_

ADDRESS: _7222 Main Street_
Johnson, NV 26401

TEL. NO: _(800) 555-7201_

ACCOUNT NO. _2012_

INVOICE DATE	INVOICE NO.	INVOICE AMOUNT		TERMS	DATE PAID	AMOUNT PAID		INVOICE BALANCE	
2/16/04	264	600	00	Net 30	3/07/04	600	00	0	00
3/16/04	326	300	00	Net 30	4/15/04	300	00	0	00
6/20/04	417	1,200	00	N30/2%10	6/26/04	1,176	00	0	00
8/26/04	816	2,000	00	N30/2%10	9/01/04	500	00	1,500	00

Ace Sporting Goods Accounts Receivable Record

Account Record

CUSTOMER: _Martin's Team Shoppe_

ADDRESS: _222 Stevens Road_

Winnemucca, NV 89502

TEL. NO: _(702) 555-2222_   ACCOUNT NO. _1024_

INVOICE DATE	INVOICE NO.	INVOICE AMOUNT		TERMS	DATE PAID	AMOUNT PAID		INVOICE BALANCE	
3/16/04	3621	240	00	Net 30	4/12/04	240	00	0	00
4/19/04	5400	316	00	Net 30	4/30/04	316	00	0	00
5/20/04	6172	525	00	N30/2%10	5/26/04	514	50	0	00
6/16/04	7511	800	00	N30/2%10	7/14/04	250	00	550	00
7/12/04	7633	386	00	N30/2%10				386	00

Ace Sporting Goods Mileage Log

NAME: _Ace Sporting Goods (John Kelley)_

DATED: From _July 1_ **To** _July 31, 2004_

DATE	CITY OF DESTINATION	NAME OR OTHER DESIGNATION	BUSINESS PURPOSE	NO. OF MILES
7-01	San Diego, CA	Convention Center	California Sports Expo	187 mi.
7-03	Cypress, CA	The Print Co.	p/u brochures	13 mi.
7-04	Long Beach, CA	Wm. Long High	Deliver Uniforms	53 mi.
7-07	Fullerton, CA	Bank of America	Loan Meeting	17 mi.
7-17	Los Angeles, CA	Moore Corp.	Negotiate inventory purchase	96 mi.
7-23	Los Angeles, CA	IDT	Consultation	113 mi.
			TOTAL MILES THIS SHEET	479

NOTE: 1. A mileage record is required by the IRS to claim a mileage deduction. It is also used to determine the percentage of business use of a car.

2. Keep your mileage log in your vehicle and record your mileage as it Occurs. It is very difficult to recall after the fact.

Ace Sporting Goods Entertainment Expense Record

NAME: _____John Kelley_____

DATED: From_____7-01-04_____ To_____7-31-04_____

DATE	PLACE OF ENTERTAINMENT	BUSINESS PURPOSE	NAME OF PERSON ENTERTAINED	AMOUNT SPENT	
7-01	The 410 Club	Sell Uniform Line	William Long	46	32
7-07	Seafood Chef	Consult w/attorney	Thomas Moore	23	50
7-18	The Cannon Club	Staff Dinner	Company Employees	384	00

NOTE: For more information on Meals and Entertainment, please refer to IRS Publication 463, *Travel, Entertainment and Gift Expenses.*

Ace Sporting Goods Travel Record

TRIP TO: _Dallas, Texas_

Dated From: _7-11-04_ To: _7-16-04_

Business Purpose: _Sports Technology Expo (show exhibitor)_

No. Days Spent on Business: _6_

DATE	LOCATION	EXPENSE PAID TO	MEALS				HOTEL	TAXIS, ETC.	AUTOMOBILE			MISC EXP
			Breakfast	Lunch	Dinner	Misc.			Gas	Parking	Tolls	
7-11	Phoenix, AZ	Mobil Gas				6 40			21 00			
7-11	Phoenix, AZ	Greentree Inn		12 50								
7-11	Chola, NM	Exxon							23 50			
7-11	Las Cruces, NM	Holiday Inn			27 00		49 00					
7-12	Las Cruces, NM	Exxon							19 00			
7-12	Taft, TX	Molly's Cafe		16 25								
7-12	Dallas, TX	Holiday Inn			18 75		54 00					
7-13	Dallas, TX	Expo Center								8 00		
7-13	Dallas, TX	Harvey's Eatery		21 00								
7-13	Dallas, TX	Holiday Inn			24 50		54 00					
7-14	Dallas, TX	Holiday Inn	9 50									
7-14	Dallas, TX	Expo Center		14 00						8 00		(Fax) 9 00
7-14	Dallas, TX	Holiday Inn			16 20		54 00					
7-15	Pokie, TX	Texaco							21 00			
7-15	Pokie, TX	Denny's		18 50								
7-15	Chola, NM	Holiday Inn			27 00		48 00					
7-16	Chola, NM	Holiday Inn	12 75									
7-16	Flagstaff, AZ	Texaco							22 00			
		TOTALS →	22 25	82 25	113 45	6 40	259 00		106 50	16 00		9 00

Attach all receipts for Meals, Hotel, Fares, Auto, Entertainment, etc. Details of your expenses can be noted on the receipts. File your travel record and your receipts in the same envelope. Label the envelope as to trip made. File all travel records together. When expenses are allocated, be sure not to double expense anything. (Ex: Gas cannot be used if you elect to use mileage as the basis for deducting your car expenses.)

Ace Sporting Goods Balance Sheet

Business Name: *Ace Sporting Goods*   *Date: September 30, 2004*

ASSETS

Current Assets

Cash	$	8,742
Petty Cash	$	167
Accounts Receivable	$	5,400
Inventory	$	101,800
Short-Term Investments	$	0
Prepaid Expenses	$	1,967

Long-Term Investments $ 0

Fixed Assets

Land (valued at cost)	$	185,000
Buildings	$	143,000
1. Cost	171,600	
2. Less Acc. Depr.	28,600	
Improvements	$	0
1. Cost		
2. Less Acc. Depr.		
Equipment	$	5,760
1. Cost	7,200	
2. Less Acc. Depr.	1,440	
Furniture	$	2,150
1. Cost	2,150	
2. Less Acc. Depr.	0	
Autos/Vehicles	$	16,432
1. Cost	19,700	
2. Less Acc. Depr.	3,268	

Other Assets

1.	$	
2.	$	

TOTAL ASSETS $ 470,418

LIABILITIES

Current Liabilities

Accounts Payable	$	2,893
Notes Payable	$	0
Interest Payable	$	1,842
Taxes Payable		
Federal Income Tax	$	5,200
Self-Employment Tax	$	1,025
State Income Tax	$	800
Sales Tax Accrual	$	2,130
Property Tax	$	0
Payroll Accrual	$	4,700

Long-Term Liabilities

Notes Payable	$	196,700

TOTAL LIABILITIES $ 215,290

NET WORTH (EQUITY)

Proprietorship	$	
or		
Partnership		
John Smith, 60% Equity	$	153,077
Mary Blake, 40% Equity	$	102,051
or		
Corporation		
Capital Stock	$	
Surplus Paid In	$	
Retained Earnings	$	

TOTAL NET WORTH $ 255,128

Assets - Liabilities = Net Worth
and
Liabilities + Equity = Total Assets

Ace Sporting Goods Profit and Loss Statement

Beginning: January 1, 2004   **Ending: December 31, 2004**

INCOME		
1. Sales Revenues		**$ 500,000**
2. Cost of Goods Sold (c-d)		**312,000**
a. Beginning Inventory (1/01)	147,000	
b. Purchases	320,000	
c. C.O.G. Avail. Sale (a+b)	467,000	
d. Less Ending Inventory (12/31)	155,000	
3. Gross Profit on Sales (1-2)		**$ 188,000**
EXPENSES		
1. Variable (Selling) (a thru h)		**67,390**
a. Advertising/Marketing	14,000	
b. Event Planning	9,000	
c. Freight	2,000	
d. Sales Salaries/Commissions	33,000	
e. Travels	3,000	
f. Vehicle	1,650	
g. Misc. Variable (Selling) Expense	390	
h. Depreciation (Prod/Serv Assets)	4,350	
2. Fixed (Administrative) (a thru h)		**51,610**
a. Financial Administration	1,000	
b. Insurance	3,800	
c. Licenses & Permits	2,710	
d. Office Salaries	14,000	
e. Rent Expense	22,500	
f. Utilities	3,000	
g. Misc. Fixed (Administrative) Expense	0	
h. Depreciation (Office Equipment)	4,600	
Total Operating Expenses (1+2)		**119,000**
Net Income from Operations (GP-Exp)		**$ 69,000**
Other Income (Interest Income)		**5,000**
Other Expense (Interest Expense)		**7,000**
Net Profit (Loss) Before Taxes		**$ 67,000**
Taxes		
a. Federal	21,000	
b. Statel	4,500	**26,000**
c. Local	500	
NET PROFIT (LOSS) AFTER TAXES		**$ 41,000**

CHAPTER 17

SUCCESS OR FAILURE: IT DEPENDS ON YOUR CASH FLOW

It is a fact that a third or more of today's businesses fail due to a lack of cash flow. What is cash flow? How do you plan ahead to ensure your chances of success? The purpose of this chapter will be to introduce you to the concept of "cash flow" and show you how careful planning can help you avoid business disaster.

WHAT IS A CASH FLOW STATEMENT?

The Pro Forma Cash Flow Statement is the financial document that **projects** what your business plan means in terms of dollars. A cash flow statement is the same as a budget. It is a pro forma (or projected) statement used for internal planning and estimates how much money will flow into and out of a business during a designated period of time, usually the coming tax year. Your profit at the end of the year will depend on the proper balance between cash inflow and outflow.

The **Cash Flow Statement** identifies when cash is expected to be received and when it must be spent to pay bills and debts. It also allows the manager to identify where the necessary cash will come from.

This statement deals only with **actual cash transactions** and not with depreciation and amortization of goodwill or other noncash expense items. Expenses are paid from cash on hand, sale of assets, revenues from sales and services, interest earned on investments, money borrowed from a lender, and influx of capital in exchange for equity in the company. If your business will require $100,000 to pay its expenses and $50,000 to support the owners, you will need at least an equal amount of money flowing into the business just to maintain the status quo. Anything less will eventually lead to an inability to pay your creditors or yourself.

Webster's New World Dictionary defines cash flow as "the pattern of receipts and expenditures of a company, government, etc., resulting in the availability or nonavailability of cash." The availability or nonavailability of cash when it is needed for expenditures gets to the very heart of the matter. By careful planning, you must try to project not only **how much** cash will have to flow into and out of your business, but also **when** it will need to flow in and out. A business may be able to plan for gross receipts that will cover its needs. However, if those sales do not take place in time to pay the expenses, your venture will soon be history unless you plan ahead for other sources of cash to tide the business over until the revenues are realized. The publishing industry is a good example of a business that has heavy cash demands as many as six to nine months before it realizes any revenues as a result of those expenditures. If a publisher cannot pay the printer, there will be no books for sale. The printer will not produce the finished product on a promise that he or she will be paid nine months later at the completion of sales and receipt of invoice payments. To keep the business going, the publisher must plan ahead for sources of cash to tide the business over until the revenues are received.

PREPLANNING WORKSHEETS

Because the cash flow statement deals with cash inflow and outflow, the first step in planning can be best accomplished by preparing two worksheets.

1. *Cash to Be Paid Out.* Cash flowing out of your business. See pages 154 and155 for an example of this worksheet that documents the cash flowing out of your business. It identifies categories of expenses and obligations and the projected amount of cash needed in each category. You may wish to approach this task by compiling several individual budgets (inventory purchases, direct expenses, administrative expenses, owner draws, etc.).

   These expenditures are not always easy to estimate. If yours is a new business, it will be necessary for you to do lots of market research. If you are an existing business, you will combine information from past financial statements with trends in your particular industry.

2. *Sources of Cash.* Cash flowing into your business. See pages 156 and 157 for examples. Use this worksheet to document the cash flowing into your business. It will help you to estimate how much cash will be available from what sources. To complete this worksheet, you will have to look at cash on hand, projected revenues, assets that can be liquidated, possible lenders or investors, and owner equity to be contributed. This worksheet will force you to take a look at any existing possibilities for increasing available cash.

On pages 154 through 157, you will see examples of the two worksheets along with accompanying information explaining each of the categories used. The worksheets are filled in for our fictitious company, **Ace Sporting Goods**, to help you understand the process. **Please**

note that the Cash to be Paid Out Worksheet shows a need for $131,000. It was necessary in projecting Sources of Cash to account for $131,000 without the projected sales because payment is not expected to be received until November and December (too late for cash needs January through October). Next year, those revenues will be reflected in cash on hand or other salable assets.

When You Do Your Own Worksheets

- Try to be as realistic as possible. *Do not overstate revenues and/or understate expenses*, a deadly error frequently made during the planning process.

- Be sure to figure all of your estimates on both worksheets for the same time period (i.e., annually, quarterly, monthly).

Cash to Be Paid Out Worksheet

Explanation of Categories

1. Start-Up Costs

These are the costs incurred by you to get your business under way. They are generally one-time expenses and capitalized for tax purposes.

2. Inventory Purchases

Cash to be spent during the period on items intended for resale. If you purchase manufactured products, this includes the cash outlay for those purchases. If you are the manufacturer, include labor and materials on units to be produced.

3. Variable Expenses (Selling or Direct)

These are the costs of all expenses that will relate directly to your product or service (other than manufacturing costs or purchase price of inventory).

4. Fixed Expenses (Administrative or Indirect)

Include all expected costs of office overhead. If certain bills must be paid ahead, include total cash outlay even if covered period extends into the next year.

5. Assets (Long-Term Purchases)

These are the capital assets that will be depreciated over a period of years (land, buildings, vehicles, equipment). Determine how you intend to pay for them and include all cash to be paid out in the current period. **Note:** Land is the only asset that does not depreciate and will be listed at cost.

6. Liabilities

What are the payments you expect to have to make to retire any debts or loans? Do you have any Accounts Payable as you begin the new year? You will need to determine the amount of cash outlay that needs to be paid in the current year. If you have a car loan for $20,000 and pay $500 per month for 12 months, you will have a cash outlay of $6,000 for the coming year.

7. Owner Equity

This item is frequently overlooked in planning cash flow. If you, as the business owner, will need a draw of $2,000 per month to live on, you must plan for $24,000 cash flowing out of your business. Failure to plan for it will result in a cash flow shortage and may cause your business to fail.

Note: Be sure to use the same time period throughout your worksheet.

* Variable and Fixed Expense Categories Must Be Determined By You *

Every business has expenses that are specific to its industry. You will have to customize your variable and fixed expense categories to match your business. We have suggested some in our examples to get you started. You will type in your own headings in the working spreadsheets. As you begin to operate your business, you will be better able to determine what your true expenditures are. You can change later if you find that your current categories do not meet your needs.

Ace Sporting Goods Cash to Be Paid Out Worksheet

Time Period Covered: January 1 thru December 31, 2004

1.	**START-UP COSTS:**		$ 1,450
	Business License	30	
	Corporation Filing	500	
	Legal Fees	920	
	Other start-up costs:		
	a.		
	b.		
	c.		
2.	**INVENTORY PURCHASES**		
	Cash out for goods intended for resale		32,000
3.	**SELLING EXPENSES (VARIABLE/DIRECT)**		
	Advertising/Marketing	6,000	
	Event Planning	2,500	
	Freight	800	
	Sales Salaries/Commissions	14,000	
	Travel	2,000	
	Vehicle	1,550	
	Miscellaneous Variable Expense	300	
	TOTAL SELLING EXPENSES		27,150
4.	**FIXED EXPENSES (ADMINISTRATIVE/INDIRECT)**		
	Financial Administration	1,800	
	Insurance	900	
	Licenses/Permits	100	
	Office Salaries	16,300	
	Rent Expenses	8,600	
	Utilities	2,400	
	Miscellaneous Fixed Expense	400	
	TOTAL OPERATING EXPENSES		30,500
5.	**ASSETS (LONG-TERM PURCHASES)**		6,000
	Cash to be paid out in current period		
6.	**LIABILITIES**		9,900
	Cash outlay for retiring debts, loans, and/or accounts payable		
7.	**OWNER EQUITY**		24,000
	Cash to be withdrawn by owner		
	TOTAL CASH TO BE PAID OUT		$ 131,000

Sources of Cash Worksheet

Explanation of Categories

1. Cash on Hand

Money that you have on hand. Be sure to include petty cash and money not yet deposited.

2. Sales (Revenues)

This includes projected revenues from the sale of your product and/or service. If payment is not expected during the time period covered by this worksheet, do not include that portion of your sales. Think about the projected timing of sales. If receipts will be delayed beyond the time when a large amount of cash is needed, make a notation to that effect and take it into consideration when determining the need for temporary financing. Include deposits you require on expected sales or services. To figure collections on Accounts Receivable, you will have to project the percentage of invoices that will be lost to bad debts and subtract it from your Accounts Receivable total.

3. Miscellaneous Income

Do you, or will you have, any money out on loan or deposited in accounts that will yield interest income during the period in question?

4. Sale of Long-Term Assets

If you are expecting to sell any of your fixed assets such as land, buildings, vehicles, machinery, equipment, etc., be sure to include only the cash you will receive during the current period.

Important. At this point in your worksheet, add up all sources of cash. If you do not have an amount equal to your projected needs, you will have to plan sources of cash covered under numbers 5 and 6.

5. Liabilities

This figure represents the amount you will be able to borrow from lending institutions such as banks, finance companies, and the SBA, etc. Be reasonable about what you think you can borrow. If you have no collateral, no business plan, or a poor financial history, you will find it difficult, if not impossible, to find a lender. This source of cash requires **preplanning.**

6. Equity

Sources of equity come from owner investments, contributed capital, sale of stock, or venture capital. Do you anticipate the availability of personal funds? Does your business have the potential for growth that might interest a venture capitalist? Be sure to be realistic in this area. You cannot sell stock (or equity) to a nonexistent investor.

Ace Sporting Goods Sources of Cash Worksheet

Time Period Covered: January 1, 2004 to December 31, 2004

1. CASH ON HAND $ 20,000

2. SALES (REVENUES)

Product Sales Income*   90,000
   Most of the sales revenue will not be received until Nov. or Dec.

Service Income   22,000

Deposits on Sales or Services   0

Collections on Accounts Receivable   3,000

3. MISCELLANEOUS INCOME

Interest Income   1,000

Payments to be Received on Loans   0

4. SALE OF LONG-TERM ASSETS   0

5. LIABILITIES

Loan Funds (Banks, Lending Inst., SBA, etc.)   40,000

6. EQUITY

Owner Investments (Sole Prop. or Partnership)   10,000

Contributed Capital (Corporation)

Sale of Stock (Corporation)

Venture Capital   35,000

TOTAL CASH AVAILABLE

A. Without product sales =   **$131,000**

B. With product sales =   **$221,000**

USING THE WORKSHEETS TO BUILD THE CASH FLOW STATEMENT

Now that you have completed the two worksheets, you are ready to use that information. You have estimated **how much** cash will be needed for the year and know what sources are available. In the next phase of cash-flow planning, you will break the time period of one year into monthly segments and predict **when** the cash will be needed to make the financial year flow smoothly. To make the job easier, you can follow these steps:

- Figure the cost of goods and the variable and fixed expenses in monthly increments. Most will vary. When do you plan to purchase the most inventory? What months will require the most advertising? Are you expecting a rent or insurance premium increase? When will commissions be due on expected sales?

- Project sales on a monthly basis based on payment of invoices, demand for your particular product or service, and how readily you can fill that demand. There will be no cash flowing in for orders that have not been filled and invoices that are not paid. If you are in a service business and have no employees other than yourself, remember that income ceases when you are on vacation.

- Determine your depreciable assets needs. When will you need them? How much will the payments be and when will they begin?

- Fill in as much of the cash flow statement as you can using these projections and any others that you can comfortably determine. Then proceed according to the directions and complete the rest.

How to Fill In the Forms

To clarify the process of filling in a cash flow statement, pages 160 and 161 have been devoted to walking you through January and part of February for Ace Sporting Goods.

Pages 162 and 163 contain the directions for completing a **Pro Forma Cash Flow Statement**. There is also a blank form located in Appendix B for you to use to make your own projection.

Remember

The pro forma cash flow statement is one of the most useful financial tools available to the small business owner. It is also the first financial projection to be examined by a lender or invester because it shows how you plan to make it through the year, repaying your loan plus interest and at the same time maintaining the necessary cash flow to operate the business for maximum profitability.

TECH TIP 22
SAVE YOUR VALUABLE TIME: USE PREFORMATTED AND PREFORMULATED SPREADSHEETS

Planning your cash flow takes time in two ways: First you will have to spend the time to research all of your information and form your organizational and marketing concepts. Once you have your ideas, you will then have to interpret everything you want to do into numbers so that you will be able to analyze the projected results.

Building your cash flow statement (budget) is a long and tedious process, especially if you are trying to do it with a pencil and a piece of paper. There are about 350+ numbers to fill in and calculate. The job becomes compounded if you make a change and have to recalculate your numbers.

Computer Spreadsheets Will Solve Your Problems

Software programs such as Excel and Lotus enable the user to build and formulate spreadsheets that will automatically perform complex calculations in an instant. Every computer user should learn to use one of these programs. Unless you are adept at using these applications, you will find yourself in over your head and bogged down in formatting and formulation.

Even more pertinent, in this instance, is the ability to access spreadsheets that have already been developed specifically for use in making cash-flow projections (e.g., Automate Your Business Plan software). These spreadsheets are already preformatted as cash flow statements, and they are preformulated to instantly perform the calculations any time that you input a number. The single word of caution is that you need one you can customize to your own chart of accounts.

What-If Scenarios

The best part about using preformatted and preformulated computer spreadsheets is that you can try out different scenarios for your business, add a product or service, buy a piece of equipment, or cut back on an expense. Input the new numbers, and you will instantly be able to see the probable financial effect on your business.

Ace Sporting Goods Cash Flow Statement

for January and February 2004

January Projections

1. Ace Sporting Goods projects a beginning cash balance of $20,000.

2. Cash Receipts: The store has not opened, so there will be no sales. However, income of $4,000 is projected on receivables from a previous location.

3. Interest on the $20,000 will amount to about $100 at current rate.

4. There are no long-term assets to sell. Enter a zero.

5. Add 1, 2, 3, and 4 above. The Total Cash Available will be $24,100.

6. Cash Payments: Inventory payment will not be due until February. However, there will be graphic design costs of $5,000 for local team uniforms.

7. Variable (Selling) Expenses: Estimated at $1,140.

8. Fixed (Administrative): Estimated at $1,215.

9. Interest Expense: No outstanding debts or loans. Enter zero.

10. Taxes: No profit for previous quarter. No estimated taxes would be due.

11. Payments on Long-Term Assets: Ace Sporting Goods plans to purchase office equipment to be paid in full at the time of purchase. Enter $1,139.

12. Loan Repayments: No loans have been received. Enter zero.

13. Owner Draws: Owner will need $2,000 for living expenses.

14. Total Cash Paid Out: Add 6 through 13. Total $10,494.

15. Cash Balance: Subtract Cash Paid Out from Total Cash Available ($13,606).

16. Loans to be Received: Being aware of the $30,000 inventory costs payable in February, a loan of $40,000 is anticipated to increase Cash Available. (This requires advance planning!)

17. Equity Deposit: Owner plans to add $5,000 from personal account.

18. Ending Cash Balance: Adding 15, 16, and 17 the sum is $58,606.

February Projections

1. Beginning Cash Balance: January's Ending Cash Balance is transferred to February's Beginning Balance. Enter $58,606.

2. Cash Receipts: Coaching clinic income of $1,000 plus $1,000 to be collected from opening sales at the end of the month. $2,000.

3. Interest Income: Projected at about $120.

4. Sale of Long-Term Assets: None. Enter zero.

5. Total Cash Available: Add 1, 2, 3, and 4 above. The result is $60,726.

6. Cash Payments: $30,000 due for store inventory. $400 due for graphic design.

7. Continue as in January. Don't forget to include payments on the loan that was received in January.

Ace Sporting Goods Partial Cash Flow Statement

	Jan	Feb
BEGINNING CASH BALANCE	**20,000**	**58,606**
CASH RECEIPTS		
A. Sales/Revenues	4,000	2,000
B. Receivables	0	0
C. Interest Income	100	120
D. Sale of Long-Term Assets	0	0
TOTAL CASH AVAILABLE	**24,100**	**60,726**
CASH PAYMENTS		
A. Cost of goods to be sold		
1. Purchases	0	30,000
2. Material	0	0
3. Labor	5,000	400
Total Cost of Goods	**5,000**	**30,400**
B. Variable Expenses (Selling)		
1. Advertising/Marketing	470	
2. Event Planning	320	
3. Freight	0	
4. Sales Salaries/Commissions	0	
5. Travel	0	
6. Vehicle	285	
7. Miscellaneous Selling Expense	65	
Total Variable Expenses	**1,140**	
C. Fixed Expenses (Administrative)		**CONTINUE as in JANUARY**
1. Financial Admin	80	
2. Insurance	125	
3. License/Permits	200	
4. Office Salaries	500	
5. Rent Expenses	110	
6. Utilities	200	
7. Miscellaneous Administrative Expense	0	
Total Fixed Expenses	**1,215**	
D. Interest Expense	0	
E. Federal Income Tax	0	
F. Other uses	0	
G. Long-term asset payments	1,139	
H. Loan payments	0	
I. Owner draws	2,000	
TOTAL CASH PAID OUT	**10,494**	
CASH BALANCE/DEFICIENCY	**13,606**	
LOANS TO BE RECEIVED	40,000	
EQUITY DEPOSITS	5,000	
ENDING CASH BALANCE	**58,606**	

Directions for Completing a Cash Flow Statement

This page contains instructions for completing the cash flow statement on the next page. A blank form for your own projections can be found in Appendix B.

VERTICAL COLUMNS are divided into 12 months and preceded by a "Total" Column.

HORIZONTAL POSITIONS on the statement contain all sources of cash and cash to be paid out. The figures are retrieved from the two previous worksheets and individual budgets.

Figures are projected for each month, reflecting the flow of cash in and out of your business for a one-year period. Begin with the first month of your business cycle and proceed as follows:

1. Project the Beginning Cash Balance. Enter under "January."
2. Project the Cash Receipts for January. Apportion your total year's revenues throughout the 12 months. Try to weight revenues as closely as you can to a realistic selling cycle for your industry.
3. Add Beginning Cash Balance and Cash Receipts to determine Total Cash Available.
4. Project cash payments to be made for cost of goods to be sold (inventory that you will purchase or manufacture). Apportion your total inventory budget throughout the year, being sure you are providing for levels of inventory that will fulfill your needs for sales projected.
5. Customize your Variable and Fixed Expense categories to match your business.
6. Project Variable, Fixed, and Interest Expenses for January. Fill out any that you can for all 12 months.
7. Project cash to be paid out on Taxes, Long-Term Assets, Loan Repayments and Owner Draws.
8. Calculate Total Cash Paid Out (Total of Cost of Goods to Be Sold, Variable, Fixed, Interest, Taxes, Long-Term Asset Payments, Loan Repayments, and Owner Draws).
9. Subtract Total Cash Paid Out from Total Cash Available. The result is entered under Cash Balance/Deficiency. Be sure to bracket this figure if the result is negative to avoid errors.
10. Look at Ending Cash Balance in each of the months and project Loans to be Received and Equity Deposits to be made. Add to Cash Balance/Deficiency to arrive at Ending Cash Balance for each month.
11. Ending Cash Balance for January is carried forward and becomes February's Beginning Cash Balance (as throughout the spreadsheet. Each month's ending balance is the next month's beginning balance).
12. Go to February and input any numbers still needed to complete that month. The process is repeated until December is completed.

To Complete the "Total" Column

1. The Beginning Cash Balance for January is entered in the first space of the "Total" column.
2. The monthly figures for each category (except Beginning Cash Balance, Total Cash Available, Cash Balance/Deficiency, and Ending Cash Balance) are added horizontally and the result entered in the corresponding Total category.
3. The Total column is then computed in the same manner as each of the individual months. If you have been accurate in your computations, the December Ending Cash Balance will be exactly the same as the Total Ending Cash Balance.

Note: If your business is new, you will have to base your projections solely on market research and industry trends. If you have an established business, you will also use your financial statements from previous years. This process may seem complicated, but as you work with, it should begin to make perfect sense and be a straightforward and reasonable task to accomplish.

Ace Sporting Goods Pro Forma Cash Flow Statement

This is the full extension of the previous form (partial cash flow statement). There is a blank form in the Appendix for your use.

Year: 2004	Jan	Feb	Mar	Apr	May	Jun	6-MONTH PERIOD	Jul	Aug	Sep	Oct	Nov	Dec	12-MONTH PERIOD
BEGINNING CASH BALANCE														
CASH RECEIPTS														
A. Sales/Revenues (Cash Sales)														
B. Receivables to be collected														
C. Interest Income														
D. Sale of Long-Term Assets														
TOTAL CASH AVAILABLE														
CASH PAYMENTS														
A. Cost of goods to be sold														
1. Purchases														
2. Material														
3. Labor														
Total Cost of Goods														
B. Variable Expenses (selling)														
1. Advertising/Marketing														
2. Event Planning														
3. Freight														
4. Sales/Salaries														
5. Travel														
6. Vehicle														
7. Misc. selling Expense														
Total Variable Expenses														
C. Fixed Expenses (admin.)														
1. Financial administration														
2. Insurance														
3. Licenses and permits														
4. Office Salaries														
5. Rent expense														
6. Utilities														
7. Misc. administrative expense														
Total Fixed Expenses														
D. Interest Expense														
E. Federal Income Tax														
F. Other uses														
G. Long-term asset payments														
H. Loan payments														
I. Owner draws														
TOTAL CASH PAID OUT														
CASH BALANCE/DEFICIENCY														
LOANS TO BE RECEIVED														
EQUITY DEPOSITS														
ENDING CASH BALANCE														

DEVELOPING A MARKETING PLAN

In Chapter 3, you researched your market and now have a good idea of the composition of your customer base or target market. You checked out the competition and have a good understanding of your industry. You determined the best way to reach your market. The development of a marketing plan builds on this information. Look at what are called the "4 Ps" of marketing. This analysis will help develop the focus needed to determine your business objectives.

More than 40 years ago, Neil Borden introduced the concept of the 4 Ps that have become the basis of traditional marketing. Basically, the concept involves **product, place, price,** and **promotion**. Take a look at these topics before moving into the development of the marketing plan. As you will see, they each play a role in how strategies and tactics will be developed.

· · · · ·

PRODUCT OR SERVICE

The first "P" stands for product or service. Basic to marketing is a clear understanding of your product or service and the unique considerations inherent in their differences. A product is a physical and tangible thing. It can be seen and touched. When you buy it, you own it. What you buy is what you get! A service is a task provided by one party for another. It is not tangible, it cannot be seen or touched, and you do not "own" it. Products are usually produced and then sold. By contrast, services are often sold first and then produced or performed. Products can be produced and stored as inventory; services can't be stored, and this can create a challenge in anticipating supply and demand.

Business owners generally think in terms of developing an individual product or service when starting a new business. You may have more success in reaching your customers by also providing related products or services. It is important to listen to your target customers what they want and develop a product or service line to meet their needs. For example, the marketing research for Ace Sporting Goods indicated that customers wanted to try equipment before purchase. Providing an area of the store where golf clubs and putters can be safely tested would be a service that could lead to a product sale. This decision is in response to customer feedback.

Throughout your marketing experience, you will hear the term **positioning**. A product or service position is determined by the image projected in terms of the competition, pricing, packaging, distribution, location, and timing of market entry. Your market research will have given you insights into the ways in which to position your product or service. You know your competition, how they advertise and who they serve. You have compared the pricing structures, the distribution channels, the packaging, and the location of the competitors. Positioning is much like a ranking system. Determine where you want to be on the ladder. Choose the most effective combination of products and/or services to offer as a product line based on feedback from your customers. Determine where you want your product line to be positioned in the marketplace. For example, Ace Sporting Goods is positioning itself to be the premier sporting goods store in the county that stocks and specializes in fishing equipment. It is also the only store to provide an area for viewing sport instructional videos.

As you develop your product or service, never lose sight of the needs and preferences of your customers. If their expectations are not met, you will lose their interest in purchasing your product or using your service.

PLACE

The second "P" stands for place. It refers to the decisions a company makes to ensure that a product or service gets to the customer at the right location and in the right manner. Place can also be expanded to include methods of distribution as well as your business location. Location was discussed in detail in Chapter 5.

Distribution is a major component of the marketing mix. The distribution process has been compared to a pipeline or channel. Information, orders, products, services, and payments flow from consumer to product manufacturer or service provider and back again. What is the normal process for order placement and delivery in the business you are developing? What are the cost factors such as commissions, delivery, shipping fees, and warehousing involved? Develop a flowchart for your product from inventory to sale to delivery and look at the time and costs involved in the process.

For example, the primary location for Ace Sporting Goods will be a retail store in Blair, New York. Sports products will be ordered from manufacturers and wholesalers at a discounted price and shipped to the store where they will be put into inventory until sold. Products can also be distributed through other methods. Fly-fishing classes can be taught off-site in order to better reach the market. Product can be presold at the time of class registration and delivered to the class. The store may wish to develop mail-order sales or an e-commerce Web site. All are ways of selling and distributing products from one location.

PRICE

The third "P" is pricing. Pricing is also a marketing decision, combining market research with financial analysis. To be successful, a business owner must establish prices for goods and services that will allow for a profit margin, be competitive with similar businesses, and will be acceptable to the customer. Pricing can "make or break" a business. If the price is wrong, it won't matter that everything else is right.

One of the problems we have as business owners is that we price a product or service at what we **want** it to sell for, rather than at what it will sell for. There are two important factors to keep in mind when developing a pricing structure.

1. *Price ceiling.* You will need to determine the price ceiling; this is the most a customer will pay for your product or service. It is "what the traffic will bear." This is the customer's perception of what you have to offer and, often, this amount has been set by the competition. The customers are used to paying a certain dollar amount. Market research will help you arrive at that figure. Your questionnaires and interview feedback will show what a customer will expect to pay. The information from trade and professional associations will indicate pricing trends and guidelines. The principle to remember is that products or services are bought on the basis of perceived value in the minds of buyers, not on the basis of what it costs you to produce or purchase a product or to provide a service. For example, the **Market Research Worksheet for Ace Sporting Goods** indicated that the market would only pay $55 for a ten-hour guided trip to the Carson River.

2. *Price floor.* Even though the cost of your product or service is not directly related to what the customer is willing to pay for it, costs are of extreme importance to you as the business owner. You must be aware of how much it cost you to produce your product or provide your service. This means you must take into account all of the operating and other expenses of the business. Evaluation of your costs and expenses allows you to establish a price floor, the price below which you cannot sell and make the necessary profit. The owner of Ace Sporting Goods looked at all the costs involved in putting his Carson River fishing trip together and determined that ten participants were needed to break even. Fewer attendees would result in a loss; more attendees would mean a profit.

Successful businesses operate between their price floor and price ceiling.

PROMOTION

The fourth "P" stands for promotion and involves using the most cost-effective and appropriate promotional methods to enable you to attract customers, make sales, and keep repeat customers. Chapter 19, "Promoting Your Business," is devoted to covering ways in which to promote and advertise your business.

Marketing is primarily what you do **before** and **after** the sale. It is everything you do to make the first sale possible and a repeat sale likely. A marketing plan is a key component in the development of a business. It is an organized system for setting up a process for reaching your market and involves determining **objectives**, developing a **strategy** for reaching those objectives, implementing the strategy through various **tactics**, and setting up an **evaluation** process to make sure your plan is working.

Determining Your Objectives

Step one involves identifying what you hope to accomplish. You have a fairly clear vision of what you want your business to be in terms of its size, service or product provided, and market to be served. Express that vision as specific, quantifiable goals and objectives. Being specific is the only way to realistically focus your business and marketing activities.

For new businesses, this may be attaining a certain sales volume or capturing a certain share of the market. Do you want to gross $60,000 during the first year of operation for Ace Sporting Goods? Do you want to capture 10 percent of the market for take-out food in your geographical area? Objectives can be formed for many aspects of your business. You may want to increase your customer base, set a goal of hiring five new employees, create three new jobs, develop a customer satisfaction program, or market on the Internet. A **Marketing Action Plan for Ace Sporting Goods** has been included on page 170 as an example.

Developing a Strategy

With your goals in mind, you want to decide on overall marketing approaches for each of your products or services and your business. A marketing strategy is the general method you will use to achieve a goal.

Once you have identified objectives and know what you want your business to accomplish, you are ready to develop a strategy for achieving those objectives. A marketing strategy is a game plan for getting products and services into the hands of your customers in a timely, cost-effective, and appropriate manner.

Tactics for Implementing a Strategy

A marketing tactic is a specific method or program you develop and implement for carrying out the strategy and quantifying the desired result. Tactics are the day-to-day actions you take to put your plan strategy into action. Use the information you developed when you worked through the four "P's." What **promotion** will work best for implementing your strategy? If you use a delivery truck as part of your distribution (**place**), signage on the truck can make your business visible. Have you considered discount coupons as part of your **pricing** plan?

Deciding on your strategies and tactics will involve looking at what you can afford to spend, what is appropriate for your particular market, product, or service, and what is likely to reach your market in the most effective way.

Evaluating the Results

To be of value, you must develop a plan for evaluating the results. If your objective was to increase revenue by 20 percent in six months, did your sales figures show the desired increase? What did it cost you to reach this goal? Was it cost-effective?

If your objectives are being met, it can mean that your strategy has been successful. You may want to continue with the same tactics. Remember that markets are dynamic and that what works now may not work in the future. Also, different markets react to different tactics. Successful businesses conduct ongoing market research throughout the life of their business. They do customer surveys, keep up with industry changes, and keep track of population changes in their target areas.

If your objectives haven't been met, look closely at your tactics. You may have to revise your plan of attack. Do more of what works and eliminate that which didn't produce the desired results.

After you have been in business for awhile, your financial statements will give a clear picture of how your business has performed financially. By comparing actual results with your objectives over a period of time, you can identify what is working and what is not. Your marketing plan is like a game plan. Basic market research and previous results are used by businesses to set new objectives and begin the cycle over again.

Marketing Action Plan for Ace Sporting Goods

Objective	Strategy	Tactic	Evaluation
Increase revenue from Carson River trips.	Offer Carson River trips twice per month during fishing season. Each trip needs 24 people with three guides.	Increase awareness of fly-fishing through: • in-store demos • in-store viewing of fly-fishing videotapes • press releases • bimonthly drawing for one free trip • direct mail to drawing participants	Keep track of sign-up at in-store demos. Monitor interest from press releases. Keep track of participation in drawing.
Increase sales of sporting goods equipment in store.	Acquire new customers. Encourage repeat business.	Hold a grand opening. Run ads in local newspaper. Saturate surrounding area with 10-percent-off coupons valid during first week of operation. Give additional discount coupon to all customers who make a purchase during first week of operation.	Keep track of percent of sales coming from advertising. Keep track of percent of sales coming from coupons. Keep track of percent of first-time customers who return.

CHAPTER 19

PROMOTING YOUR BUSINESS

Advertising is the means for getting information about your product or service to the buying public. The first step in developing an advertising plan is to define potential customers in the geographic area served by your business. Do some preliminary surveys and interviews to determine which means of advertising will reach them. What newspapers do they read? Which radio stations do they listen to? Do they use discount coupons? Do they respond to direct mail? Do they have access to the Internet? Tailor your advertising efforts to your market.

By now you will have identified what is **unique** about your business and how that uniqueness will **benefit the customer**. This theme or image for your product or service should carry through all of your advertising. It is what sets you apart from the competition and what will attract the customer.

When you know which audience you want to target, where they are located, and what you want to tell them, it is time to look at how you will reach them. There are a variety of ways to accomplish this through the media, with publicity, and by alternative methods of advertising.

• • • • •

MEDIA ADVERTISING

Media advertising and publicity can be obtained through interviews, articles, and paid advertisements in newspapers and magazines and on radio and television.

Newspaper advertising. This form of promotion usually reaches a large audience, has a short life span, is relatively inexpensive, and is quickly and easily changed. Tailor your ad to the editorial "mood" of the paper. Determine what special feature sections are being planned by calling the newspaper's editorial staff. If the paper is planning to do a special feature on "desktop publishing" and you will be opening a mobile repair service for such equipment, you may want to advertise in that section. Your ad can be placed to reach a selected audience; the people reading that section will be interested in desktop publishing and your business. The cost of the ad will vary according to frequency of publication and area of circulation. Ads are available in various sizes and several formats such as display or classified ads. Analyze the advertising of your competition regarding size, placement, and frequency. Your question-naires and market research will have indicated the newspapers read by your target market. Those are the papers in which you will place your advertising.

Magazine advertising. This is often overlooked by small business owners because ads are thought to be too costly to prepare and run. You don't have to run your ad in the entire edition of a magazine. You can reach specific geographic and demographic markets by placing your ad in a regional edition. You may be able to cut down your cost by making use of "remnant space." Sometimes a magazine will not have sold all of its advertising space prior to press time. These remnant spaces are often sold at a deep discount in order to fill the page. Contact the publication well in advance of the date when you wish your ad to appear and determine its policies. Some magazines will provide extra services such as reader response cards that enable you to develop a mailing list of individuals interested in what you have to offer.

One of the disadvantages of magazine advertising is that your ad must be placed well in advance of the issue's publication, which does not allow for last-minute changes. You also have very little control over where your ad will appear in the magazine. Expensive items gen-erally do not sell well through magazine ads. This type of advertising is best suited for mail-order businesses and name-brand merchandise.

Magazine ads carry a large degree of credibility and prestige and are worth considering as an advertising option.

Radio advertising. Advertising by radio is usually local, reaches a preselected audience, can be changed frequently, is limited to brief copy, is relatively expensive, and can be repeated frequently. It is priced according to length of message, time of broadcast, and fre-quency of broadcast. It is either read live by broadcasters or taped in advance.

There are two types of radio programming: background and foreground. Background programs are on the music stations. Foreground programs are on the news/talk stations. Foreground pro-grams involve more active listeners who will probably pay more attention to your commercials.

It has been proven that you must catch the listener's attention in the first three seconds. Your ad will be done live or taped in advance. The three biggest complaints about radio commer-cials are that they are noisy, have inane humor, and lack sincerity. Keep that in mind if you write your own commercial. Be simple and straightforward. Another approach to radio cover-age of your business would be to offer your service as an expert in your field on a radio talk show. You can answer questions from listeners and tell about your business.

Television advertising. This medium reaches large marketing areas, is relatively expensive, and is limited to brief copy. This form of advertising is usually highly professional and priced according to length of message, time of broadcast, frequency of broadcast, time of year, and whether the station is an independent or a member of a network.

Cost of advertising is based on gross rating points (GRP). One point equals one percent of the television sets in the TV marketing area. The GRP unit cost is determined by the competitive situation, size of area, and time of year. Advertising costs may be higher during the holiday season, which is considered to be October through December. Prime time covers the period from 8:00 to 11:00 PM and is more costly. The "fringe time" before and after prime time may be more cost-effective for you. Don't discount cable television. This medium is becoming very useful to the small business owner. In many communities, low-cost seminars are presented to instruct you in developing your own cable television ads or programs.

You need to know which media are most likely to influence your target audience and which reporters cover your kind of business. The public library has media source books available that list newspapers, magazines, radio, and television stations. Find out what shows your customers watch. Television stations will have demographic and psychographic breakdowns of their viewing audiences. Most use market studies to effectively help position advertising where it will be seen by those interested in the products or services offered.

Advertising takes planning, time, persistence, and money. The true effectiveness of advertising is measured over time. Your target market must be repeatedly reminded of the benefits of doing business with you. This repetition has a cumulative effect. Customers will see you as an established business. Use the **Advertising Worksheet** on page 180 as you plan which types of advertising methods will be used, how much they will cost, and when they will be used. The planning process is like drawing a blueprint. First design the framework, next fill in the details, and then begin to build the advertising plan.

TECH TIP 23
LOCATING AND EVALUATING MEDIA ADVERTISING SOURCES

Standard Rate and Data Service (SROS) publishes print and online versions of media directories that are available by subscription or for use in many business libraries. Resource titles include: Newspaper Advertising Source, Radio Advertising Source, Print Media Production Source, and TV and Cable Source. Both versions provide complete reports on the media entities you wish to consider for advertising or publicity placement; complete contact information as well as a description of the publication's market are available. The online version offers links directly to a listed media entity's Web site, allows e-mail to be sent to advertising personnel, and links directly to the newspaper's media kit. Log onto the SRDS Web site to learn more about these directories: <www.srds.com>.

PUBLICITY

In addition to paid advertising, don't overlook publicity. Publicity has been defined as "free advertising." Research print media, television, and radio stations in your area with the help of your local library. Media references available in the library will provide you with a listing of sources and contact names. Call programmers for the radio and television talk programs and editors of the newspapers and magazines in your area. Ask if they will be doing a feature on your area of expertise. If they are, offer your services as an expert working in that field. You may be interviewed and profiled, you may be able to submit an article for publication, or you may wish to place some targeted advertising to coincide with the feature. If no feature is being planned, explain why this would be a timely topic and of interest to their audiences.

It is not enough to just tell about your business. You must be prepared to present a unique angle. You must convince the editor or programmer that what you have to say will appeal and be of interest to readers, listeners, and viewers. The information you submit and the ideas you approach the media with must be timely, important, and interesting to a large segment of the audience.

You may wish to submit a **news release** in order to let people know who you are and what you have to offer. When preparing a press release, the two primary concerns are content and structure. News releases should be as short as possible while containing all of the important facts. Make every effort to write it in good journalistic style. Read news releases in your target news outlets and study format and content. News writing follows the "inverted pyramid" style in which every paragraph is considered more important than the ones following it. The story is written in descending order of importance. That means the news is up front. A busy reader whose interest is not caught in the first paragraph will not read the second one. **News Release Information**, a **News Release Format** sheet, and a **Sample News Release** are included on pages 181, 182, and 183, respectively.

ALTERNATIVE METHODS

In addition to advertising and publicity, there are other means of getting the message about your business to your customers. **Displays** may be set up at community-oriented functions such as city fairs, community events, and civic meetings. This is a good way to present your product or service to the buying public. You can also get valuable feedback. **Community involvement** can be an effective means of advertising. Membership in civic organizations can pave the way to being a guest speaker. Active membership affords you the opportunity for networking. **Networking** is the exchange of ideas and information that takes place every day of your life. You are going to direct that exchange to your benefit and the benefit of those around you. The more you meet with people, the more you will be able to promote your business, learn more about the business community around you, and become more self-confident. Membership in civic and business organizations such as the chamber of commerce is an excellent means of accomplishing this.

Trade show and **exhibit** participation allows you to take advantage of promotional campaigns that would be too expensive for a small business to undertake alone. You can request listings of trade events from malls and convention centers. Participation in trade shows and membership in trade organizations give you visibility in your business field. These shows are usually attended only by those interested in your particular field. This is an excellent way to reach your target market. You may choose to participate in a co-op display to cut costs.

Direct mail. This is an effective way to deliver specific information in a personal way to large numbers of people. Direct mail can take the form of inexpensive fact sheets, letters, promotional give-aways, contests, discount coupons, and brochures. It can be used to solicit mail-order or phone-order business, announce new products or services, notify customers of price changes, welcome new customers, thank current customers, and announce special events such as sales. To be cost-effective, you must target your market. Rent a good list from a list broker.

Direct e-mail. Ask potential and existing customers for their e-mail addresses and permission to provide them with information. Send them industry news, monthly product updates, announcements of special sales, and hyperlinks to your Web site and other sites of interest. Encourage them to bookmark your Web site; let them know you frequently update the site and provide timely and useful information that will benefit them. This is the fastest, most cost-effective, cutting edge method for reaching customers.

Telemarketing. Telephone selling has been well established in business-to-business marketing. In the past, telemarketing from business to consumer was also an effective method for contacting new customers. In October 2003, the Federal Trade Commission instituted the National Do Not Call Registry that gives individuals the opportunity to limit telemarketing calls by placing their phone numbers on the Do Not Call list. Telemarketers are required to monitor the list and remove numbers on the registry from their call lists. Businesses that cold call individuals who have listed their phone numbers on the Do Not Call list are in violation and risk fines. Political organizations, charities, telephone surveyors, or companies with an existing business relationship to the caller will be exempt. This form of promotion can still be an effective method for maintaining contact with current clients.

Cold calling of new clients or customers will be replaced with "warm calling." Many companies are finding a pre-introduction effective.

- Determine the key decision maker you want to reach.
- Send an introductory letter, send a sample, or make an offer. State in the cover letter that you will be contacting them.
- Call within one week of their receipt of the mailing. (The post office can give you an estimate of delivery time.)
- If you get a positive response, close the deal, and send a thank-you message.
- If you get a negative response, send a thank-you note indicating your appreciation for their time and letting them know your company may be able to meet their needs at some future time.

Use your best judgment regarding the use of telemarketing in view of the new restrictions.

Contact the Federal Trade Commission at <www.ftc.gov> for information on the procedure for identifying phone numbers that have been registered with the National Do Not Call Registry.

Yellow page listings. Listings are an effective means of advertising. Every person with a phone has a copy of the yellow pages. You have a captive audience; potential customers are looking at the directory because they are interested in what you have to offer. This is the most widely used form of advertising. One business owner states that, in any given week, 50 percent of her customers are directed to her clock repair shop through her yellow pages ad.

The telephone company advertising staff is very knowledgeable and will give you help in designing an ad that will present your business in an effective manner. Be aware that directories are published at various times of the year. Call the phone company to determine publication deadlines.

Discounts. This is another way to get additional customers. Discounts can be given to new customers and customers who bring in referrals. They may also be offered through coupons and brochures. Everyone likes to think they are saving money.

TECH TIP 24
DOWNLOADABLE DISCOUNTS

You can publish coupons on your Web site that can be downloaded and printed. Your site can let customers know these coupons are only available at the site and encourage your customers to bring them to your store for a discount. This is a good way to track the type of customers who are accessing your site and the frequency of their return to the site. Restaurants, grocery stores, and boutiques are some of the types of businesses that are utilizing this type of promotion.

Promotional gimmicks. T-shirts, pens, key rings, plastic shopping bags, calendars, balloons, and bumper stickers can also get your name in front of the public. The most effective promotional materials are useful items. They should be appropriate to the business they represent. For example, a logo or business name on a T-shirt is an effective way of advertising a business dealing with the out-of-doors, such as a bicycle shop or a kite maker. Pens would be a good item for a manufacturer of note cards and stationery. Balloons could represent a company specializing in children's items. Be creative in your use of this advertising form.

Customer contact. Contact with your customers has never been easier. New technology enables you to develop a computer database of your customer files. A tickler file can be set up to alert you to special events in the lives of your customers; birthday cards, discount coupons, and industry news can be sent via regular or electronic mail. An 800 phone number makes it easy for customers to reach you at no cost to them. Cellular phones and pagers enable you, the business owner, to be in contact with your market at all times, wherever you may be, and allow you to respond immediately. No matter what type of business you are in, technology can enable you to work more efficiently, better meet the needs of your customer base, and increase your profits.

MARKETING ON THE INTERNET

Technology is affecting virtually every business. People go on the World Wide Web (www) for a variety of reasons; to conduct research, communicate via electronic mail (e-mail), seek out education and training sites, and make purchases (e-commerce). Many companies are rushing to develop Web sites and to put their brochures and catalogs online so customers can browse, select products, ask questions, and place orders through their home or office computers. This technology has opened up many new marketing opportunities for businesses.

A business can set up a virtual storefront and market its products and services through a Web site located on the Internet. The Internet has been described as "the yellow pages of cyberspace." Consumers surf the Web looking for products and services they need. Before deciding on the value of a Web site for your business, answer the following questions:

- *Why do you need a Web site?* Before investing time and money into the development of your site, answer a few questions. Is your competition marketing over the Internet? To remain competitive, do you also need a presence? Look at your competitor's Web site and evaluate it. Do you want to expand geographically? Marketing on the Internet will allow your marketing materials to be viewed internationally. Are you ready for such wide exposure? If you want to remain fairly local, link up with a local identity for inclusion of your Web page. For example, many chambers of commerce are hosting sites that include information on local businesses.

- *What do you hope to accomplish through your site?* Do you want to provide information? Do you want an interactive site so you can gather information from your customers? Do you want to make sales? If so, how are you going to be paid? If you are going to take orders online, you will need to establish a secure server. This is technology that will encrypt or code your customers' credit card information so they may complete payment for the transaction over the Internet.

- *Who will be accessing your material?* Do your potential or existing customers own computers? Do they have modems and online services? Do they purchase over the Internet? Make sure the market you have researched can be reached through this medium.

- *How will they reach your site?* Will individuals just stumble upon your site or do you have a plan for leading them to it? Your Web site must be on all of your marketing materials and listed in all directories. When composing your Web pages, use words or terms that your potential customers might use when searching for your product or service.

Even though your initial research may indicate your market is not now computerized, does not order via the Internet, or would not expect to find you on this medium, markets change. Keep up-to-date on new technology and the changing marketplace.

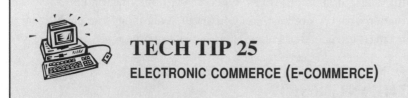

TECH TIP 25
ELECTRONIC COMMERCE (E-COMMERCE)

For a detailed look at what e-commerce is all about, visit: <www.howstuffworks.com/ecommerce.htm>.

To view examples of effective, interactive Web pages, access the following sites: <www.jellybelly.com> and <www.ragu.com>.

Note that the use of the company's name as the domain name enables the customer to remember the site. The Jelly Belly site enables the user to order online, find a local retailer, and learn about special events. By filling out a questionnaire, the user can receive a free sample. This interactive site allows the company to track product interest geographically for future retail placement. The Ragu site provides recipes, a recipe search function, and a subscription to an online newsletter. While these sites are expensive to develop, monitor, and maintain, they illustrate what can be done to capture and keep a customer's interest. They are changed frequently to keep customers coming back.

One of the major concerns for businesses offering goods for sale over the Internet has been a secure method for the transfer of payment. PayPal is a money transfer system that acts as a neutral intermediary offering low risk to both the seller/receiver and the buyer/sender of the money. To learn more about this technology and service, go to: <www.paypal.com>.

About Web Pages

Like when using the yellow pages and other directories, consumers don't want to spend a lot of time reading detailed text. A well-designed Web site can capture the interest of a potential customer and keep an existing customer returning to your site. Following are some considerations when developing your Web site:

- *Be consistent.* Just like your other promotional materials, your Web site must project your company's image.

- *Keep it simple.* You have 15 seconds to capture the customer's interest. The text should be simple and easy to read. Avoid an abundance of graphics; the page will take too long to come up on the screen, and your customers will move on before your message can be fully viewed. Use a background color that does not compete with or drown out the information.

- *Be information-based*. Potential customers have come to your site to find out about your product or service. Give them the information they need in as short a time as possible.

- *Make navigation easy*. Develop a home page with icons that can be clicked on to go to subsequent pages with additional information. The home page of Ace Sporting Goods would briefly give information regarding the nature of the business, the e-mail address, 800-phone number, and address. Icons would be included for sporting goods categories. Separate icons could be included for in-store programs and special sales. If a potential or existing customer was only interested in fly-fishing, a few clicks would take that customer to a listing of equipment for sale, special promotions, and in-store programs. The customer would not have to wade through baseball, golf, and tennis information.

Contact your nearest SBA office, SBDC, or local college to find out about low-cost workshops and seminars on e-commerce and Web page development. Your decision to market in this medium should be an educated one.

Summary

In summary, pay attention to advertising and promotions that attract your attention. Try to analyze successful advertising done by professionals for tips on designing your own ads. Your advertising should be the highest quality you can afford and as professional as possible. Your advertising represents you and your business and conveys an impression to the public.

All promotion costs something. Advertising is a necessary expense for establishing, maintaining, and expanding your business. Deciding how much money to spend to advertise your product or service can be difficult. The size of your advertising budget should be determined by long-range as well as immediate sales objectives. Although the proportion of income spent on advertising varies according to the type of business, the average is 1.5 percent. The SBA suggests that it is not the amount that is spent but how it is spent that counts. The rule of thumb is that the cost of advertising must be offset by the increase in its resulting profits. View advertising costs as an investment in your company's future and choose the methods that will best reach your target market. Advertising must be cost-effective.

All forms of advertising and publicity must be evaluated for effectiveness. To help you with this analysis, an **Advertising Response Record** and a **Publicity Tracking Record** have been included on pages 184 and 185. From this information, determine which form of advertising has worked best for your business. Eliminate those methods that have not proven effective and transfer those funds to a more productive area. After evaluating the different methods of advertising, work up an individual plan for your business.

Advertising Worksheet

Name of business: ___Ace Sporting Goods_____

1. What are the features and benefits of my product or service? ___Knowledgeable trained staff;___ _open until 9 PM weekdays, 1-5 PM Sunday; full sports product line, specializing_ _in fishing gear; offer fly-tying and fly-fishing classes; in-house guarantee of sports_ _equipment._____

2. Who is my audience? _____
   Youth, high school, university students_____
   Active, middle-income sports enthusiasts_____
   Live within ten-mile radius_____

3. Who is my competition and how do they advertise? _____
   Smith Sporting Goods—radio ads KLXY_____
   Mailing of flyers—newspaper ad—Sunday supplement_____
   Promotions—caps, T-shirts_____

4. What are the goals of my advertising campaign? _____
   Reach high school and university market_____
   Reach youth market_____
   Reach fishing enthusiasts_____

5. How much do I plan to invest for advertising? _____$1,300 per month_____
   _____
   _____
   _____
   _____

6. What advertising methods will I use? _____

x Newspapers	__ Magazines	x Yellow Pages
__ Radio	__ Television	x Direct mail
__ Telemarketing	x Flyers	__ Brochures
x Coupons	__ Press release	x Promo items
x Other ___youth team sponsorship_____		

7. When will I use them and what will they cost? _____
   Newspaper: start 1/3/04 weekly ad x 5 $300/mo.
   Direct mail flyers: 1/7/04 and 1/14/04 $550 total
   Youth team: 1/26/04 $150/mo.
   Promo items: 1/16/04 $100/mo.
   Yellow page ad: 1/25/04 (March directory) $200/mo.

8. How will I measure the effectiveness of the advertising plan? _____
   a. Ask customers how they heard about the store._____
   b. Compare cost/income on Advertising Response Record._____
      1. Change or delete methods that cost more than income generated.___
      2. Adjust or increase budget to include radio ad, brochure, larger yellow page_ and newspaper ads._____

News Release Information

Identification

The business sending the release should be plainly identified. Use your letterhead or printed news release forms. The name and telephone number of a contact person for additional information must appear at the top of the page.

Release date

Most releases should be "immediate" or "for use upon receipt." Designate a release time only if there is a specific reason, such as a scheduled speech, meeting, news announcement, or planned event.

Margins

Leave wide margins and space at the top so the editor can edit and include notations.

Headlines

The headline you submit should be to summarize your writing. The media will generally create their own headlines.

Length

Most press releases are one page in length. If you have a longer release, write the highlights into an attached news memo and include the news release as background material.

Style

Use the summary lead and the five W's (who, what, when, where, why, and, sometimes, how). Double-space. Use short sentences with active verbs. Make sure it is accurate, timely, and not self-serving. Try to use an objective style of writing. If you must use more than one page, do not split a paragraph from the first to second page. Center the word "more" at the bottom of the first page.

Check and Doublecheck

Proofread names, spellings, numbers, and grammar carefully.

Placement

Your news release should be in the hands of editors well in advance of deadlines. Contact the city desk, assignment editor, or feature editor with whom you are working to clarify deadlines and publication schedules.

End

Put "30" or ### at the end of the press release.

News releases should be cleanly typed on 8½ x 11-inch white paper. They should be hand-delivered or mailed first-class to the designated media contact.

News Release Format

(Print on Company Letterhead or News Memo Form)

TO: Addressed to editor or reporter.

FROM: Your name, address, and phone number.

RE: A one or two sentence statement regarding the story you are suggesting, the event to which you are inviting reporters, the meeting, class or seminar you have scheduled, or other purpose of the news release.

TIME AND DATE: Specific time, date, year of event, or of submission release.

LOCATION: Specific location, including directions if the location is not well-known or easily found.

WHY: You must have a reason for the news release or event.

CONTACT: The name and phone number of someone the news editor or reporters can contact with questions about the news release.

NOTE: Go to <www.constantcontact.com> for help with creating electronic fliers, brochures, and press releases.

Sample News Release

(Print on Company Letterhead or Press Release Form)

PRESS RELEASE

September 6, 2004   Contact: David Blair

For Immediate Release   555-613-7965

Fly-Fishing Demonstration and Contest

John Bacon, well-known local fly-fisherman, will demonstrate techniques for dry and wet fly casting and judge a contest to be held in the parking lot of Ace Sporting Goods on Saturday, September 26, 2004 from 10 AM to 4 PM.

Ace's owner, David Blair, reports that the popularity of the 1992 movie, *A River Runs Through It*, led to an increased interest in the sport of fly-fishing. This interest has continued to grow. The Leisure Trends Group reports that U.S. fly-fishing sales in 2000 amounted to $678 million, compared to $572 million in 1998.

Blair announced that the fee for participation in the contest is $5, with all of the proceeds going to the Memorial Hospital Children's Wing. All contestants will receive a ten percent discount coupon from the sporting goods store.

After receiving instructions from Mr. Bacon, contestants will be judged on form, distance, and accuracy. Prizes include theater passes, dinner coupons, and sporting event tickets. The contest is open to everyone. Information and preregistration are available at Ace Sporting Goods, 271 Adams St., Blair, NY or by phoning 555-613-7965.

-30-

Advertising Response Record

Company name: _Ace Sporting Goods—January 2004_

Type of Ad	Date Run	Cost	Circulation	Number of Responses	Income Generated
Register newspaper 2" x 4" in sports section	Weekly 1/3, 1/10, 1/17, 1/24, 1/31	$300.00	15,000	end of month coupon responses— 264 phone orders— 26	$6,600.00 $520.00
Flyers with 10% discount coupon—high school, university	Mailed 1/7/04	$350.00	750	10	$260.00
Flyers with 10% discount for fishermen	Mailed 1/14/04	$200.00	500	96	$1,152.00
Youth team sponsorship caps/shirts with store name	1/26/04	$150.00	12	Six team members purchased equipment at 20% discount	$135.00

In this example, the newspaper ad, which included the 10-percent-off coupon, generated income of $7,120 with an expense of $300. By analyzing the response to newspaper advertising over time, the owner of Ace Sporting Goods can determine whether the initial interest was due to curiosity about a new store or if there is continued response to this form of advertising. The discount flyers mailed to the high school and university students were not cost-effective. The flyers mailed to a targeted mailing list of fishermen were more effective: at a cost of $200, 96 new customers responded and spent $1,152. The sponsorship of a youth sports team may appear to lose money, but the goodwill and visibility generated is worth the small loss. The response to your advertising must be analyzed throughout the lifetime of a business. This type of analysis will help you determine the most effective use of your advertising dollars.

Publicity Tracking Record

Company name: _Ace Sporting Goods_

Media Name	Contact Person	Address	Date	Material Sent	Follow-up	Response	Results	Notes
KRTZ Radio "News About Town"	Jim Bell, Prog. Dir., 555-8120	722 Main Baker, MD 20601	9/9/04	News Memo Promo Kit	9/16 phoned	9/18 booked for 10/2 talk show 7–8 PM	15 calls taken on air 160 requests for brochure	Focus: Opening of fishing season. Fly-tying and fishing
Tribune newspaper	Ann Mead, Sports Ed., 555-6124	621 6th St. Baker, MD 20603	9/10/04	Press Release Promo Kit	9/17 phoned	9/20 submit 500 word article	Article printed 9/27 200 requests for brochure	Focus: Current interest in alternative sport
Orange City magazine	Karen Brown, Reporter, 555-7093	724 Adams Baker, MD 20603	9/10/04	Promo Kit Photo	10/22 phoned	not interested at this time		Focus: New business opens
Metro Cable Evening News	David Kim, Prog. Dir., 555-6201	2664 Bryan Baker, MD 20601	10/15/04	Promo Kit Photo		will film fly-tying 6 PM 10/25		Focus: Unique local business

Evaluating the results of your publicity campaign will help you decide the most effective use of your advertising dollars. The appearance on KRTZ radio netted 15 calls on air and 160 off-air requests for brochures. The material sent to listeners should be coded so that responses can be traced. If coupons are used or class registrations taken from this group, you may consider advertising on the station. The same follow-up should be considered with the newspaper article. Although Orange City magazine is not interested at this time, keep in touch and present a new angle at a later date.

BUSINESS PLANNING: THE KEY TO YOUR SUCCESS

The purpose of this chapter is to convince you that you need to write a business plan and give you some basic information about business planning. We will also provide you with a basic outline listing the components of a well-written plan. If you decide to go ahead with the project (we hope you will!), there is a comprehensive, step-by-step guide that will take you through the entire process. It is titled *Anatomy of a Business Plan* (Linda Pinson, Dearborn Trade). If you are computer-oriented, we have also developed an IBM or compatible software version of the book, complete with word processing and preformatted and preformulated spreadsheets. It is titled Automate Your Business Plan 11.0 for Windows® (Out of Your Mind...and Into the Marketplace, Tustin, CA). You can also take classes through most colleges, SBDCs, or the U.S. SBA.

Lack of adequate planning is one of the principal reasons that most businesses fail. When the concept of business planning is considered, three critical facts always seem to emerge:

1. All lenders and investors require a business plan.

2. All businesses would operate more profitably with a business plan.

3. Most business owners do not know how to write a winning business plan.

We have been teaching business workshops to entrepreneurs for several years now and have found that no task seems to cause more consternation and dread than that of preparing a business plan. In fact, most new business owners will forge ahead, sure that a good idea, enthusiasm, and the desire to achieve their goals are enough to ensure business success.

Unfortunately, there is a major flaw in this type of thinking. Many business owners are not proficient in all phases of their particular industries and, therefore, do not have enough knowledge to make the best decisions and see what changes will have to be implemented in the future. Business planning is the most effective way to overcome this deficiency and enable you to organize the making of business decisions into a logical process. Unfortunately, most business owners would love it if they could spend all of their time practicing their skills and avoid anything that resembles paperwork.

You will soon learn that about 20 percent of your time as a business owner will be spent directly working with your product or service. The other 80 percent of the time you will be kept busy doing all of the managerial and miscellaneous chores needed to keep your business functioning.

WHY SHOULD YOU WRITE A BUSINESS PLAN?

There are two main purposes for writing a business plan. What are they, and why are they important enough to make you decide to write one?

1. ***To serve as a guide during the lifetime of your business.*** This is the most important reason for writing a business plan. Writing a business plan will force you to consider everything that will come into play to make a success out of your business. It will also provide you with a means to periodically analyze what is happening in your business and give you a solid basis upon which to make decisions and implement changes. In short, it is the blueprint of your business and will serve to keep you on the right track. If you spend the time to plan ahead, many pitfalls will be avoided and needless frustrations eliminated.

2. ***To fulfill the requirement for securing lenders and investors.*** If you are planning to seek loan funds or venture capital, you will be required to submit solid documentation in the form of a business plan.

   The days are gone when your local banker would extend a loan because you were a good trustworthy person with an entrepreneurial idea that sounded great. The world is more complex, the economy is tight, and the banker has to have complete documentation that will justify your loan. Remember, a banker is the caretaker of his clients' monies. If your business plan is realistic and has complete financial documentation that indicates you will be able to repay your loan plus interest, there is a basis on which to lend you the funds you need to operate or expand your business. This also applies to venture capitalists who invest in your business in return for a share of it.

   Your business plan will provide potential lenders and investors with detailed information on all aspects of the company's past and current operations and future projections. It will detail how the desired investment or loan will further the company's goals. Every lender and investor wants to know how the loan will improve the worth of your company. Your business plan will detail how the money will be used and how it will enhance the company's profitability.

REVISING YOUR BUSINESS PLAN

Writing a business plan does not mean you can never vary from that plan. In fact, if your plan is going to be effective either to the business or a potential lender, it will be necessary for you to update it on a regular basis.

Changes are constantly taking place in your industry, in technology, and with your customers. You, as the owner, must be aware of everything that is happening in relation to your business in particular and your industry in general. You must be prepared to take the necessary steps to stay ahead of your competition. Every quarter, you will want to look at what has happened in your business, make decisions about what you can do better, and revise your plan to reflect the changes you want to implement.

A WINNING BUSINESS PLAN FORMAT

Most business planning workshops focus heavily on why you should hire a professional planner (usually their company). Since getting into the software business, we have also been confronted with a lot of hype claiming that you can install particular business planning software and create a business plan in a few hours.

The fact is that writing a business plan requires many days and possibly months, depending on the complexity of your business. But you can write it yourself—and if you do, you will know your business better before you finish. There is a lot of research to be done. Even if you hire a professional planner, you will be required to supply the information and statistics that will go into your business plan. This phase will be about 80 percent of the job. The other 20 percent is a matter of knowing how to put the information together into a readable plan.

Much of the confusion seems to stem from the fact that most business owners do not know what elements to include or how to organize their information in a logical sequence. As one student so aptly put it,

> *If God had boxes of arms, legs, heads, and other parts, and no instructions for putting a human being together, we might be pretty funny looking and not very functional. I think a business plan is the same.*

He was right! In order to be effective, a business plan must not only have all the necessary parts, it must also be put together in a functional pattern. When you write your business plan, you will want to cover specific subjects in a particular order. You will also need to maintain 100 percent continuity between all sections of the plan. Whatever you include in the text sections must be reflected in the financial documents.

ANATOMY OF A BUSINESS PLAN OUTLINE

To help make your task easier, we have included a condensed outline (based on the book, *Anatomy of a Business Plan*, and the software, Automate Your Business Plan) for you to follow when you write your business plan. Your plan should include all of the elements listed on pages 191 and 192.

TECH TIP 26

BUSINESS PLANNING SOFTWARE: USING TECHNOLOGY TO STREAMLINE THE PROCESS

There is no quick fix when it comes to writing a business plan. However, utilizing the proper tools can make your job easier and save you valuable time. Combining the research capabilities of the Internet and the use of a good business planning software package can help you to create a credible and defensible business plan for your new company.

Unfortunately, in today's world full of over-hyped products, much of the software purchased does not live up to everything promised on the outside of the package. One popular package says on its box front, "Fill in the numbers and write a business plan in a few hours." This should be your clue to run—not walk—to the nearest exit.

What Should You Look for in Business Planning Software?

Remember that your business plan is only as good as the information you are able to put into the program. It's the old "Garbage In—Garbage Out" adage. Keeping the desired result in mind, look for software that will enable you to completely customize your plan to your particular business. This means staying away from templates that create canned plans.

Good software will guide you step by step through your business plan, giving you instructions and examples for each piece, but it will not generate the text by having you fill in the blanks. Especially important is your financial plan. Be sure all of your spreadsheets can be completely customized to your chart of accounts. Generic financial statements will not help you run your business.

We Have a Preference—of Course!

Automate Your Business Plan for Windows is the companion software to the award-winning book, *Anatomy of a Business Plan*. It will walk you through the entire business planning process with instructions, examples, and templates. The Chart of Accounts Wizard will quickly customize all of your spreadsheets to your specific chart of accounts. You will then work in the Integrated (Linked) Spreadsheet Workbook where all of the spreadsheets are preformatted and preformulated. Information and numbers that you input (or change) will automatically be reflected on all related spreadsheets. As a bonus, there is an International Research Web Page (available only to our users) that will guide you through your research and hot link you via the Internet directly to the marketing and financial information you will need to write your business plan. The software also includes an amortizing program that will calculate principal and interest payments on your loans. For more information: <www.business-plan.com>.

Business Plan Outline

adapted from: *Anatomy of a Business Plan*, 5th Edition
Dearborn Trade, Chicago, IL
and
Automate Your Business Plan 11.0
Out of Your Mind...and Into the Marketplace, Tustin, CA

THE COVER SHEET

(The title page of your plan)

The cover sheet should contain the name, address, and telephone number of the business and the names, addresses, and telephone numbers of all owners or corporate officers. It should also tell who prepared the business plan and when it was prepared or revised. To help you keep track of copies out to lenders, mark each cover sheet with a copy number. You may also opt to include a confidentiality statement.

THE EXECUTIVE SUMMARY

(The summary of your plan)

The executive summary summarizes your plan and states your objectives. If you are seeking loan funds or investment capital, it will list your capital needs, how you intend to use the money, the benefit of the loan or investment funds to the business, and how you intend to repay the loan plus interest to the lender—or generate profits to the investor. Investors will be specifically interested in your exit strategy.

While you are writing your plan, many previous ideas will change and new ideas will develop. Therefore, the executive summary is most effectively formulated after writing your plan. This statement should be concise and effectively address the key points of interest to the reader.

TABLE OF CONTENTS

(Listing of contents of your plan with page numbers)

Having a table of contents will help the reader to move smoothly from one section of the plan to another when verifying information.

For example: If a lender is reading financial information regarding advertising on a pro forma cash flow statement, he can use the table of contents to locate the advertising section for specifics on where you will be advertising and how the advertising dollars will be spent. The table of contents will also refer to the page in the supporting documents section that contains advertising rate sheets backing up the plan.

Business Plan Outline, continued

PART I: THE ORGANIZATIONAL PLAN

(The first main section of your business plan)

This section contains information on how your business is put together administratively. It will include such things as a summary description of your business, a list of products and services you will sell, description of your intellectual property, choice of legal structure, management and personnel information, accounting and legal provisions, insurance considerations, and planned security measures. It will also address your location if it is not tied to your marketing.

PART II: THE MARKETING PLAN

(The second main section of your business plan)

Your marketing plan is based on the overview and goals you establish for your business. The plan defines all of the components of your marketing strategy; it addresses the details of your market analysis, sales, advertising, and public relations campaigns. The marketing plan should integrate traditional (offline) programs with new media (online) strategies. It is completed by addressing customer service, implementation of your marketing strategy, and plans for assessing your marketing effectiveness.

PART III: FINANCIAL DOCUMENTS

(The third major section of your business plan)

Your financial documents translate the information in the first two sections of your plan into financial figures that can be used to analyze your business and make decisions for higher profitability.

You will have pro forma (projected) financial statements, actual (historical) statements, and a financial statement analysis. Include a pro forma cash flow statement, three-year income projection, breakeven analysis, quarterly budget analysis, profit and loss statement, balance sheet, and a financial statement analysis ratio summary. If you are going to a lender or investor, you will also need a summary of financial needs and loan fund dispersal statement (sources and uses of funds) and business financial history.

PART IV: SUPPORTING DOCUMENTS

(Documents referred to and used to back up statements made in the three main sections of your business plan)

This section will include: owner/manager resumes, personal financial statements, articles of incorporation/partnership agreements, legal contracts, lease agreements, proprietary papers (copyrights, trademarks, and patents), letters of reference, demographics, and any other documents that are pertinent to the support of your plan.

RESOURCES FOR SMALL BUSINESS

THE SMALL BUSINESS ADMINISTRATION

The U. S. Small Business Administration was established in 1953 to provide financial, technical, and management assistance to entrepreneurs. Statistics show that most small business failures are due to poor management. For this reason, the SBA places special emphasis on business management training that covers such topics as planning, finance, organization, and marketing. Often, training is held in cooperation with educational institutions, chambers of commerce, and trade associations. Prebusiness workshops are held on a regular basis for prospective business owners. Other training programs are conducted that focus on special needs such as rural development and international trade. One-on-one counseling is provided through the Service Corp of Retired Executives (SCORE) and Small Business Development Centers (SBDC). The SBA strives to match the needs of a specific business with the expertise available.

To access the SBA: Online   <www.sba.gov>
                                 SBA Answer Desk   800-827-5722

SCORE is a volunteer program that helps small business owners solve their operating problems through free one-on-one counseling and through a well-developed system of low-cost workshops and training sessions. To locate a SCORE counseling center in your area or to consult online, access the following site: <www.score.org>.

SBDCs are generally located or headquartered in academic institutions and provide individual counseling and practical training for prospective and current business owners. To locate a center near you, log on to <www.sba.gov/sbdc>.

OTHER FEDERAL RESOURCES

Many federal agencies offer publications of interest to business owners. There is a nominal fee for some, but most are free. Below is a partial list of government agencies that provide publications and other services targeted toward small businesses. The easiest and most effective way to review available information is via the agency's Web site; phone numbers have also been included for some agencies.

Consumer Product Safety Commission	\<www.cpsc.gov\>
Environmental Protection Agency	\<www.epa.gov\>
Patent and Trademark Office	\<www.uspto.gov\>
U. S. Copyright Office	\<www.loc.gov/copyright\>
U. S. Department of Agriculture	\<www.usda.gov\>
Economic Research Service	\<www.ers.gov\>
National Agricultural Statistics Service	\<www.usda.gov/nass\>
U. S. Department of Commerce	\<www.commerce.gov\>
U. S. Census Bureau	\<www.census.gov\>
Bureau of Economic Analysis	\<www.bea.gov\>
International Trade Administration	\<www.ita.doc.gov\>
U. S. Department of Energy	\<www.energy.gov\>
U. S. Department of Homeland Security	\<www.dhs.gov\>
U. S. Department of Labor	
Occupational Safety and Health Administration (OSHA)	\<www.osha.gov\>
Bureau of Labor Statistics	\<www.stats.bls.gov\>
Employment and Training Administration	\<www.doleta.gov\>
U. S. Department of the Treasury	
Internal Revenue Service:	\<www.irs.gov\>
Information Help Desk	800-876-1715
Forms and Publications via Fax-on-Demand	703-368-9694
Forms and Publications by phone	800-829-3676

ASSOCIATIONS AND AGENCIES

Direct Marketing Association (DMA)   \<www.the-dma.org\>
The oldest and largest trade association for users and suppliers of direct, database, and interactive marketing. Its Web site offers a wide range of information on direct marketing.

International Franchise Association   \<www.franchise.org\>
Membership-based association represents franchisers, franchisees, and suppliers. Provides information on start-up, operations, legislation, etc.

National Association for the Self-Employed   <www.nase.org>

Serves the needs of small business owners by helping obtain competitive employee benefits, offering discounts on items such as office equipment and telephone service, and providing a small business advice hotline.

National Association of Home-Based Business   <www.aahbb.org>

Membership-based association works to assist entrepreneurs in the start-up and operation of home-based businesses.

National Federation of Independent Business   <www.nfib.com>

The largest advocacy organization representing small and independent businesses in Washington, DC, and all 50 state capitals. The organization provides timely informational resources designed to help business owners succeed.

National Association of Manufacturers   <www.nam.org>

Membership-based association of manufacturing firms that represents the interests of small manufacturers.

National Association of Women Business Owners   <www.nawbo.org>

Membership-based organization represents women's business interests to government. Local chapters provide counseling and technical assistance for the woman business owner.

BOOKS

Bangs, David H. Jr. *The Business Planning Guide: Creating a Winning Plan for Success*, 9th Edition. Chicago: Dearborn Trade, 2002.

———. *The Market Planning Guide: Creating a Plan to Successfully Market Your Business, Product, or Service,* 6th Edition. Chicago: Dearborn Trade, 2002.

———. *The Start-Up Guide: A One-Year Plan for Entrepreneurs*, 3rd Edition. Chicago: Dearborn Trade, 1998.

Daily, Frederick. *Tax Savvy for Small Business*, 6th Edition. Berkeley, CA: Nolo Press, 2002.

Fishman, Stephen. *The Copyright Handbook*, 5th Edition. Berkeley, CA: Nolo Press, 2002.

———. *Hiring Independent Contractors,* 3rd Edition. Berkeley, CA: Nolo Press, 2000.

Godin, Seth. *If You're Clueless about Starting Your Own Business and Want to Know More.* Chicago: Dearborn Trade, 1998.

Hall, Stephen. *From Kitchen to Market: Selling Your Gourmet Food Specialty,* 3rd Edition. Chicago: Dearborn Trade, 2000.

Kamaroff, Bernard. *Small Time Operator: How to Start Your Own Small Business, Keep Your Books, Pay Your Taxes, and Stay out of Trouble!* 25th Edition. Willitts, CA: Bell Springs Publishing, 2000.

Mancuso, Anthony and Beth Lawrence. *Form Your Own Limited Liability Company*, 3rd Edition. Berkeley, CA: Nolo Press, 2002.

McKeever, Mike. *How to Write a Business Plan*, 5th Edition. Berkeley, CA: Nolo Press, 2002.

Norman, Jan. *What No One Ever Tells You about Starting Your Own Business*. Chicago: Dearborn Trade, 1999.

Pakroo, Peri and Twila Slasnick. *The Small Business Start-up Kit: a Step-by-Step Legal Guide*. Berkeley, CA: Nolo Press, 2000.

Pinson, Linda. *Anatomy of a Business Plan: A Step-by-Step Guide to Building a Business and Securing Your Company's Future*, 5th Edition. Chicago: Dearborn Trade, 2001.

———. *Keeping the Books: Basic Record Keeping and Accounting for the Successful Small Business*, 6th Edition. Chicago: Dearborn Trade, 2004.

Schiffman, Stephan. *Sales Don't Just Happen: 26 Proven Strategies to Increase Sales in Any Market*. Chicago: Dearborn Trade, 2002.

Sitarz, Daniel, *The Complete Book of Small Business Legal Forms*, 3rd Edition. Carbondale, IL: Nova Publishing Company, 2000.

Steingold, Fred and Janet Portman. *Leasing Space for Your Small Business*. Berkeley, CA: Nolo Press, 2001.

Steingold, Fred. *Legal Guide for Starting and Running a Small Business,* 6th Edition. Berkeley, CA: Nolo Press, 2001.

Stoltze, William. *An Entrepreneur's Guide to Launching and Managing a New Business*. Franklin Lakes, NJ: Career Press, 1999.

Strauss, Steven D. *The Business Start-Up Kit*. Chicago: Dearborn Trade, 2003.

Sundt, Peter. *Business Start-up Handbook: Guidelines and Pitfalls*. Houston, TX: Cibolo Press, 1999.

LIBRARY RESOURCES

Almanac of Business and Industrial Financial Ratios (Prentice Hall). Provides ratios and industry norms in actual dollar figures derived from IRS data. Each industry includes performance indicators such as total assets, cost of operations, wages, and profit margins.

American Wholesaler and Distributor Directory (Gale Research). Provides listings of wholesalers and distributors sorted by product category and state.

Catalog of Catalogs (Woodbine House). Contains descriptions and contact information for more than 14,000 catalogs, indexed by subject and company name.

Directory of Manufacturers' Sales Agencies (Manufacturing Agents National Association). Lists manufacturers' sales agencies alphabetically and by state. Also has information on how to select a sales agent.

Encyclopedia of Associations (Gale Research). Guide to national and international associations; contains contact information and descriptions; indexed by name, key word, and geographic area.

Financial Studies of the Small Business (Financial Research Associates). Organized by industry; contains financial ratios and indicators for small and microbusinesses.

Lifestyle Market Analyst (Standard Rate & Data Service). Reference book containing demographic and psychographic statistics for metropolitan statistical areas in the United States.

Small Business Profiles (Gale Research). Provides profiles of selected small businesses with statistics and contact information for associations and franchise opportunities.

Small Business Sourcebook (Gale Research). Contains sources of information related to starting specific types of small businesses. Typical entries include start-up information, trade associations and publications, statistics, and supply sources.

Thomas Food Industry Register. Directory of food manufacturers and suppliers to the food industry.

Thomas Register of Manufacturing. Directory of most manufacturing firms; includes company profile and contact information.

WORKSHEETS

READY TO COPY FOR YOUR OWN USE

The blank forms and worksheets on the following pages have been provided for you to copy and use for your own business.

When you use the recordkeeping forms, you will notice that categories under fixed and variable expenses in the financial statements (profit and loss statement and cash flow statement) have been left blank. The categories are developed by using the categories from your revenue and expense journal. Those expenses that are frequent and/or sizable will have a heading of their own (i.e., advertising, rent, salaries, etc.). Those that are very small will be included under the heading "miscellaneous" in either the variable or fixed expense sections of each of your financial statements.

Personal Assessment Worksheet 1

Skills	Interests	Personal Qualities	Business Ideas

Personal Assessment Worksheet 2

Strengths	Weaknesses	Action Plan	Cost	Time

Buying a Business Worksheet

Name of business: _____

Type of business: _____

Address: _____

_____

Contact person: _____

Why is this business for sale? _____

What is the history of this business? _____

_____

_____

Has this business been profitable? _____

_____

_____

_____

What will I be buying? _____

   Accounts payable/liabilities: _____

   Accounts receivable: _____

   Business name: _____

_____

   Customer list: _____

   Fixed assets: _____

   Inventory: _____

   Lease: _____

   Personnel: _____

_____

   Proprietary rights (copyright, patent, trademark): _____

_____

   Unpaid taxes: _____

What is the selling price of this business? _____

How will I finance this purchase? _____

_____

Buying a Franchise Worksheet

Name of franchise: _____

Type of business: _____

_____

_____

Address: _____

Contact person: _____

What is the reputation of the franchisor? _____

_____

_____

Is the company involved in litigation? _____

_____

_____

What is the reputation of the individual business? _____

_____

_____

What training and start-up assistance is offered by the franchisor? _____

_____

_____

_____

What continuing assistance is offered by the franchisor? _____

_____

_____

_____

What is the management structure of the organization? _____

_____

_____

_____

Are the location and territory protected? _____

_____

_____

Buying a Franchise Worksheet, continued

What are the operating practices of the franchise? _____

_____

_____

What are the operating control policies? _____

_____

_____

What are the franchise costs? _____

_____

_____

Initial license fee: _____

_____

_____

Continuing royalty fees: _____

_____

_____

Other fees: _____

_____

_____

How will the sale be financed? _____

_____

_____

Do I have the right to sell the franchise? _____

_____

_____

What are the terms of renewal and termination? _____

_____

_____

_____

_____

_____

Competition Evaluation Form

1. Competitor: _____

2. Location: _____

   _____

3. Products or services offered: _____

4. Methods of distribution: _____

5. Image: _____

   Packaging: _____

   Promotional materials: _____

   Methods of advertising: _____

   Quality of product or service: _____

6. Pricing structure: _____

   _____

7. Business history and current performance: _____

   _____

8. Market share (number, types, and location of customers): _____

   _____

9. Strengths (the strengths of the competition become your strengths): ___

   _____

10. Weaknesses (looking at the weaknesses of the competition can help you find ways of being unique and benefiting the customer): _____

    _____

    _____

    _____

    _____

    _____

    _____

    _____

    _____

Target Market Worksheet

1. Who are my customers?

   Profile: _____

   _____

   Economic level: _____

   _____

   Psychological make-up (lifestyle): _____

   _____

   Age range: _____

   Sex: _____

   Income level: _____

   _____

   Buying habits: _____

   _____

2. Where are my customers located?

   Where do they live: _____

   _____

   Where do they work: _____

   _____

   Where do they shop: _____

   _____

3. Projected size of the market:

   _____

   _____

   _____

   _____

   _____

   _____

   _____

Target Market Worksheet, continued

4. What are the customers needs?

_____

_____

_____

_____

_____

_____

_____

_____

_____

5. How can I meet those needs?

_____

_____

_____

_____

_____

_____

_____

_____

_____

6. What is unique about my business?

_____

_____

_____

_____

_____

_____

_____

_____

Market Research Worksheet

Questions	Information Source	Results	Effect on Plan

Location Analysis Worksheet

1. Address: _____

2. Name, address, phone number of realtor/contact person: _____

_____

3. Square footage/cost: _____

_____

_____

4. History of location: _____

_____

_____

5. Location in relation to target market: _____

_____

_____

6. Traffic patterns for customers: _____

_____

_____

7. Traffic patterns for suppliers: _____

_____

_____

8. Availability of parking (include diagram): _____

_____

_____

9. Crime rate for the area: _____

_____

_____

10. Quality of public services (e.g., police, fire protection): _____

_____

_____

11. Notes from walking tour of the area: _____

_____

_____

Location Analysis Worksheet, continued

12. Neighboring shops and local business climate: _____

_____

_____

13. Zoning regulations: _____

_____

_____

14. Adequacy of utilities (get information from utility company representatives): _____

_____

_____

_____

15. Availability of raw materials/supplies: _____

_____

16. Availability of labor force: _____

_____

_____

17. Labor rate of pay for the area: _____

_____

_____

_____

18. Housing availability for employees: _____

_____

_____

_____

19. Tax rates (state, county, income, payroll, special assessments): _____

_____

_____

20. Evaluation of site in relation to competition: _____

_____

_____

_____

_____

Choosing a Bank

	Name of Potential Financial Institution		
	A.	B.	C.
1. Have you already established a working relationship with a. the management? b. the personnel?			
2. What kind of business bank accounts are available?			
3. Does this bank offer merchant credit card services?			
4. Does the business participate in business loan programs?			
5. Is the bank a federal depository bank?			
6. Is the bank a stable financial institution?			
7. How many branches does the bank have?			
8. Is the location of the bank convenient for your business?			
9. What are the bank's hours of operation? Are they open on Saturdays?			
10. Will the bank place a holding period on your deposits?			
11. What will it cost you to have a business checking account?			
12. What other services does the bank have: a. electronic banking? b. safe deposit? c. notary public? d. electronic transfer? e. other?			
13. What is your overall feeling about the bank?			

Revenue and Expense Journal

Month: _____ _____ 20___, page _____

CHECK NO.	DATE	TRANSACTION	REVENUE	EXPENSE	Customize headings to match the business									MISC
		Balance forward----												
		TOTALS												

Petty Cash Record

PETTY CASH - 20___				Page ___	
DATE	PAID TO WHOM	EXPENSE ACCOUNT DEBITED	DEPOSIT	AMOUNT OF EXPENSE	BALANCE
	BALANCE FORWARD				

Inventory Record—Nonidentifiable

DEPARTMENT/CATEGORY: _____

PRODUCTION OR PURCHASE DATE	INVENTORY PURCHASED OR MANUFACTURED		NUMBER OF UNITS	UNIT COST	VALUE ON DATE OF INVENTORY (Unit Cost X Units on Hand)	
	Stock #	Description			Value	Date

Inventory Record—Identifiable

WHOLESALER:_____ **Page**___

PURCH DATE	INVENTORY PURCHASED		PURCH. PRICE	DATE SOLD	SALE PRICE	NAME OF BUYER (Optional)
	Stock #	Description				

Fixed Assets Log

COMPANY NAME: _____

ASSET PURCHASED	DATE PLACED IN SERVICE	COST OF ASSET	% USED FOR BUSINESS	RECOVERY PERIOD	METHOD OF DEPRECIATION	DEPRECIATION PREVIOUSLY ALLOWED	DATE SOLD	SALE PRICE

Accounts Payable Record

CREDITOR: _____

ADDRESS: _____

_____

TEL. NO: _____   ACCOUNT NO._____

INVOICE DATE	INVOICE NO.	INVOICE AMOUNT	TERMS	DATE PAID	AMOUNT PAID	INVOICE BALANCE

Accounts Receivable Record

CUSTOMER: _____

ADDRESS: _____

_____

TEL. NO: _____   ACCOUNT NO._____

INVOICE DATE	INVOICE NO.	INVOICE AMOUNT		TERMS	DATE PAID	AMOUNT PAID		INVOICE BALANCE	

Mileage Log

NAME: _____

DATED: From_____To_____

DATE	CITY OF DESTINATION	NAME OR OTHER DESIGNATION	BUSINESS PURPOSE	NO. OF MILES
			TOTAL MILES THIS SHEET	

Entertainment Expense Record

NAME: _____

DATED: From_____To_____

DATE	PLACE OF ENTERTAINMENT	BUSINESS PURPOSE	NAME OF PERSON ENTERTAINED	AMOUNT SPENT

Travel Record

TRIP TO: _____

Dated From: _____ To: _____

Business Purpose: _____

No. Days Spent on Business _____

DATE	LOCATION	EXPENSE PAID TO	MEALS				HOTEL	TAXIS, ETC.	AUTOMOBILE			MISC EXP
			Breakfast	Lunch	Dinner	Misc.			Gas	Parking	Tolls	
TOTALS →												

Balance Sheet

Business Name: _____   Date: _____ ____, 20____

ASSETS

Current Assets

Cash $ _____
Petty Cash $ _____
Accounts Receivable $ _____
Inventory $ _____
Short-Term Investments $ _____
Prepaid Expenses $ _____

Long-Term Investments $ _____

Fixed Assets

Land (valued at cost) $ _____

Buildings $ _____
  1. Cost   _____
  2. Less Acc. Depr. _____

Improvements $ _____
  1. Cost   _____
  2. Less Acc. Depr. _____

Equipment $ _____
  1. Cost   _____
  2. Less Acc. Depr. _____

Furniture $ _____
  1. Cost   _____
  2. Less Acc. Depr. _____

Autos/Vehicles $ _____
  1. Cost   _____
  2. Less Acc. Depr. _____

Other Assets

1. $ _____
2. $ _____

TOTAL ASSETS $ _____

LIABILITIES

Current Liabilities

Accounts Payable $ _____
Notes Payable $ _____
Interest Payable $ _____

Taxes Payable
  Federal Income Tax $ _____
  Self-Employment Tax $ _____
  State Income Tax $ _____
  Sales Tax Accrual $ _____
  Property Tax $ _____

Payroll Accrual $ _____

Long-Term Liabilities

Notes Payable $ _____

TOTAL LIABILITIES $ _____

NET WORTH (EQUITY)

Proprietorship $ _____
or
Partnership
_____ % Equity $ _____
_____ % Equity $ _____
or
Corporation
Capital Stock $ _____
Surplus Paid In $ _____
Retained Earnings $ _____

TOTAL NET WORTH $ _____

Assets - Liabilities = Net Worth
and
Liabilities + Equity = Total Assets

Profit and Loss Statement

Company: _____

Beginning: _____ ____, 20___   Ending: _____ ___, 20___

INCOME		
1. **Sales Revenues**		$
2. **Cost of Goods Sold (c-d)**		
a. Beginning Inventory (1/01)		
b. Purchases		
c. C.O.G. Avail. Sale (a+b)		
d. Less Ending Iventory (12/31)		
3. **Gross Profit on Sales (1-2)**		$
EXPENSES		
1. **Variable (Selling) (a thru h)**		
a.		
b.		
c.		
d.		
e.		
f.		
g. Misc. Variable (Selling) Expense		
h. Depreciation (Prod/Serv. Assets)		
2. **Fixed (Administrative) (a thru h)**		
a.		
b.		
c.		
d.		
e.		
f.		
g. Misc. Fixed (Administrative) Expense		
h. Depreciation (Office Equipment)		
Total Operating Expenses (1+2)		
Net Income from Operations (GP-Exp)		$
Other Income (Interest Income)		
Other Expense (Interest Expense)		
Net Profit (Loss) Before Taxes		$
Taxes		
a. Federal		
b. Statel		
c. Local		
NET PROFIT (LOSS) AFTER TAXES		$

Cash to Be Paid Out Worksheet

(Cash Flowing Out of the Business)

Business Name: _____   **Time Period:** _____ to _____

1. **START-UP COSTS:**
    Business License $ _____
    Corporation Filing   _____
    Legal Fees   _____
    Other start-up costs:
      a.   _____
      b.   _____
      c.   _____

2. **INVENTORY PURCHASES**
    Cash out for goods intended for resale   _____

3. **SELLING EXPENSES (VARIABLE/DIRECT)**
      a.   _____
      b.   _____
      c.   _____
      d.   _____
      e.   _____
      f.   _____
    Miscellaneous Variable Expense   _____
        TOTAL SELLING EXPENSES   _____

4. **FIXED EXPENSES (ADMINISTRATIVE/INDIRECT)**
      a.   _____
      b.   _____
      c.   _____
      d.   _____
      e.   _____
      f.   _____
    Miscellaneous Fixed Expense   _____
        TOTAL OPERATING EXPENSES   _____

5. **ASSETS (LONG-TERM PURCHASES)**   _____
    Cash to be paid out in current period

6. **LIABILITIES**   _____
    Cash outlay for retiring debts, loans, and/or
    accounts payable

7. **OWNER EQUITY**   _____
    Cash to be withdrawn by owner

    TOTAL CASH TO BE PAID OUT $ _____

Sources of Cash Worksheet

Business Name: _____

Time Period Covered: _____ ___, _____ to _____ ___, _____

---

   1. CASH ON HAND $ _____

   2. SALES (REVENUES)

     Product Sales Income   _____

     Service Income   _____

     Deposits on Sales or Services   _____

     Collections on Accounts Receivable   _____

   3. MISCELLANEOUS INCOME

     Interest Income   _____

     Payments to be Received on Loans   _____

   4. SALE OF LONG-TERM ASSETS   _____

   5. LIABILITIES

     Loan Funds (Banks, Lending Inst., SBA, etc.)   _____

   6. EQUITY

     Owner Investments (Sole Prop. or Partnership)   _____

     Contributed Capital (Corporation)   _____

     Sale of Stock (Corporation)   _____

     Venture Capital   _____

   TOTAL CASH AVAILABLE $ _____

Pro Forma Cash Flow Statement

Company Name: _____

Year: _____

	Jan	Feb	Mar	Apr	May	Jun	6-MONTH PERIOD	Jul	Aug	Sep	Oct	Nov	Dec	12-MONTH PERIOD
BEGINNING CASH BALANCE														
CASH RECEIPTS														
A. Sales/Revenues														
B. Receivables														
C. Interest Income														
D. Sale of Long-Term Assets														
TOTAL CASH AVAILABLE														
CASH PAYMENTS														
A. Cost of goods to be sold														
1. Purchases														
2. Material														
3. Labor														
Total Cost of Goods														
B. Variable Expenses														
1.														
2.														
3.														
4.														
5.														
6.														
7. Misc. Variable Expense														
Total Variable Expenses														
C. Fixed Expenses														
1.														
2.														
3.														
4.														
5.														
6.														
7. Misc. Fixed Expense														
Total Fixed Expenses														
D. Interest Expense														
E. Federal Income Tax														
F. Other uses														
G. Long-term asset payments														
H. Loan payments														
I. Owner draws														
TOTAL CASH PAID OUT														
CASH BALANCE/DEFICIENCY														
LOANS TO BE RECEIVED														
EQUITY DEPOSITS														
ENDING CASH BALANCE														

Questionnaire Coding Log

Code	Date	Number Sent	Destination/ Recipient	Response Rate	Evaluation

Marketing Action Plan

Objective	Strategy	Tactic	Evaluation

Advertising Worksheet

Name of business: _____

1. What are the features and benefits of my product or service? _____
   _____
   _____
   _____

2. Who is my audience? _____
   _____
   _____
   _____

3. Who is my competition and how do they advertise? _____
   _____
   _____
   _____

4. What are the goals of my advertising campaign? _____
   _____
   _____
   _____

5. How much do I plan to invest for advertising? _____
   _____
   _____
   _____

6. What advertising methods will I use? _____
   __ Newspapers   __ Magazines   __ Yellow pages
   __ Radio   __ Television   __ Direct mail
   __ Telemarketing   __ Flyers   __ Brochures
   __ Coupons   __ Press release   __ Promo items
   __ Other _____

7. When will I use them, and what will they cost? _____
   _____
   _____
   _____
   _____
   _____

8. How will I measure the effectiveness of the advertising plan? _____
   _____
   _____
   _____
   _____
   _____

Advertising Response Record

Company name: _____

Type of Ad	Date Run	Cost	Circulation	Number of Responses	Income Generated

Publicity Tracking Record

Company name: _____

Media Name	Contact Person	Address	Date	Material Sent	Follow-up	Response	Results	Notes

GLOSSARY

account A record of a business transaction. A contract arrangement, written or unwritten, to purchase and take delivery with payment to be made later as arranged.

account balance The difference between the debit and the credit sides of an account.

accountant One who is skilled at keeping business records. Usually, a highly trained professional rather than one who keeps books. An accountant can set up the books needed for a business to operate and help the owner understand them.

accounting period A time interval at the end of which an analysis is made of the information contained in the bookkeeping records. Also the period of time covered by the profit and loss statement.

accounts payable Money you owe to an individual or business for goods or services that have been received but not yet paid for.

accounts receivable Money owed to your business for goods or services that have been delivered but not yet paid for.

accrual basis A method of keeping accounts that shows expenses incurred and income earned for a given fiscal period, even though such expenses and income have not been actually paid or received in cash.

actuary A professional expert in pension and life insurance matters, particularly trained in mathematical, statistical, and accounting methods and procedures, and in insurance probabilities.

administrative expense Expenses chargeable to the managerial, general administrative, and policy phases of a business in contrast to sales, manufacturing, or cost of goods expense.

advertising The practice of bringing to the public's notice the good qualities of something in order to induce the public to buy or invest in it.

agent A person who is authorized to act for or represent another person in dealing with a third party.

amortization To liquidate on an installment basis; the process of gradually paying off a liability over a period of time.

analysis Breaking an idea or problem down into its parts; a thorough examination of the parts of anything.

annual report The yearly report made by a company at the close of the fiscal year, stating the company's receipts and disbursements, assets, and liabilities.

appraisal Evaluation of a specific piece of personal or real property. The value placed on the property evaluated.

appreciation The increase in the value of an asset in excess of its depreciable cost due to economic and other conditions, as distinguished from increases in value due to improvements or additions made to it.

arrears Amounts past due and unpaid.

Articles of Incorporation A legal document filed with the state that sets forth the purposes and regulations for a corporation. Each state has different regulations.

assets Anything of worth that is owned. Accounts receivable are an asset.

audiotaping The act of recording onto an audiotape.

audit An examination of accounting documents and supporting evidence for the purpose of reaching an informed opinion concerning their propriety.

bad debts Money owed to you that you cannot collect.

balance The amount of money remaining in an account.

balance sheet An itemized statement that lists the total assets and liabilities of a given business to portray its net worth at a given moment in time.

bank statement A monthly statement of account that a bank renders to each of its depositors.

benchmarking Rating your company's products, services, and practices against those of the front-runners in the industry.

bill of lading A document issued by a railroad or other carrier. It acknowledges the receipt of specified goods for transportation to a certain place, sets forth the contract between the shipper and the carrier, and provides for proper delivery of the goods.

bill of sale Formal legal document that conveys title to or interest in specific property from the seller to the buyer.

board of directors Those individuals elected by the stockholders of a corporation to manage the business.

bookkeeping The process of recording business transactions into the accounting records. The "books" are the documents where the records of transactions are kept.

bottom line The figure that reflects company profitability on the income statement. The bottom line is the profit after all expenses and taxes have been paid.

brand A design, mark, symbol, or other device that distinguishes one line or type of goods from those of a competitor.

brand name A term, symbol, design, or combination thereof that identifies and differentiates a seller's product or service.

breakeven The point of business activity when total revenue equals total expenses. Above the breakeven point, the business is making a profit. Below the breakeven point, the business is incurring a loss.

budget An estimate of the income and expenditures for a future period of time, usually one year.

business venture Taking financial risks in a commercial enterprise.

capital Money available to invest or the total of accumulated assets available for production.

capital equipment Equipment you use to manufacture a product, provide a service, or sell, store, and deliver merchandise. Such equipment will not be sold in the normal course of business but will be used and worn out or consumed in the course of business.

capital gains (and losses) The difference between purchase price and selling price in the sale of assets.

cash Money in hand or readily available.

cash discount A deduction that is given for prompt payment of a bill.

cash flow The actual movement of cash within a business; the analysis of how much cash is needed and when that money is required by a business within a period of time.

cash receipts The money received by a business from customers.

Certified Public Accountant (CPA) An accountant who has met prescribed requirements designed to ensure competence on the part of the public practitioner in accounting as directed by the state. The designation is that of a certified public accountant, commonly abbreviated as CPA.

chamber of commerce An organization of business people designed to advance the interests of its members. There are three levels: national, state, and local.

choice A decision to purchase that is based on an evaluation of alternatives.

cosigners Joint signers of a loan agreement who pledge to meet the obligations of a business in case of default.

collateral Something of value given or held as a pledge that a debt or obligation will be fulfilled.

commission A percentage of the principal or income that an agent receives as compensation for services.

contract An agreement regarding mutual responsibilities between two or more parties.

controllable expenses Those expenses that can be controlled or restrained by the business person.

corporation A voluntary organization of persons, either actual individuals or legal entities, legally bound together to form a business enterprise; an artificial legal entity created by government grant and treated by law as an individual entity.

cost of goods sold The direct cost to the business owner of those items that will be sold to customers.

credit Another word for debt. Credit is given to customers when they are allowed to make a purchase with the promise to pay later. A bank gives credit when it lends money.

credit line The maximum amount of credit or money a financial institution or trade firm will extend to a customer.

current assets Valuable resources or property owned by a company that will be turned into cash within one year or used up in the operations of the company within one year. Generally includes cash, accounts receivable, inventory, and prepaid expenses.

current liabilities Amounts owed that will ordinarily be paid by a company within one year. Generally includes accounts payable, current portion of long-term debt, interest, and dividends payable.

debt That which is owed. Debt refers to borrowed funds and is generally secured by collateral or a cosigner.

debt capital The part of the investment capital that must be borrowed.

default The failure to pay a debt or meet an obligation.

deficit The excess of liabilities over assets; a negative net worth.

depreciation A decrease in value through age, wear, or deterioration. Depreciation is a normal expense of doing business that must be taken into account. There are laws and regulations governing the manner and time periods that may be used for depreciation.

desktop publishing Commonly used term for computer-generated printed materials such as newsletters and brochures.

differentiated marketing Selecting and developing a number of offerings to meet the needs of a number of specific market segments.

direct mail Marketing goods or services directly to the consumer through the mail.

direct selling The process whereby the producer sells to the user, ultimate consumer, or retailer without intervening middlemen.

discount A deduction from the stated or list price of a product or service.

distribution channel All of the individuals and organizations involved in the process of moving products from producer to consumer. The route a product follows as it moves from the original grower, producer, or importer to the ultimate consumer.

distributor Middleman, wholesaler, agent, or company distributing goods to dealers or companies.

downsize Term currently used to indicate employee reassignment, layoffs, and restructuring in order to make a business more competitive, efficient, and/or cost-effective.

entrepreneur An innovator of business enterprise who recognizes opportunities to introduce a new product, a new process, or an improved organization, and raises the necessary money, assembles the factors for production, and organizes an operation to exploit the opportunity.

equipment Physical property of a more or less permanent nature ordinarily useful in carrying on operations, other than land, buildings, or improvements to either of them. Examples are machinery, tools, trucks, cars, ships, furniture, and furnishings.

equity A financial investment in a business. An equity investment carries with it a share of ownership of the business, a stake in the profits, and a say in how it is managed. Equity is calculated by subtracting the liabilities of the business from the assets of the business.

equity capital Money furnished by owners of the business.

exchange The process where two or more parties give something of value to one another to satisfy needs and wants.

facsimile machine (fax) Machine capable of transmitting written input via telephone lines.

financial statements Documents that show your financial situation.

fixed expenses Those costs that don't vary from one period to the next. Generally, these expenses are not affected by the volume of business. Fixed expenses are the basic costs that every business will have each month.

franchise Business that requires three elements: franchise fee, common trade name, and continuous relationship with the parent company.

fundraising Events staged to raise revenue.

gross profit The difference between the selling price and the cost of an item. Gross profit is calculated by subtracting cost of goods sold from net sales.

guarantee A pledge by a third party to repay a loan in the event that the borrower cannot.

home page The "table of contents" to a Web site, detailing what pages are on a particular site. The first page one sees when accessing a Web site.

income statement A financial document that shows how much money (revenue) came in and how much money (expense) was paid out.

interest The cost of borrowing money.

Internet The vast collection of interconnected networks that provide electronic mail and access to the World Wide Web.

inventory A list of assets being held for sale.

invest To lay out money for any purpose where a profit is expected.

keystone Setting a retail price at twice the wholesale price.

lead The name and address of a possible customer.

lease A long-term rental agreement.

liability insurance Risk protection for actions where a business is liable.

license Formal permission to conduct business.

lifestyle A pattern of living that comprises an individual's activities, interests, and opinions.

limited partnership A legal partnership where some owners are allowed to assume responsibility only up to the amount invested.

liquidity The ability of a business to meet its financial responsibilities. The degree of readiness where assets can be converted into cash without loss.

loan agreement A document that states what a business can and cannot do as long as it owes money to the lender.

loan Money lent with interest.

long-term liabilities The liabilities (expenses) that will not mature within the next year.

management The art of conducting and supervising a business.

market A set of potential or real buyers or a place where there is a demand for products or services. Actual or potential buyers of a product or service.

market demand Total volume purchased in a specific geographic area by a specific customer group in a specified time period under a specified marketing program.

market forecast An anticipated demand that results from a planned marketing expenditure.

market niche A well-defined group of customers that are interested in what you have to offer.

market positioning Finding a market niche that emphasizes the strengths of a product or service in relation to the weaknesses of the competition.

market share A company's percentage share of total sales within a given market.

market targeting Choosing a marketing strategy in terms of competitive strengths and marketplace realities.

marketing mix The set of product, place, promotion, price, and packaging variables that a marketing manager controls and orchestrates to bring a product or service into the marketplace.

marketing research The systematic design, collection, analysis, and reporting of data regarding a specific marketing situation.

mass marketing Selecting and developing a single offering for an entire market.

merchandise Goods bought and sold in a business. "Merchandise" or stock is a part of inventory.

microbusiness An owner-operated business with few employees and less than $250,000 in annual sales.

middleman A person or company that performs functions or renders services involved in the purchase and/or sale of goods in their flow from producer to consumer.

multilevel sales Also known as network marketing. Rather than hiring sales staff, multilevel sales companies sell their products through thousands of independent distributors. Multilevel sales companies offer distributors commissions on both retail sales and the sales of their "downline" (the network of other distributors they sponsor).

need A state of perceived deprivation.

net What is left after deducting all expenses from the gross.

net worth The total value of a business in financial terms. Net worth is calculated by subtracting total liabilities from total assets.

niche A well-defined group of customers for whom what you have to offer is particularly suitable.

nonrecurring One time; not repeating. Nonrecurring expenses are those involved in starting a business, and which only have to be paid once and will not occur again.

note A document that is recognized as legal evidence of a debt.

operating costs Expenditures arising out of current business activities. The costs incurred to do business such as salaries, electricity, and rental. Also may be called "overhead."

organizational market A marketplace made up of producers, trade industries, governments, and institutions.

outsourcing Term used in business to identify the process of subcontracting work to outside vendors.

overhead A general term for costs of materials and services not directly adding to or readily identifiable with the product or service being sold.

partnership A legal business relationship of two or more people who share responsibilities, resources, profits, and liabilities.

payable Ready to be paid. One of the standard accounts kept by a bookkeeper is "accounts payable." This is a list of those bills that are current and due to be paid.

perception The process of selecting, organizing, and interpreting information received through the senses.

prepaid expenses Expenditures that are paid in advance for items not yet received.

price The exchange value of a product or service from the perspective of both the buyer and seller.

price ceiling The highest amount a customer will pay for a product or service based on perceived value.

price floor The lowest amount a business owner can charge for a product or service and still meet all expenses.

price planning The systematic process for establishing pricing objectives and policies.

principal The amount of money borrowed in a debt agreement and the amount interest is calculated on.

pro forma A projection or estimate of what may result in the future from actions in the present. A pro forma financial statement is one that shows how the actual operations of the business will turn out if certain assumptions are achieved.

producers The components of the organizational market that acquire products, services that enter into the production of products, and services that are sold or supplied to others.

product Anything capable of satisfying needs, including tangible items, services, and ideas.

product life cycle (PLC) The stages of development and decline through which a successful product typically moves.

product line A group of products related to each other by marketing, technical, or end-use considerations.

product mix All of the products in a seller's total product line.

profit and loss statement A list of the total amount of sales (revenues) and total costs (expenses). The difference between revenues and expenses is your profit or loss.

profit Financial gain, returns over expenditures.

profit margin The difference between your selling price and all of your costs.

promotion The communication of information by a seller to influence the attitudes and behavior of potential buyers.

promotional pricing Temporarily pricing a product or service below list price or below cost in order to attract customers.

psychographics The system of explaining market behavior in terms of attitudes and lifestyles.

publicity Any nonpaid, news-oriented presentation of a product, service, or business entity in a mass media format.

quantitative forecasts Forecasts that are based on measurements of numerical quantities.

questionnaire A data-gathering form used to collect information by a personal interview, with a telephone survey, or through the mail.

ratio The relationship of one thing to another. A ratio is a shortcut way of comparing things, which can be expressed as numbers or degrees.

receivable Ready for payment. When you sell on credit, you keep an accounts receivable ledger as a record of what is owed to you and who owes it. In accounting, a receivable is an asset.

retail Selling directly to the consumer.

retailing Businesses and individuals engaged in the activity of selling products to final consumers.

revenue Total sales during a stated period.

sales potential A company's expected share of a market as marketing expenditures increase in relation to the competition.

sales promotion Marketing activities that stimulate consumer purchasing in the short term.

sales representative An independent salesperson who directs efforts to selling your products or service to others but is not an employee of your company. Sales reps often represent more than one product line from more than one company and usually work on commission.

sample A limited portion of the whole of a group.

security Collateral that is promised to a lender as protection in case the borrower defaults on a loan.

service business A retail business that deals in activities for the benefit of others.

share One of the equal parts that the ownership of a corporation is divided into. A share represents part ownership in a corporation.

short-term notes Loans that come due in one year or less.

sole proprietorship Business legal structure where one individual owns the business.

stock An ownership share in a corporation; another name for a share. Another definition would be accumulated merchandise.

suppliers Individuals or businesses that provide resources needed by a company in order to produce goods and services.

survey A research method in which people are asked questions.

takeover The acquisition of one company by another.

target market The specific individuals, distinguished by socioeconomic, demographic, and interest characteristics, who are the most likely potential customers for the goods and services of a business.

target marketing Selecting and developing a number of offerings to meet the needs of a number of specific market segments.

telemarketing Marketing goods or services directly to the consumer via the telephone.

terms of sale The conditions concerning payment for a purchase.

trade credit Permission to buy from suppliers on open account.

undifferentiated marketing Selecting and developing one offering for an entire market.

venture capital Money invested in enterprises that do not have access to traditional sources of capital.

volume An amount or quantity of business; the volume of a business is the total it sells over a period of time.

wholesaling Businesses and individuals engaged in the activity of selling products to retailers, organizational users, or other wholesalers. Selling for resale.

working capital The excess of current assets over current liabilities. The cash needed to keep the business running from day to day.

INDEX

A

accounting professional, hiring an, 132–33
accounting software, 132, 138
    and sales tax reporting, 102
accounts payable, 134, 138, 144
    record, sample of, 144
accounts receivable, 134, 138, 145
    record, sample of, 145
address code, 23
advertising, 171–85
    Internet, 176–79
    response record, sample of, 184
    worksheet, 180
Anatomy of a Business Plan, 189, 190, 191, 196
angel investors, 123
assets, 154, 156, 157
associations and agencies, 194–95
attorney, hiring an, 83–84
Automate Your Business Plan, 189, 190, 191–92
    Web site, 190

B

balance sheet, 136
    sample of, 149
bank
    account, setting up a, 109–13
    choosing a, 113
boiler and machinery coverage, 117
bookkeeping system, establishing a, 131–50
borrowing money, 121–22
brochures, promotional, 75

business
    books and publications, 195–96
    buying an existing, 10–11, 14
    cards, 70–71, 74
    checkbook, 135
    developing your own, 9–10
    failure, reasons for, 187–88
    feasibility, determining, 17–33
    financing your, 121–29
    finding a, 9–16
    ideas, 2–3, 17–18
    incubators, 41
    legal structure, 59–68
    loans, 121–29
    location, choosing a, 39–45
    opportunity, Web site addressing pitfalls of, 13
    owners, Internet connections, 3, 11
    planning software, 190
    planning, as key to success, 187–92
    presenting your, 69–76
    protecting your, 77–85
    resources, 193–97
    start-up, Internet information, 3
business interruption insurance, 117
business license
    applying for a, 89, 90
    posting your, 89–90
    sample application, 91–92
    securing a, 87–92
    via Internet, 89

business name
  choosing a, 35–38
  domain name, Internet, 36
  Internet availability search, 38
  registering a fictitious (DBA), 93–97
business plan
  outline, sample of, 191–92
  writing a, 187–92
buying a business worksheet, sample of, 14
buying a franchise worksheet, sample of, 15–16
buying an existing business, 10–11
  Internet information regarding, 11

C

cash flow
  preformatted spreadsheets, 159
  statement, 151, 158, 160–64
cash to be paid out, 152–53
  sample worksheets, 154, 155
checking account, 111–12
colors, company, 70
community involvement as networking opportunity, 174
competition
  evaluating the, 21–22, 24
  evaluation form, sample of, 30
contracts, 82–83
copyright, 78–80
  Internet information, 80
corporation, forming a, 63–66
  bylaws, 65
  certificate of incorporation, 64
  S corporation, 65–66
customer
  contact, 177
  discounts, 176
  records, 135

D

data collecting
  general (or secondary), 20–21
  personal (or primary), 22–23
database
  customer, 135
  software, 135
debt financing, 122–23
demographics, 20, 24
direct mail advertising, 175
disclosure letter, 77
discounts, customer, 176
displays, advertising, 174
doing business as (DBA), 37, 93–97

E

e-mail advertising, 175
earthquake and flood insurance, 116–17
electronic commerce (e-commerce), 178
employee benefits, 118–19
entertainment records, 134
Entrepreneur magazine Web site, 3
equity, 156, 157
equity financing, 123, 127–28
exit strategy, 128
expense record, sample of, 147

F

federal resources, 194
fictitious business name, 37, 93–97
  statement, sample of, 96
fidelity bonds, 117
finances, separating business and personal, 111
financial statements, 135–37
financing, 121–29
  costs, calculating, 128–29
finding a business, 9–16
fire insurance, 116
fixed assets log, 134
  sample of, 143
fixed expenses, 154
forms, blank, 199–231
franchise
  buying a, 11–13
  Web site for buyer information, 13
  worksheet for buying, 15–16

G

general liability insurance, 116
glossary, 233–241
graphic/visual identity, business, 69–70

H

health insurance, 118
home-based business
  calculating your deductions, 50–51, 56, 57
  developing a, 47–57
  expenses for business use of home, sample form, 57
  IRS Internet publication, 51
  licensing a, 88–89
  office deductions, 48–52
  tax avoidance schemes, 51–52

I

ideas, exploring business, 3

insurance
    fact sheet, 120
    selecting, 115–20
interests, personal, 1–8
Internal Revenue Service
    form: expenses for business use of your
        home, 57
    Internet electronic bulletin board systems,
        137
    publications, forms, information, 51, 137
inventory purchases, 154
inventory record, 134
    sample of, 141–42

J
journal
    keeping a, 78
    revenue and expense, 133–34
    sample page, 85

L
lease considerations, and location, 42–43
    Internet information, 42
liabilities, 154, 156, 157
liability insurance, 116–17
library resources, 196–97
licensing your business, 87–92
    sample application, 91–92
life insurance, 118
limited liability company (LLC), 66–67
loans, business, 121–29
location
    analysis worksheet, sample of, 44–45
    business, 39–45
    considerations and business license,
        87–89
    evaluation, 39–45
logo, company, 70
    using technology to test, 70
logotype, 70

M
magazine advertising, 171, 172
market research, 18–32
    Internet resources, 21
    worksheet, sample of, 33
marketing
    action plan, sample of, 170
    objectives, 168, 169
    on the Internet, 177–79
    plan, developing a, 165–70
    strategy, implementing, 168
media advertising, 171–74

locating and evaluating sources of, 173
media directories, print and online, 173
mileage
    log, sample of, 146
    records, 134
MYOB (Mind Your Own Business) software, 132

N
networking, 174–75
news release, 174
    format, 182
    information, 181
    sample of, 183
newspaper advertising, 171, 172

O
One-Write Plus software, 132
order form, guidelines for developing worksheet,
        76
overhead insurance, 117
owner equity, 2, 154

P
page distribution, trends in, 20
partnership, 61–62
    agreements, 62–63
patent, 80, 81–82
    Internet information, 80
Paypal, 178
payroll records, 135
Peach Tree software, 132
personal assessment worksheet, sample of,
        7, 8
personal monthly expense worksheet, sample of,
        6
personal objectives, examining, 1–2
personal qualities, 4–5
    assessment worksheet, 7–8
petty cash record, 134
    sample of, 140
place, in marketing, 166–67
price, in marketing, 167
printer, choosing a, 72–73
product liability, 117
product or service, developing, 165–66
profit and loss statement (P&L or income state-
        ment), 136–37
    sample of, 150
promoting your business, 171–85
promotion, in marketing, 167–68
promotional
    gimmicks, 176–77
    materials, 71–72

property insurance, 116–17
publication certificate, example of, 97
publicity, 171, 174
    tracking record, sample of, 185
pyschographics, 20

Q

questionnaire
    coding log, sample of, 29
    format worksheet, sample of, 26
    product, sample of, 27
    service, sample of, 28
    use of, 23–24
Quickbooks Pro software, 132

R

radio advertising, 171, 172–73
recordkeeping, 131–50
    general, 133–35
    schedule, example of, 138
resale certificate, 101
    sample of, 108
resources for small business, 193–97
revenue and expense journal, sample of, 139

S

S corporation, 65–66
sales (revenues), 156, 157
sales tax
    flowchart, sample of, 103
    reporting, 101–02, 103
sellers permit, obtaining a, 99–108
    sample application, 104–05
Service Corp of Retired Executives (SCORE),
    193
    Web site, 193
skills, personal, 4–5, 7–8
Small Business Administration (SBA)
    guaranteed loans, 123–27
    Internet workshops, 179
    Small Business Development Centers
        (SBDC), 193
    Small Business Investment Companies
        (SBIC), 127–28
    Web site, 3, 126, 127, 193
sole proprietorship, 60–61
sources of cash, 152–53
    sample worksheets, 156, 157
spreadsheets, preformatted and preformulated,
    159
start-up costs, 154
state board of equalization report, sample of,
    106–07

strengths and weaknesses, evaluating your, 4–5

T

target market, 13
    finding your, 19–20
    worksheet, sample of, 31–32
tax information, Internet, 51, 137
telemarketing, 175–76
television advertising, 171, 172
theft insurance
trade shows and exhibits, 175
trademark, 80–81
    Internet information, 80
travel records, 134
    sample of, 148

U

U.S. Patent and Trademark Web site, 80
umbrella insurance, 117

V

variable expenses, 154
vehicle insurance, 117
venture capital, 128, 129

W

Wall Street Journal Center for Entrepreneurs,
    Web site, 3
Web pages, developing, 178–79
Web site
    and marketing, 175
    as marketing tool, 177–79
    "bookmarking," 3
    offering discount coupons through your, 176
workers' compensation, 117
worksheets, blank, 199–231

Y

Yellow Pages advertising, 176